For Sue —

The Same God?

Other titles from the author:

Non-fiction:
  In This Land of Eve
  Outlaw for God
  The Plains Brood Alone

Fiction:
  Brainchild
  Pan
  The Taking of Hill 1052

The Same God?

Comparing the Bible
with the Koran

J. Birney Dibble, M.D.

VANTAGE PRESS
New York

Cover design by Susan Thomas

FIRST EDITION

Published by Vantage Press, Inc.
419 Park Ave. South, New York, NY 10016

Manufactured in the United States of America

ISBN: 0-533-15281-X

Library of Congress Catalog Card No.: 2005908809

0 9 8 7 6 5 4 3 2 1

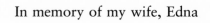

In memory of my wife, Edna

Contents

Notes on the Text

I have used *The New American Bible* as the biblical source of quotes.

I have used two translations of the Koran. One is from *Everyman's Library*, translated by Rev. J. M. Rodwell, M. A., and published by E. P. Dutton and Co. The suras are arranged in chronological order, that is, in the order in which they were revealed to Mohammed. It is written in Jacobean English, the same as used in the King James Version of the Christian Bible.

The other is from *Penguin Classics*, translated by N. J. Dawood, and published by Penguin Books. The suras are arranged in the classic manner, that is, in the order in which they were arranged shortly after Mohammed's death. This is the translation used by Salman Rushdie in his controversial book, *The Satanic Verses*. It is written in modern English; therefore all the passages quoted in this work were taken from this translation unless otherwise noted.

I have also used the numbering of the verses found in Dawood's translation. They are often slightly different in not only Rodwell's translation, but in other translations that I have seen.

The reader should know that the entire Koran is in the archangel Gabriel's words, and Gabriel is speaking for God. So, when you read, "After We had destroyed the first generation . . . ," The "We" is God using the royal pronoun. When you read, "All will return to Us . . . ," God is again using the royal pronoun. This will be taken up in more detail in the INTRODUCTION.

When you read, "Say: 'Bring down from God a scripture . . . ' " it is Gabriel telling Mohammed what to say to the people.

Italics are used in transition passages and in parenthetical explanations. Bold type is used for quotes from the Bible.

Introduction

The Life of Mohammed, and the Origin of the Koran

Mohammed was born in Mecca in the year 570, the posthumous son of Abdullah bin Abd al-Muttalib of the Quaraysh (Koreisch) tribe. His mother, Aminah, died in 576 when Mohammed was six. He was brought up first by a loving grandfather and then by his uncle Abu Talib. As a youth he traveled with the trading caravans from Mecca to Syria. At the age of twenty-five he married forty-year-old Khadijah, who had become rich in the caravan trade.

It was a time of great change in his tribe. Only two generations earlier they had lived a harsh nomadic life in the desert, always in a grim struggle for survival. Now they had become extremely successful in trade and had settled in Mecca. Their drastically altered lifestyle meant that the old tribal values had been superseded by a ruthless capitalism where the rich no longer shared with the poor and where the tribal members no longer depended on each other for mere survival.

Karen Armstrong in *History of God* says that "Mohammed was convinced that unless the Quaraysh learned to put another transcendent value at the center of their lives and overcome their egotism and greed, his tribe would tear itself apart morally and politically in internecine strife."

Although his tribe worshiped many gods, they did believe that al-Lah was the chief god. But there were 360 others whose idols sat in the sand around the Ka'bah.

The Ka'bah was already of great antiquity. Arabs had been making a pilgrimage ("hajj") to it for centuries, circumambulating it like present-day Muslims. The Koran states that Abraham and Ishmael built it. Muslim tradition holds that it was actually *re*built on the exact spot where Adam had built the first one which was destroyed by the Flood.

(For further details of the Ka'bah, see Chapter 16, Section 3, ABRAHAM.)

It was Mohammed's habit to periodically retire to a cave on Mount Hira, near Mecca, to pray and meditate. According to Muslim tradition, on the 17th night in the month of Ramadan—the 9th month in the Muslim year—Mohammed was in the cave and was torn from sleep by the angel Gabriel, who said to him, "Recite!"

At first, Mohammed refused. He said to Gabriel, "I am no reciter!"

Gabriel enveloped him in an overpowering embrace three times before Mohammed agreed. He suddenly began reciting with these words:

> "Recite in the name of your Lord who created, created man from clots of blood. Recite! Your Lord is the Most Bountiful One, who by the pen taught man what he did not know. Indeed, man transgresses in thinking himself his own master: for to your Lord all things return. Observe the man who rebukes Our servant (*Mohammed*) when he prays." (Sura #1 in Rodwell, #96 in Dawood.)

The word of God had been spoken for the first time in Arabic, and ultimately further recitations would be called the Koran. The root of the word "Koran" (sometimes transliterated as "Qu'ran") is *karaa,* which means "to address" or "to recite" or "to cry aloud." The speaker in all Suras is Gabriel, speaking to Mohammed, speaking for God, telling Mohammed what to recite to his fellow Arabs.

There is a parallel in Isaiah 58:1—(*God speaking to Isaiah*):

> Cry out full-throated and unsparingly, lift up your voice like a trumpet blast; tell my people their wickedness and the house of Jacob their sins.

Mohammed was terrified, thinking he had been possessed by a jinn, a capricious spirit that could lead a person into error. He rushed from the cave, determined to kill himself by leaping from the mountain. But then he had another vision, which he later described to his new converts:

> When I was midway on the mountain, I heard a voice from heaven saying, "Mohammed! You are the apostle of God and I am Gabriel."
> I raised my head towards heaven to see who was speaking, and lo,

Gabriel in the form of a man with feet astride the horizon . . . I stood gazing at him, moving neither backward or forward; then I began to turn my face away from him, but towards whatever region of the sky I looked, I saw him as before.

Mohammed returned home, and, still trembling violently, crawled on hands and knees to Khadija and flung himself into her lap. "Cover me! Cover me!" he cried, begging her to throw her cloak over him to shield him from the divine presence. A controversial tradition holds that Gabriel then came to Mohammed and made him recite the second sura—74th in Dawood—which starts out like this:

You that are wrapped up in your cloak, arise and give warning. Magnify your Lord, purify your garments, and keep away from uncleanness. Bestow no favors expecting gain. Be patient for your Lord's sake. The day the Trumpet sounds shall be a hard and joyless day for the unbelievers.

Later, then, Khadijah convinced him that he had not been possessed by a jinn and suggested that he consult with her Christian cousin Waraqa ibn Nawfal. Waraqa had no doubt at all that Mohammed had received a revelation from the God of Moses and the prophets and would become an envoy to the Arabs.

He was 40 years old when he received this first revelation.

Mohammed firmly believed that he was the messenger of God, sent to confirm previous scriptures (the Torah, the first five books of the Hebrew Bible and Christian Old Testament), and the gospels (the first four books of the New Testament). Sura 10:37 quotes Gabriel as saying to Mohammed:

This Koran could not have been devised by any but God. It confirms what was revealed before it and fully explains the scriptures. It is beyond doubt from the Lord of the Universe.

In Sura 2:129, Gabriel quotes Abraham as saying:

"Lord, send forth to them (*the Arabs*) as apostle of their own who shall declare to them Your revelations, and shall instruct them in the Book and in wisdom, and shall purify them of sin. You are the Mighty, the Wise."

This is almost identical to a declaration by Moses to the Israelites in Deuteronomy 18:15, which is considered to be messianic prophecy by both Christians and Jews:

"A prophet like me will the Lord, your God, raise up for you from among your own kinsmen; to him you shall listen."

Mohammed believed that God had revealed His will to the Jews and the Christians through chosen apostles, but they disobeyed God's commandments and divided themselves into sects. God had expressly commanded them to worship none but Him, but they had gone astray. It was Mohammed's duty then to bring them—and his own tribesmen—back to the true religion preached by Abraham.

He was aware that for at least 100 years—perhaps as long as 200 years—there had been a sect of "Hanyfs" in Syria. (The root from which *Hanyf* is derived means *to turn* from good to bad, or vice versa, and is equivalent to *convert* or *pervert*.) These people claimed to have rediscovered the religion of Abraham, who, having lived before either the Old or the New Testament was revealed, was neither Christian nor Jew, and who believed in the One True God. Mohammed himself at first claimed to be a Hanyf, being unable to accept either Judaism or Christianity, but was intent upon giving up idolatry. He later exchanged that term for "Muslim," one who surrenders himself to God.

For three years Mohammed had no more visions. He labored in comparative privacy for those three years and made forty converts. His wife Khadijah was the first. Abu Bekr, Khadijah's father, was the most important; he became the first caliph after Mohammed died. About 25 years after Mohammed's death he founded the Sunni division of Islam. The Shiite division was formed by Ali ibn Abi Talib, Mohammed's cousin and his daughter Fatimah's husband.

Then the visions began again and lasted for 20 years. Most present-day Muslims insist that all of the Koran was dictated by Gabriel and memorized by Mohammed. Since Mohammed was illiterate, his recitations were written down by others. Mohammed himself professed ignorance of other sources. Most Muslims hold that in those passages that seem to show Mohammed's knowledge of the Bible, it is God who has that knowledge and is passing it on to Mohammed through Gabriel. In contrast, most non-Muslims believe that the Meccan Suras show that during the three-year interval Mohammed gained a more intimate acquaintance with the Bible, both Jewish and Christian scriptures.

Originally the verses were written down in four separate collections, but in 644, twelve years after Mohammed's death, Zaid ibn Thabit collected all the known written verses into an authorized version of the Koran. He wrote that he gathered them "from date leaves, tablets of white stone, and from the breasts of men."

In ten places in the Koran, Mohammed explains why the Koran must be written and read in Arabic. Here is one of them:

43:2—We have revealed the Koran in the Arabic tongue that you may understand its meaning.

Zaid was scrupulously honest as a compiler. Not in any way did he dare tamper with the sacred text. He made no attempt to put the Suras in any chronological order, nor did he try to suppress contradictory or inaccurate statements. Modern Muslims concede that there are 225 verses that contradict others in the Koran.

Attempts have been made by Noldeke, Grimme, Rodwell, and Bell to arrange the Suras in chronological order. Although not entirely successful, one does note striking and interesting contrasts between the earlier, middle and later Suras. Rodwell writes in the Preface to his translation, "In the Suras as far as the 54th, we cannot but notice the entire predominance of the poetical element, a deep appreciation of the beauty of natural objects, brief fragmentary and impassioned utterances, denunciations of woe and punishment . . . With a change, however, in the position of Mohammed when he openly assumes the office of 'public warner,' the Suras begin to assume a more prosaic and didactic tone, though the poetical ornament of rhyme is preserved throughout. We gradually lose the Poet . . . make way for gradually increasing historical statements . . . while in the 29 Suras revealed at Medina, we no longer listen to vague words, but to the earnest disputant with the enemies of the faith."

Most Muslims and non-Muslim commentators agree that the poetical parts are Mohammed's own creation. But most non-Muslims think that there were certainly other sources: the legends of his time and country, Jewish traditions based on the Talmud and the

Hebrew Bible, and the Christian traditions of Arabia, Persia, and southern Syria. For example, he may have owed his descriptions of Heaven and Hell to Salman the Persian for they are analogous to those of the Zendavesta. He may have learned about the Hebrew Bible from the Jewish clans in and around both Mecca and Medina. He may well have learned of both the canonical and apocryphal Christian scriptures from many sources: the monk Sergius (such as the Infancy Gospel of James and the Infancy Gospel of Thomas), from the Christian slaves in Mecca, from his wife's Christian cousin Waraqa ibn Nawfal, and from members of several Christian Arab tribes near Mecca.

As we may have noted above, Mohammed firmly believed that he was chosen by God to reveal his visions to his idolatrous tribesmen. This is stated innumerable times in the Koran. One example:

> 33:7–8, 40—We made a covenant with you (*Mohammed*) as We did with the other prophets: with Noah and Abraham, with Moses and Jesus, the son of Mary. A solemn covenant We made with them, so that He might question the truthful about their truthfulness . . . Mohammed is the father of no man among you (*Mohammed left no male heirs*). He is the Apostle of God and the Seal of the Prophets. (See also 53:1–4 and 17:105–107 for two other examples.)

Mohammed therefore became the **fifth—and last—major prophet,** the **seal** of the prophets.

The final rupture between Mohammed and his tribe, the Quaraysh, dates from the incident of the Satanic verses. Three female Arabian deities—"the daughters of God"—were particularly dear to the Arabs of the Hijaz: al-Lat, al-Uzza, and Manat. Mohammed's converts at first assumed that they could continue to worship these goddesses. Mohammed forbade them, then became distressed when this proscription caused a rift between him and his tribe. So unknowingly inspired by Satan, he uttered some verses which allowed the "daughters of God" to be venerated as intercessors.

But then Gabriel recognized—and told Mohammed—that these verses were of Satanic origin and ordered them to be replaced by the following, in Sura 53:19–26:

> Have you, then, ever considered al-Lat, al-Uzza, as well as Manat, the third and last of this triad? . . . These (*allegedly divine beings*) are

nothing but empty names which you have invented—you and your forefathers—for which God has bestowed no warrant from on high. They (*who worship them*) follow nothing but surmise and their own wishful thinking—although right guidance has now indeed come unto them from their Sustainer.

Now Mohammed did lose most of his converts. The remnant who remained loyal became a despised minority. In fact, in 616—six years after his first revelation—Mohammed was forced by the Meccans to flee for his life to Ethiopia. It is not known how long he stayed there. It must have been less than a year because it is recorded that in 617 he converted a certain Omar back in Arabia. From this point, Mohammed became a jealous monotheist and idolatry became the greatest sin in Islam.

Khadijah died in 619 and Mohammed married many times after that, despite his edict in the Koran that a Muslim man could not have more than four wives at any one time. This is discussed more thoroughly in Chapter 12, ATTITUDES TOWARDS FEMALES.

In 620, he had a vision of a night journey:

Sura 17:1–2—Glory be to Him who made His servant go by night from the Sacred Temple (*the Ka'bah in Mecca*) to the farther Temple (*the Jewish Temple in Jerusalem*), whose surroundings We have blessed, that We might show him some of Our signs.

Since the Koran does not give the details of the journey, most Muslims believe that it was a spiritual journey, a vision. Some Muslims believe that Mohammed actually did make this journey to the Temple Mount in Jerusalem on the back of the flying horse Borak, accompanied by Gabriel. There he was greeted by Abraham, Moses, Jesus and a crowd of other prophets who all confirmed that Mohammed had indeed been called by God to be a prophet with the mission of leading his people back to the one true God. Then he and Gabriel ascended on a ladder to the throne of God above the seventh heaven. Each of the seven heavens was presided over by a prophet. From God's throne they flew back to Mecca. The Koran does not record these details nor what was said at the meeting between God and Mohammed.

In 622 he was again forced by the hostile Meccans to flee for his life. This time he went to the city of Yathrib, which became known as Medinat-en-nabi, "The City of the Prophet," or El Medina, "The City," and it is now known simply as Medina. He made treaties with the Christian tribes there. He also was well accepted by the three clans of Jews because they recognized at once that he worshiped the One True God. It is believed by non-Muslims that it was here that Mohammed learned more of the stories of the Hebrew Bible. Mohammed now adapted Islam to bring it closer to Judaism. He prescribed a fast on the Jewish Day of Atonement. He commanded prayers three times a day instead of two. He allowed Muslims to marry Jewish converts to Islam. He commanded Muslims to pray towards Jerusalem.

It was a short-lived truce, for when the Jews insisted that the era of the prophets had ended with their own prophets, and that their laws had been the end of God's revelations, they became bitter enemies. It was perhaps the greatest disappointment in Mohammed's life. Some Jews did remain friendly and it was from them that he may have learned the biblical stories.

Especially interesting to him was the Jewish legend that when Sarah drove Hagar and Ishmael out of Abraham's camp, they went to southern Arabia where the angel Gabriel answered their plea for water by causing the spring of Zamzam to gush forth where little Ishmael had kicked his heels. Mecca was later built around Zamzam as a stopping place for the caravans passing from Yemen to Syria along the Red Sea.

So Mohammed learned that Ishmael was the ancestor of the Arabs, music to his ears for he was now bringing the Arabs their own scripture. Later, however, when he recited the story of Ishmael's birth, Sarah is clearly his mother. There is no mention of Hagar in the Koran. (See the story of Abraham in Chapter 16.)

Meanwhile the tension grew between the Muslims in Medina and Mohammed's own tribe of the Quaraysh back in Mecca. The Battle of Bedr probably took place in 622, a fight between the Muslims and Quarayshis. A thousand men marched from Mecca to Medina and were vanquished by 319 Muslim followers of Mohammed. (For further details of that battle, see Chapter 11, ANGELS.)

Five years later, in 627, the Muslims in Medina were placed in siege by a coalition of Jews and idolatrous Arabs. The attackers were driven off, and Mohammed retaliated by killing or capturing the entire Jewish tribe of Quarayzah. In 628, a truce was signed with the Quaraysh in Mecca, giving Mohammed the right to proselytize without hindrance. Mohammed responded by putting the Jewish tribe of Khaybar to the sword.

In 630 the Quaraysh broke the truce. So, Mohammed attacked Mecca and took it. The entire population converted and the Ka'bah was established as the religious center of Islam. In the next year all of the Arabian tribes accepted Islam.

Mohammed died on 8 June, 632, in Medina, three months after a triumphant farewell pilgrimage to Mecca.

The Same God?

1

There Is One God and He Cannot Have a Son

In the Name of God the Compassionate the Merciful

Throughout the Koran, Mohammed reminds us dozens of times that there is only one God and tells us in eighteen places that God cannot have a son. Specifically this means that there can be no Trinity as most Christians believe. In most places, Mohammed repeats the same phrase, "God is One." But occasionally there are variations, some of which we shall now look at.

Since the concepts of One God and No Son are frequently intertwined in the Koran, I have opted to collect those sayings into this one chapter. Where there is clear agreement or disagreement in the Bible, I shall quote that passage in the appropriate spot.

Koran 73:8–9—Remember the name of your Lord and dedicate yourself to Him utterly. He is the Lord of the East and of the West: there is no god but Him.

Exodus 20:2—**You shall not have other gods besides me.** (*This is the second of the Ten Commandments given Moses on Mt. Sinai/Horeb.*)

Mark 12:28–29—**One of the scribes, when he came forward and heard them disputing and saw how well he (*Jesus*) had answered them, asked him, "Which is the first of all the commandments?" Jesus replied, "Hear, O Israel! The Lord our God is Lord alone!"**

Koran 38:7—"We have not heard of this (*monotheism*) in the Christian faith. It is nothing but a false invention. Was the Word revealed to him (*Jesus*) alone among us?" (*Mohammed implies here that Christians in "worshiping" the Trinity do not believe in Monotheism.*)

John 14:6—**Jesus said, "I am the way, the truth, and the life. No one comes to the Father except through me. If you know me,**

1

then you will also know my Father. From now on you do know him and have seen him."

1 Corinthians 8:4b–6—(*Paul writing to the church in Corinth*) There is no God but one.

1 Timothy 2:5—(*Paul writing pastoral instructions to Timothy*) For there is one God and one mediator between God and the human race. Christ Jesus, himself human, who gave himself as ransom for all.

Koran 57:3—He is the First and the Last, the Visible and the Unseen.

Revelation 21:6—(*Jesus speaking in John's vision*) I am the Alpha and the Omega, the beginning and the end.

Koran 4:171, 173—The Messiah, Jesus the son of Mary, was no more than God's apostle . . . So believe in God and His apostles and do not say "Three." God is but one God. God forbid that He should have a son.

Colossians 1:15, 19–20a—(*Paul writing to the church in Colossae*) He (*Jesus*) is the image of the invisible God, the firstborn of all creation. For in him all the fullness (*of the deity*) was pleased to dwell, and through him to reconcile all things for him. (*Most Christians believe that God was in Jesus, so they do not believe that they are worshiping more than one God.*)

Luke 4:21–22—After all the people had been baptized and Jesus also had been baptized and was praying, heaven was opened and the holy Spirit descended upon him in bodily form like a dove. And a voice came from heaven, "You are my beloved Son; with whom I am well pleased."

John 1:1–3—In the beginning was the Word, and the Word was with God, and the Word was God. He (*Jesus*) was in the beginning with God. All things came to be through him, and without him nothing came to be.

Matthew 16:15–17—He (*Jesus*) said to them, "But who do you say that I am?" Simon Peter said in reply, "You are the Messiah, the Son of the Living God."

Koran 59:23—He is God, besides whom there is no other deity. He is the Sovereign Lord, the Holy One, the Giver of Peace, the Keeper of Faith; the Guardian, the Mighty One, the All-powerful, the Most High! Exalted be He above their idols. He is God, the

Creator, the Originator, the Modeler. He is the Mighty, the Wise One. His are the most gracious names.

God is called by 99 names in the Koran. Many Muslims carry a rosary to help them remember all the names. The Old Testament uses 17 different names for God, some of which are Adonai, El and its plural Elohim, Shaddai, Jehovah and Yahweh, the latter always written as the tetragammaton YHWH.

The following prophecy was written by Isaiah in the 8th century BCE. *It is considered by both Christians and Jews as messianic, but Jews do not believe that Jesus fulfilled the prophecy and are still waiting.*

Isaiah 9:5–6—For a child is born to us, a son is given us; upon his shoulder dominion rests. They name him Wonderful, Counselor, the Mighty God, the Everlasting Father, the Prince of Peace. His dominion is vast and forever peaceful.

Koran 5:114–116—Then God will say: "Jesus, son of Mary, did you ever say to mankind, 'Worship me and my mother as gods besides God?' " "Glory to You," he will answer, "how could I ever say that to which I have no right? If I had ever said so, You would have surely known it."

Koran 19:88–90—Those who say: "The Lord of Mercy has begotten a son," preach a monstrous falsehood, at which the very heavens might crack, the earth break asunder, and the mountains crumble to dust. That they should ascribe a son to the Merciful, when it does not become the Lord of Mercy to beget one! (See also 23:90–91, 21:26–28, 17:111, 39:4, 6:102.)

Luke 1:30–32, 35—Then the angel (*Gabriel*) said to her, "Do not be afraid, Mary, for you have found favor with God. Behold, you will conceive in your womb and bear a son, and you shall name him Jesus. He will be great and will be called Son of the Most High, and the Lord God will give him the throne of David his father . . . Therefore the child to be born will be called holy, the Son of God."

Mark 15:37, 39—(*Jesus is dying on the cross*) Jesus gave a loud cry and breathed his last . . . When the centurion who stood facing him saw how he breathed his last, he said, "Truly, this man was the Son of God."

2
Praise Be to God

In the Name of God the Compassionate the Merciful

In Dawood's version of the Koran, the first Sura is the "Exordium," the beginning of the speech, or in this case, the recitation. According to Rodwell, it was probably the eighth Sura to be revealed to Mohammed. A prayer of praise and supplication, it is recited several times in each of the five daily prayers and also on many other occasions, such as in concluding a bargain. Muslims call it by many names, some of which are "the Opening of the Book," "the Completion," "the Sufficing Sura," "the Sura of Praise, Thanks, and Prayer," "the Healer," "the Remedy," "the Basis," "the Treasure," "the Mother of the Book," "the Seven Verses of Repetition." It always ends with "Amen," Mohammed having been instructed by Gabriel to do so.

THE EXORDIUM—FATIHAH

Praise be to God, Lord of the Universe,
The Compassionate, the Merciful,
Sovereign of the Day of Judgement!
You alone we worship, and to You alone
we turn for help.
Guide us to the straight path.
The path of those whom You have favored,
Not of those who have gone astray.
Amen

The following transliteration of this Sura from Arabic script into English letters will give the reader some idea of the rhyming poetry in which the entire Koran is written:

4

Bismillahi 'rahhmani 'rrahheem
El-hamdu lillahi rabi 'lalameen
Arrahhmani raheem
Maliki yowmi-d-deen
Eyaka nabudu, waéyaka nestāeen
Ihdinat 'ssirat almostakeen
Sirat alezeena anhamta aleihim
Gheiri-l mughdubi aleihim
Wala dsaleen. Ameen.

The closest parallel in the Bible is the prayer that Jesus taught his disciples, which Christians call the Lord's Prayer. It is found in Matthew 6:9–13:

**Our Father in heaven
hallowed be your name,
your kingdom come,
your will be done, on earth as it is in heaven.
Give us today our daily bread,
and forgive us our debts
as we forgive our debtors,
and do not subject us to the final test
but deliver us from evil.
Amen**

Later redactors added the words to the KJV, **"For thine is the kingdom, the power, and the glory, forever."**

Giving praise and glory to God is a major theme in both the Koran and the Bible. First, some examples from the Koran:

Koran 87:1–7—Praise the Name of your Lord, the Most High, who has created all things and proportioned them; who has ordained their destinies and guided them; who brings forth the green pasture, then turns it to withered grass.

Koran 24:35–38—God is the light of the heavens and the earth. His light may be compared to a niche that enshrines a lamp, the lamp within a crystal of star-like brilliance. It is lit from a blessed olive tree neither eastern nor western. Its very oil would almost shine forth, though no fire touched it. Light upon light; God guides to His light whom He will. (See also 21:19, 21:41, 22:18a.)

And from the Bible:

Isaiah 9:1—The people who walked in darkness have seen a great light; upon those who dwelt in the land of gloom a light has shone.

Psalm 150—Praise God in his holy sanctuary, give praise in the mighty dome of heaven. Give praise for his mighty deeds, praise him for his great majesty. Give praise with blasts upon the horn, praise him with harp and lyre. Give praise with tambourines and dance, praise him with flutes and strings. Give praise with crashing cymbals, praise him with sounding cymbals. Let everything that has breath give praise to the Lord! Hallelujah. (See also Matthew 5:14–16, and Psalms 30:1–4.)

3

The Five Pillars of Islam

In the Name of God the Compassionate the Merciful

In this and the next chapter we shall look at what the Koran and the Bible say about the duties of believers. Wherever possible I shall correlate the duties of Muslim believers with the duties of Christian believers. There are, of course, many similarities, but also many differences.

Nowhere in the Koran does Mohammed say anything about "pillars of Islam," but he is reported to have said to his followers, "Islam is based on five pillars." The passages that describe these "pillars" are not collected in one place but are distributed throughout the Koran. So therefore I have collected passages that illustrate the Five Pillars and have matched them with passages from the Bible.

The Five Pillars are:

1) Witness to the belief that there is one God and Mohammed is His apostle
2) Alms-giving
3) Fasting
4) Prayer
5) A pilgrimage to Mecca

Subsumed under "Witness" are five elements:

a) Belief in one God
b) Belief in angels which do the will of God
c) Belief in the Torah and the Gospel
d) Belief in the prophets as examples to follow
e) Belief in the Day of Judgment and the Resurrection.

7

There are many other duties (injunctions, orders, prescriptions, proscriptions, etc.) distributed throughout the Koran. I have collected these and will correlate them with the Bible in the next chapter.

The five pillars of Islam:

Pillar #1—Witness

a) Belief that there is one God and Mohammed is his apostle (or prophet):

> Koran 51:51—Set up no deity besides God. I come from Him to warn you plainly. (See also 73:8–9.)
> Koran 33:40—He (*Mohammed*) is the Apostle of God and the Seal of the Prophets. (See also 17:105–107.)
> *Several references to "one God" in the Bible have been quoted in Chapter 1, THERE IS ONE GOD. One more is quoted here to round out the comparison of the Bible with this section of the Five Pillars:*
> **Isaiah 45:5–6—I am the Lord and there is no other, there is no God besides me. It is I who arm you, though you know me not, so that toward the rising and the setting of the sun, men may know that there is none besides me.**

b) Belief in angels that do the will of God:

> Koran 41:30–31—As for those who say: "Our Lord is God," and take the straight path to Him, the angels will descend to them, saying: "Let nothing alarm or grieve you. Rejoice in the Paradise you have been promised. We are your guardians in this world and in the hereafter." (See also 81:10.)
> **Matthew 4:11—(*Jesus has just successfully resisted the devil's temptation in the wilderness*) Then the devil left him and, behold, angels came and ministered to him.**
> **Luke 22:41–43—(*Jesus is on the Mount of Olives on the night he was betrayed*) After withdrawing about a**

stone's throw from them and kneeling, he prayed, saying, "Father, if you are willing, take this cup away from me; still, not my will but yours be done." And to strengthen him an angel from heaven appeared to him.

c) Belief in the Torah and the Gospel:

Koran 3:2–4—He has revealed to you the Book of Truth, confirming the scriptures which preceded it, for He has already revealed the Torah and the Gospel for the guidance of mankind. (See also 5:46.)

Acts 17:2—Following his usual custom, Paul joined them and for three sabbaths he entered into discussions with them from the scriptures. (See also 17:11a.)

d) Belief in the prophets as examples to follow:

Koran 33:7–8—We made a covenant with you (*Mohammed*) as We did with the other prophets: with Noah and Abraham, with Moses and Jesus, the son of Mary.

Malachai 2:4–5—(*The Lord speaking through Malachi*) Then you will know that I sent you (*the priests*) this commandment because I have a covenant with Levi, says the Lord of hosts. My covenant with him was one of life and peace; fear I put in him and he feared me, and stood in awe of my name.

e) Belief in the Day of Judgment and in the Resurrection: This is discussed in Chapter 23, THE RESURRECTION, and Chapter 24, THE FINAL DAY.

Pillar #2—The giving of alms

Koran 9:60–61—Alms shall be only for the poor and the destitute, for those that are engaged in the management of alms and those whose hearts are sympathetic to the Faith, or the freeing of slaves and debtors, for the advancement of God's cause, and for the traveler in need. That is a duty enjoined by God.

Koran 2:261—Those that give their wealth for the cause of God can be compared to a grain of corn which brings forth seven ears, each bearing a hundred grains.

Koran 1:271—To be charitable in public is good, but to give alms to the poor in private is better and will atone for some of your sins.

Matthew 6:4—(*Jesus preaching*) When you give alms, do not let your left hand know what your right hand is doing, so that your almsgiving may be secret. And your Father who sees in secret will repay you.

Koran 2:273—Whatever alms you give shall rebound to your own advantage, provided that you give them for the love of God. And whatever alms you give shall be paid back to you in full; you shall not be wronged.

Ecclesiastes 11:1—Cast your bread upon the waters; after a long time you may find it again.

Koran 3:93—You shall never be truly righteous until you give in alms what you dearly cherish (See also 2:267.)

Luke 21:1–3—When he (*Jesus*) looked up he saw some wealthy people putting their offerings into the treasury and he noticed a poor widow putting in two small coins. He said, "I tell you truly, this poor widow put in more than all the rest, for those others have all made offerings from their surplus wealth, but she, from her poverty, has offered her whole livelihood." (See also Luke 11:39–42, Luke 12:32–34, and Acts 8:18–22.)

Koran 2:195—Give generously for the cause of God and do not with your own hands cast yourselves into destruction. (*Rodwell notes that this passage seems to indicate that man does have free will, in contradiction of the doctrine of predestination, which I will discuss in Chapter 6.*)

1 Timothy 6:10—For the love of money is the root of all evils, and some people in their desire for it have strayed from the faith and have pierced themselves with many pains.

Pillar #3a.—Fasting as an obligation

Koran 2:183–185—Believers, fasting is decreed for you as it was decreed for those before you; perchance you will guard yourselves against evil. Fast a certain number of days, but if any among you is

10

ill or on a journey, let him fast a similar number of days later, and for those that cannot endure it there is a ransom: the feeding of a poor man . . . In the month of Ramadan the Koran was revealed . . . God desires your well-being, not your discomfort. He desires you to fast the whole month (*of Ramadan*) so that you may magnify God and render thanks to Him for giving you His guidance. (*The fast is for daylight hours only, and includes drinking no liquids and abstinence from sex.*)

Isaiah 58:3b—Would that today you might fast so as to make your voice heard on high!

Matthew 4:1—Then Jesus was led by the Spirit into the desert to be tempted by the devil. He fasted for forty days and forty nights, and afterwards he was hungry.

Matthew 6:16–18—(*Jesus teaching the disciples*) "When you fast, do not look gloomy like the hypocrites. They neglect their appearance, so that they may appear to others to be fasting. Amen, I say to you, they have received their reward. But when you fast, anoint your head and wash your face, so that you may not appear to be fasting, except to your Father who is hidden. And your Father who sees what is hidden will repay you."

Pillar #3b—Fasting as a penalty

Koran 5:89—The penalty for a broken oath is the feeding of ten needy men with such food as you normally offer to your own people; or the clothing of ten needy men; or the freeing of one slave. He that cannot afford any of these must fast three days.

Koran 58:3–4—Those that divorce their wives by so saying (*by declaring them to be their mothers*), and afterwards retract their words, shall free a slave before they touch each other again . . . He that has no slave shall fast two successive months before they touch one another. (*Presumably this was a daytime fast only, as during Ramadan.*)

Koran 4:92—He that accidentally kills a believer must free one Muslim slave and pay blood-money to the family of the victim. If the victim be a Muslim from a hostile tribe, the penalty is the freeing of one Muslim slave. But if the victim be a member of an allied tribe, then blood-money must be paid to his family and a Muslim slave set free. He that lacks the means must fast two consecutive months.

11

Leviticus 16:29—This shall be an everlasting ordinance for you: on the tenth day of the seventh month every one of you, whether a native or a resident alien, shall mortify himself (*which included fasting*) and shall do no work.

1 Samuel 7:3, 6—Samuel said to them (*the Israelites*), "If you wish with your whole heart to return to the Lord, put away your foreign gods and your Ashtaroth (*the Syrian goddess of love and fertility*), devote yourselves to the Lord, and worship him alone." . . . When they were gathered at Mizpah, they drew water and poured it out on the ground before the Lord, and they fasted that day, confessing, "We have sinned against the Lord."

1 Samuel 31:11–13—When the inhabitants of Jabesh-gilead heard what the Philistines had done to Saul, all their warriors set out, and after marching throughout the night, removed the bodies of Saul and his sons from the wall of Beth-shan, and brought them to Jabesh, where they cremated them. Then they took their bones and buried them under the tamarisk tree in Jabesh, and fasted for seven days. (See also 2 Samuel 12:15b–17 and Joel 1:13–14.)

Pillar #4—Prayers

Koran 17:78—Recite your prayers at sunset, at nightfall, and at dawn; the dawn prayer has its witnesses. Pray during the night as well; an additional duty, for the fulfillment of which your Lord may exalt you to an honorable station.

Koran 2:238–239—Attend regularly to your prayers, including the middle prayer (*between noon and nightfall*), and stand up with all devotion before God.

Modern Muslims have combined these two passages to determine when they are to pray. The first times are: before dawn, noon, mid-afternoon, dusk, and any time after dark before retiring.

Psalm 55:17—But I will call upon God, and the Lord will save me. At dusk, dawn, and noon I will grieve and complain, and my prayer will be heard.

Koran 17:110–112—Pray neither with too loud a voice nor in silence, but between these extremes, seek a middle course.

Koran 7:56—Pray to the Lord with humility and in secret. Pray to Him with fear and hope; His mercy is within reach of the righteous.

Matthew 6:5–13—(*Jesus teaching the disciples*) "When you pray, do not be like the hypocrites, who love to stand and pray in the synagogues and on street corners so that others may see them. Amen, I say to you, they have received their reward. But when you pray, go to your inner room, close the door and pray to your Father in secret. And your Father who sees in secret will repay you. In praying, do not babble like the pagans, who think that they will be heard because of their many words. Do not be like them. Your Father knows what you need before you ask him." (He then taught them the "Lord's Prayer." See Chapter 2, PRAISE BE TO GOD, for that prayer.)

Matthew 14:22–23—(*Jesus has just fed the five thousand with five loaves and two fish.*) Then he made the disciples get into the boat and precede him to the other side, while he dismissed the crowds. After doing so, he went up on the mountain by himself to pray.When it was evening he was there alone. (*Note that this was also Mohammed's custom.*) (See also Luke 11:9, 11–13, Luke 18:9–14, and Mark 9:28–29.)

Koran 62:9–10—Believers, when you are summoned to Friday prayers, hasten to the remembrance of God and cease your trading. That would be best for you, if you but knew it. Then, when the prayers are ended, disperse and go your ways in quest of God's bounty. (*"Friday prayers" are different from the Sabbath observed by Christians and Jews. Every Muslim who is able to do so, leaves whatever he/she is doing and goes to the mosque at noon on Friday for a 30-60 minute service of lengthy prayers, reading from the Koran, and often a homily. Then he/she returns to his/her usual occupation. It is said that Friday was chosen because Mohammed first entered Medina on a Friday, and also, creation was finished on a Friday. Most Jews observe the Sabbath from 6 PM Friday to 6 PM Saturday. Most Christians observe the Sabbath on Sunday.*)

Koran 4:43–45—Believers, do not approach your prayers when you are drunk, but wait till you can grasp the meaning of your words, nor when you are polluted—unless you are traveling the road—until you have washed yourselves; or, if you have relieved yourselves or had intercourse with women while traveling and can find no water, take some clean sand and rub your faces and your hands with it. Gracious is God and forgiving.

13

1 Thessalonians 5:16–18—(*Paul writing to the church in Thessalonika*) Rejoice always. Pray without ceasing. In all circumstances give thanks, for this is the will of God for you in Christ Jesus.

Mark 11:24–25—(*Jesus teaching*) Therefore I tell you, all that you ask for in prayer, believe that you will receive it and it shall be yours. When you stand to pray, forgive anyone against whom you have a grievance, so that your heavenly Father may in turn forgive you your transgressions.

Koran 2:186a—When My servants question you about Me, tell them that I am near. I answer the prayer of the suppliant when he calls to Me; therefore let them answer My call and put their trust in Me, that they may be rightly guided.

Jeremiah 29:12–14a—(*Jeremiah in Jerusalem sending the words of the Lord by letter to the Israelites in exile in Babylon*) Thus says the Lord: When you call me, when you go to pray to me, I will listen to you. When you look for me, you will find me. Yes, when you seek me with all your heart, you will find me with you, says the Lord, and I will change your lot.

Philippians 4:6—(*Paul writing to the church in Philippi*) Have no anxiety at all, but in everything, by prayer and petition, with thanksgiving, make your requests known to God. Then the peace of God that surpasses all understanding will guard your hearts and minds in Christ Jesus.

James 5:13–16—(*The brother of Jesus, in Jerusalem, writing to the "twelve tribes of the dispersion," a euphemism for all Jews throughout the world*) Is anyone among you suffering? He should pray. Is anyone in good spirits? He should sing praise. Is anyone among you sick? He should summon the presbyters of the church, and they should pray over him and anoint him with oil in the name of the Lord, and the prayer of faith will save the sick person, and the Lord will raise him up. (*One of the key verses for members of the Christian Scientist faith.*)

Acts 2:13–14—(*After the resurrection of Jesus*) When they entered the city they went to the upper room where they were staying, Peter and John and James and Andrew, Philip, and Thomas, Bartholomew and Matthew, James son of Alphaeus, Simon the Zealot, and Judas, son of James. All these devoted themselves with one accord to prayer, together with some women, and Mary the mother of Jesus, and his brothers. (*James, son of Alphaeus, is to be distinguished from James, brother of Jesus. The latter was not a disciple during Jesus' lifetime, but did become an apostle after Jesus was crucified. Note, too, that Judas, son of James, is to be distinguished from Judas Iscariot, betrayer of Jesus.)*

Pillar #5—The pilgrimage (hajj)

Koran 2:196a, 197—Make the pilgrimage and visit the Sacred House (*Ka'bah*) for His sake. If you cannot, send such offerings as you can afford and do not shave your heads until the offerings have reached their destination. Make the pilgrimage in the appointed months. He that intends to perform it in those months must abstain from sexual intercourse, obscene language, and acrimonious disputes while on pilgrimage. (*The "greater pilgrimage"—the one obligatory pilgrimage that every Muslim must do once in his life if he possibly can—is made during the month of Ramadan. The "little pilgrimage" may be done at any time; its ceremonies are much fewer.*)

A pilgrimage resembling the Hajj developed in ancient Israel and continued until the destruction of the Temple by the Romans in 70 C.E. It began in Egypt as the culmination of the Israelites' escape from captivity. I shall now trace the development of this ritual.

In Exodus 12:21–25, we read the story of God "passing over" the Israelites and striking down the firstborn of the Egyptians. This first Passover observance was not a pilgrimage, but it gradually developed into one, as we shall see in the passages below.

Deuteronomy 16:1, 13, 15b, 16a—(*Moses has just come down from Mt. Sinai with detailed instructions from the Lord for the Israelites to follow. The following ordinances concern the three feasts that later became occasion for pilgrimages to Jerusalem.*) Observe the month of Abib (*later, in the exile in Babylon, renamed Nisan*) by keeping the Passover of the Lord, your God, since it was in the month of Abib that he brought you by night out of Egypt. You shall offer the Passover sacrifice from your flock or your herd to the Lord, your God, in the place which he chooses as the dwelling place of his name. (*Later this became Solomon's temple in Jerusalem, and remained so until its destruction*) . . . You shall count off seven weeks, computing them from the day when the sickle is first put to the standing grain. You shall then keep the Feast of Weeks in honor

15

of the Lord, your God . . . in the place which the Lord, your God, chooses as the dwelling place of his name (*later, Solomon's temple*) . . . You shall celebrate the Feast of Booths for seven days, when you have gathered in the produce from your threshing floor and wine press . . . in the place where He chooses . . . Three times a year, then, every male among you shall appear before the Lord, your God, in the place which he chooses: at the Feast of Unleavened Bread (*Passover*), at the Feast of Weeks, and at the Feast of Booths.

2 Chronicles 30:1, 13—Hezekiah sent a message to all Israel and Judah, and even wrote letters to Ephraim and Manasseh saying that they should come to the house of the Lord in Jerusalem to celebrate Passover in honor of the Lord, the God of Israel . . . Thus many people gathered in Jerusalem to celebrate the feast of Unleavened Bread in the second month: it was a very great assembly.

Luke 2:41–42—Each year his (*Jesus's*) parents went to Jerusalem for the feast of the Passover, and when he was twelve years old, they went up according to festival custom.

Luke 22:1–2, 7, 14—Now the Feast of Unleavened Bread, called the Passover, was drawing near, and the chief priests and the scribes were seeking a way to put him (*Jesus*) to death . . . When the day of the Feast of Unleavened Bread arrived . . . he (*Jesus*) sent out Peter and John, instructing them, "Go and make preparations for us to eat the Passover . . . " When the hour came, he took his place at table with apostles. He said to them, "I have eagerly desired to eat this Passover with you before I suffer, for I tell you, I shall not eat it again until there is fulfillment in the kingdom of God." (*This was the "Last Supper," celebrated by Christians as "Holy Communion," or the "Eucharist"*)

4

Further Duties of Believers

In the Name of God the Compassionate the Merciful

If you except the passages that tell stories about people, it could almost be said that the entire Koran deals with the duties of believers. Even Mohammed's poetry, aphorisms, proverbs, and flights of fancy illustrate in most cases some point in the religious life of a Muslim. So, to include all of them in this work would be impossible. My purpose is not to create a shortened version of the Koran and the Bible, but to juxtapose passages that have similar content. Therefore this chapter does not claim to include *all* the duties of believers in either Koran or Bible. Rather, just those that have counterparts in the other Book.

Nor have I listed these duties in any order of importance, but only as I found them in the Koran:

1) **Patience:**

Koran 70:20–35—Indeed, man was created impatient. When evil befalls him he is despondent; but, blessed with good fortune, he grows niggardly. Not so the worshippers, who are steadfast in prayer.

Hebrews 6:11–12—We earnestly desire each of you to demonstrate the same eagerness for the fulfillment of hope until the end, so that you may not become sluggish, but imitators of those who, through faith and patience are inheriting the promises.

2) **Treatment of parents:**

Koran 17:22–23—Your Lord enjoined you to worship none but Him, and to show kindness to your parents. If either or both of them attain old age in your dwelling, show them no sign of impatience, nor rebuke them, but speak to them kind words. Treat them with humility and tenderness and say: "Lord, be merciful to them. They nursed me when I was an infant."

Exodus 12:20—Honor your father and your mother, that you may have a long life in the land which the Lord, your God is giving you.

3) Suicide:

Koran 4:29—Do not kill yourselves. God is merciful to you, but he that does that through wickedness and injustice shall be burned in fire. That is easy enough for God.

Suicides occur in both Testaments:

1 Samuel 31:1–4—(Summary) At the battle of Mount Gilboa, King Saul is mortally wounded. He orders his armor-bearer to kill him. 1 Samuel 31:5—But his armor-bearer, badly frightened, refused to do it. So Saul took his own sword and fell upon it. When the armor-bearer saw that Saul was dead, he too fell upon his sword and died with him. (*There seems to be no recrimination by God for Saul's act.*)

There is a well-known suicide in the New Testament:

Matthew 27:3–5—Then Judas (Iscariot), his betrayer, seeing that Jesus had been condemned, deeply regretted what he had done. He returned the thirty pieces of silver to the chief priests and elders, saying, "I have sinned in betraying innocent blood." They said, "What is that to us? Look to it yourself." Flinging the money into the temple, he departed and went off and hanged himself. Did God punish him? We don't know.

Finally, there is a tradition in Judaism called "kiddush ha-Shem," suicide in the name of the Lord, "blessed by Abraham and all the prophets, solely for the triumph and everlasting glory of the Creator." The classic example is the mass suicide on Masada, during the final days of the Jewish Revolt against the Romans in 67-72 CE. The entire population, estimated by Josephus at 960 people, committed mass suicide rather than be captured alive by the Romans. (*The story can be found in the Works of Josephus, The Jewish War, Book 7, Chapters 8 and 9. It can also be found in a novelized version in* The Tenth Measure, *by Brenda Lesley Segal.*)

4) Stewardship of money:

Koran 17:26—Give to the near of kin their due, and also to the destitute and to the traveler in need. Do not squander your substance wastefully, for the wasteful are Satan's brothers; and Satan is ever ungrateful to his Lord.

Matthew 25:14ff—(Summary) A man leaving on a journey gives gold talents to three servants: five, two and one respectively. The first two double the money while the third buries his one talent for fear of losing it. The master is angry with the third servant for not using the money wisely. He praises the other two for being good stewards of his money.

1 Timothy 6:10—For the love of money is the root of all evils and some people in their desire for it have strayed from the faith.

5) Infanticide:

Koran 17:31—You shall not kill your children for fear of want. We will provide for them and for you. To kill them is a great sin. (*It was common practice at that time in Arabia to bury alive unwanted babies, especially females. See Chapter 12, ATTITUDES TOWARDS FEMALES, for more details on this practice.*)

Leviticus 20:1–3—The Lord said to Moses, "Tell the Israelites: Anyone, whether an Israelite or an alien residing in Israel, who gives any of his offspring to Molech, shall be put to death. Let his fellow citizens stone him." (*Molech was a Canaanite god who required sacrifice of infants by burning them alive. Despite this command, the practice was revived time and again at least up to the time of Jeremiah, in the 6th century* BCE.)

Jeremiah 32:35—They built high places to Baal in the Valley of Ben-hinnon, and immolated their sons and daughters to Molech; this I (*Jeremiah*) never commanded them, nor did it even enter my mind that they should practice such abominations.

6) Adultery:

Koran 17:32—You shall not commit adultery.

Exodus 20:14—You shall not commit adultery.

7) Homicide:

Koran 17:32—You shall not kill any man whom God has forbidden you to kill, except for a just cause.

Koran 4:92a, 93—It is unlawful for a believer to kill another believer except by accident. He that accidentally kills a believer must free one Muslim slave and pay blood-money to the family of the victim . . . He that kills a believer by design shall burn in Hell forever.

Exodus 20:13—You shall not kill.

Leviticus 24:17, 22—Whoever takes the life of any human being shall be put to death (*by stoning*) . . . You shall have but one rule for alien and native alike. I, the Lord, am your God.

Exodus 21:12–13—Whoever strikes a man a mortal blow must be put to death. He, however, who did not hunt a man down, but caused his death by an act of God, may flee to a place which I will set apart for this purpose.

The following tells how this should be done:

Numbers 35:9–13—The Lord said to Moses, "Tell the Israelites: When you go across the Jordan into the land of Canaan, select for yourselves cities to serve as cities of asylum, where a homicide who has killed someone unintentionally may take refuge. These cities shall serve you as places of asylum from the avenger of blood, so that a homicide shall not be put to death unless he is first tried before the community. Six cities of asylum shall you assign . . ."

8) Theft:

Koran 5:39—As for the man or woman who is guilty of theft, cut off their hands to punish them for their crimes. That is the punishment enjoined by God. (*This has been modified in modern-day Saudi Arabia: the left hand is cut off for the first offense, the right hand for the second.*)

Exodus 20:15—You shall not steal.

9) Honesty in business:

Koran 17:35–39—Give full measure and weigh with even scales. That is fair, and better in the end.

Deuteronomy 25:13–16—You shall not keep two differing weights in your bag, one large and the other small; nor shall you keep two different measures in your house, one large and the other small. But use a true and just weight, and a true and just measure, that you may have a long life on the land which the Lord, your God, is giving you. Everyone who is dishonest in any of these matters is an abomination to the Lord, your God.

10) Bearing true witness:

Koran 5:8–9—Believers, fulfill your duties to God and bear true witness. Do not allow your hatred for other men to turn you away from justice. Deal justly; that is nearer to true piety. Have fear of God; God is cognizant of all your actions.

Exodus 20:16—You shall not bear false witness against your neighbor.

11) Concerning pride:

Koran 31:18–19—Do not treat men with scorn, nor walk proudly on the earth: God does not love the arrogant and the vainglorious. Rather let your gait be modest and your voice low: the most hideous of voices is the braying of the ass.

1 Peter 5:5— (*Peter, or one of his disciples, teaching*) Clothe yourselves with humility in your dealings with one another, for "God opposes the proud but bestows favor on the humble." (*The quote is a paraphrase of Proverbs 3:34.*)

Micah 7:8—You have been told, O man, what is good, and what the Lord requires of you: Only to do the right and to love goodness, and to walk humbly with your God. (See also Matthew 5:3, 5.)

12) Sober worship:

Koran 4:43—Believers, do not approach your prayers when you are drunk, but wait till you can grasp the meaning of your words.

Leviticus 10:8–11—The Lord said to Aaron, "When you are to go to the meeting tent, you and your sons are forbidden under pain of death, by a perpetual ordinance throughout your generations, to drink any wine or strong drink."

13) Dress in worship, real and metaphorical:

Koran 7:25, 31—Children of Adam! We have given you clothes to cover your nakedness, and garments pleasing to the eye; but the finest of these is the robe of piety . . . Children of Adam, dress well when you attend our mosques. Eat and drink but avoid excess. (*The pagan Quaraysh tribe had forbidden food during the pre-Islamic processions around the Ka'bah and required that the only clothing that could be worn was that borrowed from Meccans. The result was that most pilgrims visited the holy places nude.*)

Ephesians 6:13–17—(*Paul writing*) Therefore, put on the armor of God, that you may be able to resist on the evil day and, having done everything, to hold your ground. So stand fast with your loins girded in truth, clothed with righteousness as a breastplate, and your feet shod in readiness for the gospel of peace. In all circumstances, hold faith as a shield, to quench all the flaming arrows of the evil one. And take the helmet of salvation and the sword of the Spirit, which is the word of God.

14) Life in this world and the next:

Koran 6:70—Avoid those that treat their faith as a sport and a pastime and are seduced by the life of this world. Admonish them with this lest their souls be damned by their own sins.

Matthew 6:19–21, 24—(*Jesus preaching*) Do not store up for yourselves treasures on earth, where moth and decay destroy, and thieves break in and steal. But store up treasures in heaven, where neither moth nor decay destroys, nor thieves break in and steal. For where your treasure is, there also will your heart be.

15) My brother's keeper?:

Koran 6:106—Avoid the pagans. Had God pleased, they would not have worshiped idols. We have not made you their keeper, nor are you their guardian.

Genesis 4:8–9—Cain said to his brother Abel, "Let us go out in the field." When they were in the field, Cain attacked his brother Abel and killed him. Then the Lord asked Cain, "Where is your brother Abel?" He answered, "I do not know. Am I my brother's keeper?" (See also Matthew 9:9–13.)

16) Keeping the commandments of God:

Koran 2:176—Righteousness does not consist in whether you face towards the East or the West. The righteous man is he who believes in God and the Last Day, in the angels and the Book (*Koran*) and the prophets; who, though he loves it dearly, gives away his wealth to kinsfolk, to orphans, to the destitute, to the traveler in need and to beggars, and for the redemption of captives; who attends to his prayers and renders the alms levy; who is true to his promises and steadfast in trial and adversity and in times of war. (*Note that this passage includes four of the five "Pillars of Islam."*)

Ecclesiastes 12:13—The last word, when all is heard: Fear God and keep his commandments, for this is man's all; because God will bring to judgement every work, with all its hidden qualities, whether good or bad.

17) Homosexuality:

Koran 4:15—If two men among you commit indecency, punish them both. If they repent and mend their ways, let them be. God is forgiving and merciful.

Koran 26:166—(*Lot speaking to the men who wanted to have sex with his two male visitors*) Will you fornicate with males and abandon your wives, whom God has created for you? Surely you are great transgressors.

Genesis 19:4–11—(Summary) The men of Sodom come to Lot's house and demand that he let them have intercourse with his two male visitors. The visitors are in fact angels who have come to rescue

Lot and his family from the coming destruction. Lot says, "I beg you, my brothers, do not do this wicked thing . . ." (See Chapter 16 for the details of Lot's story.)

Leviticus 20:13—(*Moses speaking*) If a man lies with a male as with a woman, both of them shall be put to death for their abominable deed; they have forfeited their lives.

1 Corinthians 6:9–10—(*Paul writing*) Do you not know that the unjust will not inherit the kingdom of God? Do not be deceived; neither fornicators nor idolaters nor adulterers nor boy prostitutes, nor sodomites nor thieves nor slanderers nor robbers will inherit the kingdom of God.

18) Interest and usury:

Koran 2:275a, 276—Those that live on usury shall rise up before God like men whom Satan has demented by his touch; for they claim that trading is no different from usury. But God has permitted trading and made usury unlawful. (*Strict modern-day Muslims interpret this verse to mean that no interest shall be charged.*)

Exodus 22:24–25—(*God speaking through Moses*) If you lend money to one of your poor neighbors among my people, you shall not act like an extortioner toward him by demanding interest. If you take your neighbor's cloak as a pledge, you shall return it to him before sunset; for this cloak of his is the only covering he has for his body. What else has he to sleep in? If he cries out to me, I will hear him; for I am compassionate.

Leviticus 25:36–37—Do not exact interest from your countryman either in money or in kind, but out of fear of God let him live with you. You are to lend him neither money at interest nor food at a profit.

Deuteronomy 23:21—You may demand interest from a foreigner.

By the time of Jesus, however, it was apparently not only okay to charge interest, but it was expected:

In Matthew 25:14–30, we read the story of the servants receiving gold talents to invest. One servant buries his talent. The story finishes with this tongue lashing, "You wicked, lazy servant! Should you not then have put my money in the bank so that I could have got it back with interest on my return?"

19) Legal witnesses to a debt:

Koran 2:282a—Believers, when you contract a debt for a fixed period, put it in writing. Let a scribe write it down for you with fairness . . . If the debtor be an ignorant or feeble-minded person, or one who cannot dictate, let his guardian dictate for him in fairness. Call in two male witnesses, but if two men cannot be found, then one man and two women, so that if either of them (*women*) commit an error, the other will remind her.

Deuteronomy 19:15—One witness alone shall not take the stand against a man in regard to any crime or any offense of which he may be guilty; a judicial fact shall be established only on the testimony of two or three witnesses. (*This presumably includes debtors, although neither Old nor New Testament contain any actual rule regarding witnesses to a debt.*)

20) Family as enemy:

Koran 64:14–16—Believers, you have an enemy in your spouses and in your children: beware of them (*because they will beguile you from your duty, especially that of contending for the faith*).

Matthew 10:34–36—(*Jesus speaking to his disciples*) Do not think that I have come to bring peace upon the earth. I have come to bring not peace but the sword. For I have come to set a man "against his father, a daughter against her mother, and a daughter-in-law against her mother-in-law; and one's enemies will be those of his household." (*A direct quote from Micah 7:6.*) Whoever loves father or mother more than me is not worthy of me, and whoever loves son or daughter more than me is not worthy of me . . .

21) God leads man astray?:

Koran 3:6–8—It is He who has revealed to you the Book (*Torah and Gospels*). Some of its verses are precise in meaning—they are the foundation (*literally, "mother"*) of the Book—and others ambiguous. Those whose hearts are infected with disbelief follow the ambiguous part, so as to create dissension by seeking to explain. But no one knows its meaning except God. Those who are well-grounded in knowledge say: "We believe in it: it is all from our Lord. But only the wise take heed. Lord, do not cause our hearts to go astray after You have guided us."

Matthew 6:13—(*Jesus praying*) New American Bible: ". . . do not subject us to the final test, but deliver us from the evil one." KJV: ". . . and lead us not into temptation, but deliver us from evil."

NIV: ". . . lead us not into temptation but deliver us from the evil one."

22) Community of the righteous:

Koran 3:104—Let there become of you a community that shall call for righteousness, enjoin justice, and forbid evil. Such men will surely triumph.

Matthew 18:20—(*Jesus teaching*) For where two or three are gathered together in my name, there am I in the midst of them.

Acts 2:42, 44—They (*the new Christians*) devoted themselves to the teaching of the apostles and to the communal life, to the breaking of the bread and to the prayers . . . All who believed were together and had all things in common.

23) No place to hide:

Koran 4:107—You shall not plead for traitors . . . nor for those who betray their own souls; God does not love the treacherous or the sinful. They seek to hide themselves from men, but they cannot hide themselves from God.

Psalm 139:7–12—(*David praying*) Where can I hide from your spirit? From your presence, where can I flee? If I ascend to the heavens, you are there; if I lie down in Sheol, you are there, too. If I fly with the wings of dawn and alight beyond the sea, even there your hand will guide me, your right hand hold me fast. If I say, "Surely darkness shall hide me, and night shall be my light"—Darkness is not dark for you and night shines as the day. Darkness and light are but one.

24) Oaths:

Koran 24:53—They (*the believers*) swear by God that if you order them, they will march forth. Say: "Do not swear: your obedience, not your oaths, will count."

The swearing of oaths was permitted and common in Old Testament times, but controlled by firm rules:

Leviticus 19:12—You shall not swear falsely by my name, thus profaning the name of your God. I am the Lord.

Deuteronomy 6:13—The Lord, your God, shall you fear; him shall you serve, and by his name shall you swear.

Joshua 23:6–8—(*Joshua speaking to the Israelites in the desert*) You must not invoke their (*Canaanites'*) gods, or swear by them, or serve them, or worship them.

25

1 Kings 2:42, 46—The king (*Solomon*) summoned Shimei and said to him: "Why, then, have you not kept the oath of the Lord and the command that I gave you?" . . . The king then gave the order to Benaiah, son of Jehoiada, who struck him dead as he left.

But Jesus turned this around:

Matthew 5:34–36—(*Jesus speaking*) I say to you, do not swear at all, not by heaven, for it is God's throne; nor by the earth, for it is his footstool; nor by Jerusalem, for it is the city of the great King (*David*).

The writer of James agrees with Jesus:

James 5:12—But above all, my brothers, do not swear, either by heaven or by earth or with any other oath.

But the writer of the letter to the Hebrews (thought to be Apollos or Barnabas) seems to disagree:

Hebrews 6:15—Human being swear by something greater than themselves; for them an oath serves as a guarantee and puts an end to all argument.

25) Loving your enemy:

Koran 60:9—(God) forbids you to make friends with those who have fought against you on account of your religion and driven you from your homes or abetted others to drive you out. Those that make friends with them are wrongdoers.

Matthew 5:43–48—(*Jesus to his disciples*) You have heard that it was said, "You shall love your neighbor and hate your enemy." But I say to you, love your enemies, and pray for those who persecute you, that you may be children of your heavenly Father, for he makes his sun rise on the bad and the good, and causes rain to fall on the just and the unjust.

The quotation Jesus uses in the previous passage is not found in the Old Testament. In fact, we read there that it is only one's fellow countrymen against whom you don't take revenge:

Leviticus 19:17–18—Take no revenge and cherish no grudge against your fellow countrymen. (*This could also be quoted under the next heading.*)

26) Retaliation:

Koran 5:45—We decreed for them a life for a life, an eye for an eye, a nose for a nose, an ear for an ear, a tooth for a tooth, and a wound for a wound. But if a man charitably forbears from retaliation, his remission shall atone for him.

Exodus 21:23–25—(*God speaking through Moses*) But if injury ensues, you shall give life for life, eye for eye, tooth for tooth, hand for hand, foot for foot, burn for burn, wound for wound, stripe for stripe. (*This ruling was advanced to prevent over-zealous retaliation, that is, taking more than an eye for an eye, etc.*)

But Jesus turned this around also:

Matthew 5:38–41—(*Jesus speaking to his disciples*) You have heard that it was said, "An eye for an eye and a tooth for a tooth." But I say to you, offer no resistance to one who is evil. When someone strikes you on your right cheek, turn the other one to him as well. If anyone wants to go to law with you over your tunic, hand him your cloak as well. Should anyone press you into service for one mile, go with him for two miles.

27) Dietary laws:

Koran 16:114—Eat of the good and lawful things which God bestowed on you and give thanks for God's favors if you truly serve Him. He has forbidden you carrion, (*running*) blood and the flesh of swine; also any flesh consecrated other than in the name of God (*such as to idols*). But whoever is compelled through necessity, intending neither to sin nor to transgress, will find that God is forgiving and merciful.

Koran 6:116—We forbade the Jews all animals with undivided hoofs and the fat of sheep and oxen, except what is on their backs and intestines and what is mixed with their bones. Such is the penalty We imposed on them for their misdeeds.

Leviticus 11—*The entire chapter lists in great detail what can and cannot be eaten. These laws came from God to Moses and Aaron while the Israelites were still in the Sinai desert between the Egyptian captivity and entering Canaan. The following animals can be eaten: cloven-footed animals that chew the cud, sea creatures that have both fins and scales, insects that walk on all fours and have jointed legs. (Neither God nor Moses noticed that insects have six legs!)*

The *following animals* cannot *be eaten*: camel, rock badger, hare, pig, water creatures that do not have fins or scales, eagle, vulture, osprey, kite, falcon, crow, ostrich, nightjar, gull, hawk, owl, cormorant, buzzard, stork, heron, hoopoe, bat, winged insects that do not have jointed feet, all quadrupeds that walk on paws, rat, mouse, lizard, gecko, chameleon, agama, skink, mole, the body of

27

any animal that "dies of itself." (*There is no indication in the Bible that these restrictions were promulgated as a "penalty for misdeeds."*)

Jesus turned this around:

Mark 7:18–20—He (*Jesus*) said to them, "Are even you likewise without understanding? Do you not realize that everything that goes into a person from outside cannot defile, since it enters not the heart but the stomach and passes out into the latrine?" (Thus he declared all foods clean.) But what comes out of a person, that is what defiles. (See also Acts 10:9–15.)

28) On sects:

Koran 30:32—Do not split up your religion into sects, each exulting in its own beliefs.

Christians, Jews, and Muslims have all *done this!*

As we noted in the Introduction, Islam split into two branches just twenty-five years after the death of Mohammed in 632. The Sunnis constitute about 90 percent of Muslims, the Shi'ites, 10 percent The Sunni are the majority in every country except Iran, Iraq, and perhaps Yemen.

Acts 23:7—For the Sadducees say there is no resurrection or angels or spirits while the Pharisees acknowledge all three.

At the time of Jesus there were three distinct sects within Judaism: 1) Pharisees, who were strict interpreters and followers of the Mosaic Law, believed in the resurrection, and actively opposed the rule of Rome. 2) Sadducees, the old priesthood and landed aristocracy, did not believe in the resurrection, and openly collaborated with Rome. 3) Zealots were revolutionaries who plotted actively against Rome. Their leaders were Sicarii, "men of the dagger," who began the Jewish revolt in 67 CE, *which ended in disaster in 72* CE.

Christianity began as a Jewish sect. It soon split into two major factions. One, the Judaizers, led by Peter, John, and James the brother of Jesus, insisted that Gentile converts learn and follow Jewish law, including circumcision, before baptism as Christians. The other faction, led by Paul and Barnabas, insisted that this was not necessary. The former faction disappeared with the death of Peter and James. During the next 1500 years many small sects appeared and disappeared. Then with the advent of Martin Luther's Protestant Reformation, two major divisions formed, Catholics and

Protestants. And Protestants have since split into major denominations which are perhaps not properly called sects. But there are groups which can be: Christian Science, Mormonism, Jehovah's Witnesses, etc.

29) Idols and idolatry:

There are some three dozen references to idols and idolatry in the Koran. There are well over a hundred references in the Bible. In both Books, most are slightly different versions of the same theme. We need to record only a few passages to illustrate Gabriel's instructions to Mohammed regarding idols and idolatry, followed by a few from the Old Testament and then from the New Testament.

Koran 13:15—The idols to which the pagans pray give them no answer. They are like a man who stretches out his hands to the water and bids it rise to his mouth. Vain are the prayers of the unbelievers.

Koran 22:73—Men, listen to this aphorism. Those idols whom you invoke besides God could never create a single fly. And if a fly carried away a speck of dust from them, they could never retrieve it. Powerless is the suppliant, and powerless he whom he supplicates.

Koran 5:3—You are forbidden (*to eat*) animals sacrificed to idols.

*   *   *

There are 39 references to idols in the book of Ezekiel alone. Ezekiel was a priest of the Jewish people during their captivity in Babylon and was so influential that he has become known as the "father of Judaism."

Ezekiel 14:6—Thus says the Lord God (*to the Israelites preparing to leave their Babylonian captors*): "Return and be converted from your idols; turn yourselves away from all your abominations."

Hosea 8:4b—With their silver and gold they made idols for themselves, to their own destruction.

Zechariah 10:2—For the teraphim (*household idols*) speak nonsense, the diviners have false visions; deceitful dreams they tell, empty comfort they offer. This is why they wander like sheep, wretched: they have no shepherd.

Leviticus 19:4—(*God speaking to Moses*) Do not turn aside to idols, nor make molten gods for yourselves. I, the Lord, am your God.

Psalm 115:4–8—Their idols are silver and gold, the work of human hands. They have mouths but do not speak, eyes but do not see. They have ears but do not hear, noses but do not smell. They have hands but do not feel, feet but do not walk, and no sound rises from their throats. Their makers shall be like them, all who trust in them.

*   *   *

One passage from the New Testament illustrates how Paul felt about idols:

1 Corinthians 10:7–8—And do not become idolaters, as some of them did, as it is written, "The people sat down to eat and drink, and rose up to revel" (*Exodus 32:6b, after Aaron made the golden calf and the people worshiped it*). Let us not indulge in immorality as some of them did, and twenty-three thousand fell within a single day. (*Paul has confused Exodus 32:28, which says 3,000 fell, with Numbers 26:62, which says that 23,000 Levites were registered in a census.*)

5

Proverbs, Aphorisms, Etc.

In the Name of God the Compassionate the Merciful

There are hundreds of pithy sayings in the Koran. No attempt can be made in this work to include them all. Therefore I shall present a sampling of those that either agree or disagree with a Biblical counterpart.

God knows our thoughts:

Koran 67:13—Whether you speak in secret or aloud, He knows your inmost thoughts. Shall He who has created all things not know them all? Gracious is He and all-knowing. (See also Koran 49:9b.)

1 Corinthians 3:19–20—(*Paul writing*) For the wisdom of this world is foolishness in the eyes of God, for it is written: "He catches the wise in their own ruses" (*a direct quote of Job 5:13*), and again, "The Lord knows the thoughts of the wise, that they are vain" (*a paraphrase of Psalm 94:11:* The Lord does know human plans; they are only puffs of air).

Hebrews 4:12—Indeed, the word of God is living and effective, sharper than any two-edged sword, penetrating even between soul and spirit, joints and marrow, and able to discern reflections and thoughts of the heart. (See also Job 42:2.)

The keys to heaven:

Koran 42:10—His are the keys of the heavens and the earth. He gives abundantly to whom He will and sparingly to whom He pleases. He has knowledge of all things.

31

Matthew 16:18–19—*(Jesus speaking)* And so I say to you, you are Peter, and upon this rock I will build my church, and the gates of the netherworld shall not prevail against it. I will give you the keys to the kingdom of heaven.

God takes care of his own:

Koran 67:19—Do they *(the disbelievers)* not see the birds above their heads, spreading their wings and closing them? None save the Merciful sustains them. He observes all things. (See also Koran 29:60.)

Matthew 6:26—Look at the birds in the sky; they do not sow or reap, they gather nothing into barns, yet your heavenly Father feeds them. (See also Luke 12:24.)

Requiting evil:

Koran 23:97—Requite evil with good.

Koran 42:39–43—Let evil be rewarded with like evil. But he that forgives and seeks reconcilement shall be rewarded by God. He does not love the wrongdoers. *(Chronologically, Sura 23 was the 64th to be revealed, Sura 42 the 83rd. Mohammed's change of mind was probably prompted by the growing antipathy of his own tribe in Mecca. The verses in Sura 42 therefore supersede those in Sura 23.)*

Luke 6:27–36—**(*From Jesus' Sermon on the Plain*)** But to you who hear, I say, love your enemies, do good to those who hate you, bless those who curse you, pray for those who mistreat you. To the person who strikes you on one cheek, offer the other as well, and from the person who takes your cloak, do not withhold even your tunic. Give to everyone who asks of you, and from the one who takes what is yours, do not demand it back. Do to others as you would have them do to you.

Truth:

Koran 21:18—Indeed, We will hurl Truth at Falsehood until Truth shall triumph and Falsehood be no more.

John 8:32—(*Jesus teaching in the Temple in Jerusalem*) Jesus then said to those Jews who believed in him, "If you remain in my word, you will truly be my disciples, and you will know the truth and the truth will set you free."

Brevity of man's time on earth:

Koran 25:47—It is He who has made the night a mantle for you, and sleep a rest. He makes each day a resurrection.

John 9:4–5—Jesus answered, "We have to do the works of the one who sent me while it is day. Night is coming when no one can work. While I am in the world, I am the light of the world."

Reward of the believer:

Koran 16:30—Good is the reward of those that do good works in this present life: but far better is the abode of the life to come. Blessed is the abode of the righteous.

Matthew 19:28–29—Jesus said to them (*his 12 disciples*), "Amen, I say to you who have followed me, in the new age, when the Son of Man is seated on his throne of glory, will yourselves sit on twelve thrones, judging the twelve tribes of Israel. And everyone who has given up (*everything*) for the sake of my name will receive a hundred times more and will inherit eternal life."

Worldly wealth is meaningless:

Koran 16:95—You shall not barter God's covenant for a trifling price. God's reward is better for you, if you but knew it. Your worldly riches are transitory, but God's reward is everlasting.

Matthew 6:19–21—(*From Jesus' Sermon on the Mount*) Do not store up for yourselves treasures on earth, where moth and decay destroy, and thieves break in and steal. But store up treasures in heaven, where neither moth nor decay destroys, nor thieves break in and steal. For where your treasure is, there also will your heart be.

Youth is transitory:

Koran 30:54—God creates you weak: after weakness He gives you strength, and after strength infirmity and grey hairs.

Ecclesiastes 12:1—Remember your Creator in the days of your youth, before the evil days come and the years approach of which you will say, I have no pleasure in them. (See also 12:2–8.)

Life is like a tree:

Korana 14:25—Do you not see how God compares a good word to a good tree? Its root is firm and its branches are in the sky; it yields its fruit in every season by God's leave. But an evil word is like an evil tree torn out of the earth and shorn of all its roots.

Psalm 1:3–6—They (*the righteous*) are like a tree planted near streams of water, that yields its fruit in season; its leaves never wither; whatever they do prospers. But not the wicked! They are like chaff driven by the wind.

Bearing one another's burdens:

Koran 35:17—No soul shall bear another's burden. If a laden soul cries out for help, not even a near relation shall share its burden.

Galatians 6:2–3—(*Paul writing*) Bear one another's burdens and so you will fulfill the law of Christ. For if anyone thinks he is something when he is nothing, he is deluding himself. (See also Philippians 2:3–4 and Exodus 18:22.)

A light from the Lord:

Koran 39:21—He whose heart God has opened to Islam shall receive light from his Lord.

Matthew 4:16—The people who sit in darkness have seen a great light, on those dwelling in a land overshadowed by death, light has arisen. (*A paraphrase of Isaiah 9:1.*)

Putting man to the test:

Koran 29:1—Do men think that once they say: "We are believers," they will be left alone and not be put to the test? We tested those who have gone before them.

Matthew 6:13—(*From "The Lord's Prayer"*) **And do not subject us to the final test.** (*The final test would be the trials just before the end of the age.*)

2 Peter 2:1–22, and the entire short letter of Jude, deal with the coming testing of Christians by "false teachers" or "false prophets." (*These would be of three kinds: the antinomial errorists, the gnostics, and the Judaizers.*) (See also Matthew 7:15–16b and Acts 20:29–31b.)

God needs man's help?:

Koran 29:6—He that fights for God's cause fights for himself. God needs no man's help.

Korana 22:39–40—Had God not defended some men by the might of others, the monasteries and churches, the synagogues and mosques in which His praise is daily celebrated, would have been utterly destroyed. But whoever helps God shall be helped by Him. (*The contradiction here between Suras 29 and 22 can be explained by a great change in Mohammed's circumstances. Sura 29 (chronologically the 81st) was revealed while Mohammed was still in Mecca. Sura 22 (chronologically the 107th) was revealed long after the flight to Medina, and near the end of Mohammed's life.*)

Genesis 19:24—**The Lord rained down sulfurous fire upon Sodom and Gomorrah. He overthrew those cities and the whole Plain, together with the inhabitants.** (*God needed no help here.*)

Exodus 14:26–28—**Then the Lord told Moses, "Stretch out your hand over the sea, that the waters may flow back upon the Egyptians, upon their chariots and their charioteers." So Moses stretched out his hand over the sea, and at dawn the sea flowed back to its normal depth.** (*God acts through Moses.*) (For further examples of God using men to accomplish his purposes, see Deuteronomy 2:24–25, Joshua 11:6–9, 1 Samuel 17, and Nehemiah 4.)

Nowhere to hide:

Koran 29:22—Neither on earth nor in heaven shall you escape His reach, nor have you any besides God to protect or help you.

Psalm 139:7–10—(*David praying*) Where can I hide from your spirit? From your presence, where can I flee? If I ascend to the heavens, you are there; if I lie down in Sheol, you are there too. If I fly with the wings of dawn and alight beyond the sea, even there your hand will guide me, your right hand hold me fast.

The good life:

Koran 29:64—The life of this world is but a sport and a pastime. It is the life to come that is the true life; if they but knew it.

Ecclesiastes 2:24—There is nothing better for man than to eat and drink and provide himself with good things by his labors.

Matthew 10:29—(*Jesus, on the conditions of discipleship*) Whoever finds his life will lose it, and whoever loses his life for my sake will find it.

Worshiping God in a foreign land:

Koran 29:57—(For) you that are true believers among My servants, My earth is vast. Therefore serve Me. (*Interpreted by Muslims to mean that if they are driven from their native city, then can find places of refuge where they can worship the true God in other parts of the earth. This passage was revealed to Mohammed when the flight from Mecca to Medina was imminent, and he and his followers were afraid that they would be unable to worship God properly so far from the Ka'bah.*)

Psalm 137:1–4—By the rivers of Babylon we sat mourning and weeping when we remembered Zion. On the poplars of that land we hung up our harps. There our captors asked us for the words of a song; our tormentors, for a joyful song: "Sing for us a song of Zion!" But how could we sing a song of the Lord in a foreign land? (*This is one of the psalms that clearly indicates that David did not write all the psalms. David lived over four hundred years* before *the Babylonian exile.*)

Jeremiah 29:4–14a—(Summary) Jeremiah answers the plea above in a letter to the Israelites in exile in Babylon. He tells them that they can worship God in a foreign land. They do not need a temple, do not need the Ark of the Covenant.

Adding to the scriptures:

Koran 31:27—If all the trees of the earth were pens, and the sea, replenished by seven more seas, were ink, the words of God could not be finished still. Mighty is God, and wise. (*This verse was revealed at Medina in answer to the Jews who had affirmed that all knowledge was contained in their own Law.*)

Revelation 22:18–19—(*John writing*) I warn everyone who hears the prophetic words in this book: if anyone adds to them, God will add to him the plagues described in this book. And if anyone takes away from the words in this prophetic book, God will take away his share in the tree of life and in the holy city described in this book. (*Many conservative Christians claim that this proscription applies to the entire Bible, not just Revelation, that there has not been and will not be any further revelations to man from God. However, despite this curse, The Revelation has been altered, distorted, and misinterpreted more than any other book in the New Testament.*)

Pride and arrogance:

Koran 16:23—Your God is one God. Those that deny the life to come have faithless hearts and are puffed up with pride. God surely knows what they hide and what they reveal. He does not love the proud.

Proverbs 8:13—Pride, arrogance, the evil way, and the perverse mouth I (Wisdom) hate.

Proverbs 16:18—Pride goes before disaster, and a haughty spirit before a fall.

Impious prayer:

Koran 107:5–7—Woe to those who pray but are heedless in their prayer; who make a show of piety and forbid almsgiving.

Luke 18:11–12—The Pharisee took up his position and spoke this prayer to himself. "O God, I thank you that I am not like the rest of humanity—greedy, dishonest, adulterous . . ."

Sowing seeds on good or bad soil:

Koran 7:58—Good soil yields fruit by God's will. But poor and scant are the fruits which spring from barren soil. Thus do We make plain Our revelations to those who render thanks.

Matthew 13:3–9—(*Jesus speaking*) "A sower went out to sow. And as he sowed, some seed fell on the path, and birds came and ate it up. Some fell on rocky ground, where it had little soil. It sprang up at once because the soil was not deep, and when the sun rose it was scorched, and it withered for lack of roots. Some seed fell among thorns, and the thorns grew up and choked it. But some seed fell on rich soil, and produced fruit, a hundred or sixty or thirtyfold. Whoever has ears ought to hear."

I think both passages are parables about what happens to the word of God when it falls on human ears.

God's straight path:

Koran 6:153—This path of Mine is straight. Follow it and do not follow other paths, for they will lead you away from Him. He thus exhorts you so that you may guard yourselves against evil.

John 1:22–23—So they (*Jews from Jerusalem*) said to him (*John the Baptist*), "Who are you, so we can give an answer to those who sent us? What do you have to say for yourself?" He said: "I am 'the voice of one crying out in the desert, make straight the way of the Lord,' as the prophet Isaiah said." (Isaiah 40:3.)

Judgment of God:

Koran 3:128—it is no concern of yours (*Mohammed's*) whether He will forgive or punish them. They are the wrongdoers.

Matthew 7:1–5—(*Jesus to his disciples*) Stop judging, that you may not be judged. For as you judge, so will you be judged, and the measure with which you measure will be measured out to you.

The omnipotence and omniscience of God:

Koran 6:59–62—He has the keys of all that his hidden: none knows them but He. He has knowledge of all that land and sea contain.

Koran 6:95–99—He brings forth living from the dead, and the dead from the living. Such is God. How then can you turn away?

Koran 14:48—Mighty is God and capable of revenge. On that day when the earth is changed into a different earth and the heavens into new heavens, mankind shall stand before God, the One, who conquers all. On that day you shall see the guilty bound with chains, their garments pitch, and their faces covered with flames.

2 Timothy 4:14—(*Paul to Timothy*) Alexander the coppersmith did me great harm; the Lord will pay him back for his deeds.

Hebrews 10:30—We know the one who said: "Vengeance is mine. I will repay," and again, "The Lord will judge his people" (*Quotes from Deuteronomy 32:35, 36*). **It is a fearful thing to fall into the hands of the living God.**

Koran 13:41—Do they (*the unbelievers*) not see how We invade their land and curtail its borders? If God decrees a thing, none can reverse it. (*This was revealed to Mohammed when the progressive conquests of the Muslims encroached more and more on the territories of the idolatrous Arabians.* **The entire book of Joshua recounts the Israelite conquest of Canaan with the direct aid of God.**)

Koran 42:49–50—He gives daughters to whom He will and sons to whom He pleases. To some He gives both sons and daughters, and He makes sterile whom He will. Omniscient is God, and mighty.

Koran 58:7—Are you not aware that God knows what the heavens and the earth contain? If three men converse in secret, He is their fourth; if five, He is their sixth; whether fewer or more, wherever they be, He is with them. Then on the day of Resurrection he will inform them of their doings. God has knowledge of all things.

Matthew 18:20—(*Jesus speaking*) For where two or three are gathered together in my name, there am I in the midst of them.

Koran 5:120—God has sovereignty over the heavens and the earth and all that they contain. He has power over all things.

1 Chronicles 29:12–13—(*David praying*) Riches and honor are from you, and you have dominion over all. In your hand are power and might; it is yours to give grandeur and strength to all.

Job 37:22–23—(*from Elihu's last speech to Job*) From the North (*a symbol for God's mysterious abode*) the splendor comes, surrounding God's awesome majesty! The Almighty! We cannot discover him, pre-eminent in power and judgment; his great justice owes no one an accounting.

Lukewarm believers:

Koran 4:143—The hypocrites seek to deceive God, but it is He who deceives them. When they rise to pray, they stand up sluggishly: they pray for the sake of ostentation and remember God but little, wavering between this and that and belonging neither to these nor those.

Revelation 3:16—(*Christ speaking in John's vision*) To the angel of the church in Laodicea, write this: "The Amen, the faithful and true witness, the source of God's creation, says this: 'I know your works; I know that you are neither cold nor hot. So, because you are lukewarm, neither hot nor cold, I will spit you out of my mouth.' " (*From this passage derives the now archaic English word "laodicean," meaning "lukewarm" or "indifferent."*)

The importance of riches:

Koran 104:1–9—Woe to every back-biting slanderer who amasses riches and sedulously hoards them, thinking his wealth will render him immortal! By no means! He shall be flung to the Destroying Flame.

Psalm 52:8–9—The righteous will look on with awe; they will jeer and say: "That one did not take God as refuge, but trusted in great wealth, relied on devious plots."

Koran 26:87–94—Do not hold me up to shame on the Day of Resurrection; the day when wealth and offspring will avail nothing.

Proverbs 11:4—Wealth is useless on the day of wrath, but virtue saves from death. (*That is, saves one from eternal damnation.*)

Koran 7:40—For those that have denied and scorned Our revelations the gates of heaven shall not be opened; nor shall they enter Paradise until a camel shall pass through the eye of a needle.

Mark 10:23–27—(*Jesus to his disciples*) "Children, how hard it is for the rich to enter the kingdom of God! It is easier for a camel to pass through the eye of a needle."

1 Timothy 6:10—For the love of money is the root of all evils, and some people in their desire for it have strayed from the faith and have pierced themselves with many pains.

God is unjust (unfair)?:

Koran 3:117—God is not unjust to them; they are unjust to their own souls.

Ezekiel 18:25—(*God speaking to Ezekiel*) You say, "The Lord's way is not fair!" Hear now, house of Israel: Is it my way that is unfair, or rather, are not your ways unfair?

Equality, inequality, amongst men:

Koran 16:70, 74—To some God has given more than He has to others . . . On the one hand there is a helpless slave, the property of his master. On the other, a man on whom We have bestowed Our bounty, so that he gives of it both in private and in public. Are the two equal? God forbid!

Colossians 3:11—(*Paul writing*) Here there is not Greek (*a metonym for "Gentile"*) and Jew, circumcision and uncircumcision, barbarian, Scythian, slave, free; but Christ is all and in all.

Leviticus 19:15b, 18b—(*Moses repeating the words of God to the Israelites*) Show neither partiality to the weak nor deference to

the mighty, but judge your fellow men justly . . . You shall love your neighbor as yourself, I am the Lord.

Koran 33:50, 52—Prophet, We have made lawful to you . . . any believing woman who gives herself to the Prophet and whom the Prophet wishes to take in marriage. This privilege is yours alone, being granted to no other believer. We grant you this privilege so that none may blame you. God is forgiving and merciful. (*He had nine wives at this time, besides slave girls: Five more than legal for other men.*)

There are two contradictory passages in the Koran concerning equality among prophets:

Koran 17:54—We have exalted some prophets above others. To David We gave the Psalms.

Koran 2:136–137—Say: "We believe in God and that which is revealed to us; in what was revealed to Abraham, Ishmael, Isaac, Jacob, and the tribes; to Moses and Jesus and the other prophets by their Lord. We make no distinction among any of them, and to God we have surrendered ourselves."

There is clear evidence in the Bible that some prophets were exalted over others. In the Old Testament the prophets are divided into "major" and "minor" prophets. Among other examples in the New Testament is this one from Matthew's gospel:

Matthew 4:11—(*John the Baptist baptizing in the Jordan*) I am baptizing you with water, for repentance, but the one who is coming after me (*Jesus*) is mightier than I. I am not worthy to carry his sandals. He will baptize you with the holy Spirit and fire.

Concerning division of the spoils of battle:

Koran 57:10—Those of you that gave of their wealth before the victory (*over the Meccans*) and took part in the fighting, shall receive greater honor than the others who gave and fought thereafter.

1 Samuel 30:21–24—(Summary) After a victorious battle, those who had fought didn't want to share the booty with those who had remained with the baggage. David insisted that they should share alike. (*Oliver Cromwell in the 17th century echoed David: "He also serves who only stands and waits."*)

Mohammed, Moses, and Jesus sent to witness and to testify:

Koran 73:15–17—We have sent forth an apostle (*Mohammed*) to testify against you, just as We sent an apostle (*Moses*) to Pharaoh before you.

Exodus 3:4, 10—When God saw him (*Moses*) coming over to look at it (*the burning bush*) more closely, God called out to him from the bush . . . "Come now! I will send you to Pharaoh to lead my people, the Israelites, out of Egypt."

John 1:17—Because while the law was given through Moses; grace and truth came through Jesus Christ.

Koran 35:23—We have sent you (*Mohammed*) with the Truth to proclaim good news and to give warning, for there is no community that has not had a warner. Their apostles came to them with veritable signs, with scriptures (*the Torah*), and with the light-giving Book (*the Gospels*). But in the end I smote the unbelievers; how terrible was the way I disowned them.

1 John 4:14—Moreover, we have seen and testify that the Father has sent his Son to be the Savior of the world.

6

Predestination

In the Name of God the Compassionate the Merciful

There is an endless number of direct and indirect references throughout the Koran to the total control that God has over humans' destiny. One Muslim commentator claims that God and Gabriel sit down together at the first of every year to determine just who will survive the next year and who won't, but this is not found in the Koran. The following selections were chosen because they clearly show just how omnipotent the Muslim God is when the life of a human is at stake. I have varied the format a bit for this chapter: I shall give the Koranic verses first, followed by passages from the Old Testament and the New Testament that deal with predestination.

From the Koran:

Koran 16:61, 70–71—If God punished men for their sins, not one creature would be left alive. He reprieves them till a time ordained; when their time arrives, not for one hour shall they stay behind: nor can they go before it . . . God created you, and He will then reclaim you. Some shall have their lives prolonged to abject old age, when all they once knew they shall know no more. (*Alzheimer's encephalopathy is not a new disease.*) All-knowing is God, and mighty.

Koran 18:46–49—Tell of the day when We shall blot out the mountains and make the earth a barren waste; when We shall gather all mankind together, leaving not a soul behind. They shall be ranged before your Lord, and He will say to them: "You have returned to Us as We created you at first. Yet you supposed We had not set for you a predestined time."

Koran 35:11—God created you from dust, then from a little germ. Into two sexes He divided you. No female conceives or is delivered without His knowledge. No man grows old or has his life cut short but in accordance with His decree. All this is easy enough for God.

Koran 7:178—We have predestined for Hell numerous jinn and men. They have hearts they cannot comprehend with; they have eyes they cannot see with; and they have ears they cannot hear with. They are like beasts—indeed, they are more misguided. Such are the heedless.

Koran 3:145—No one dies unless God permit. The term of every life is fixed. (*Rodwell's translation: No one can die without God's permission, according to the Book that fixes the time of life.*)

Koran 3:153–54—(*God, through Gabriel and Mohammed, chastises the people who ran away rather than continuing to fight in the Battle of Ohod, and assures those who fought and died that it was not their decision.*) They complain: "Had we had any say in the matter we should not have been slain here." Say to them: "Had you stayed in your homes, those of you who were destined to be slain would have gone to their graves nevertheless." . . . Believers, do not follow the example of the infidels, who say of their brothers when they meet death or abroad or in battle: "Had they stayed with us they would not have died, nor would they have been killed."

Koran 57:22—Every misfortune that befalls the earth, or your own persons, is ordained before We bring it into being.

Koran 22:6—We cause to remain in the womb whatever We please, then we bring you forth as infants, that you may grow up and reach your prime. (*Rodwell's translation: We cause one sex or the other at our pleasure to abide in the womb until the appointed time.*)

Koran 9:51—Say: "Nothing will befall us except what God has ordained. He is our Guardian. In God let the faithful put their trust."

From the Bible:

The Old Testament:
There are no direct references to predestination in the Old Testament such as we find in the Koran. There are, however, numerous

references to "the chosen" and to "the elect," from which some might infer that God has foreordained the future for a given person or a given people. Others will disagree with that interpretation. Though in some of the following passages it may be stretching things a little to call them examples of belief in predestination, I present them for consideration:

Malachi 2:4–5—(*The Lord speaking through Malachi*) Then you will know that I sent you (*the priests*) this commandment because I have a covenant with Levi, says the Lord of hosts. My covenant with him was one of life and peace; fear I put in him and he feared me, and stood in awe of my name.

Deuteronomy 30:15–18, 46–47—(*from Moses' farewell speech to the Israelites*) Here, then, I have today set before you life and prosperity, death and doom. If you obey the commandments of the Lord, your God, which I enjoin on you today, loving him, and walking in his ways, and keeping his commandments, statutes and decrees, you will live and grow numerous, and the Lord, your God, will bless you in the land you are entering to occupy. If, however, you turn away your hearts and will not listen, but are led astray and adore and serve other gods, I tell you now that you will certainly perish; you will not have a long life on the land which you are crossing the Jordan to enter and occupy . . . Take to heart all the warning which I have now given you and which you must impress on your children, that you may carry out carefully every word of this law. For this is no trivial matter for you; rather, it means your very life, since it is by this means that you are to enjoy a long life on the land which you will cross the Jordan to occupy.

Psalm 21:5–6—He (*David*) asked life of you; you gave it to him, length of days forever. Great is his glory in your victory; majesty and splendor you confer upon him.

Daniel 8:16, 19—(*Daniel telling of his vision*) . . . and on the Ulai (*River*) I heard a human voice that cried out, "Gabriel, explain the vision to this man." . . . "I will show you," he said, "what is to happen later in the period of wrath; for at the appointed time, there will be an end."

Habakkuk 2:2–3—(*Habakkuk speaking*) Then the Lord answered me and said: Write down the vision clearly upon the tablets, so that one can read it readily. For the vision still has its time, presses on to fulfillment, and will not disappoint; if it delays, wait for it, it will surely come, it will not be late.

Psalm 139:15–16—My very self you knew; my bones were not hidden from you, when I was being made in secret, fashioned as in the depths of the earth. Your eyes foresaw my actions; in your book all are written down; my days were shaped, before one came to be.

The New Testament:

In the New Testament there are very few references to God's control over every human being on earth. But the disciples, the Gospel writers and Paul clearly believed that Jesus was predestined to fulfil the prophecies in the Old Testament.

Matthew 1:22–23—*(Joseph has just been told by an angel that Mary's child has been conceived by the Holy Spirit)* All this took place to fulfil what the Lord had said through the prophet *(Isaiah)*: "Behold, the virgin shall be with child and bear a son, and they shall name him Emmanuel," which means "God is with us."

Matthew 2:23—He *(Joseph)* went and dwelt in a town called Nazareth, so that what had been spoken through the prophets might be fulfilled, "He *(Jesus)* shall be called a Nazorean."

And an example from the Book of Acts:

Acts 2:23—*(Peter speaking at Pentecost to the Jews)* "This man, delivered up by the set plan and foreknowledge of God, you killed, using lawless men to crucify him."

Jesus himself believed that he had come to fulfil the prophecies:

Matthew 5:17—*(Jesus speaking)* Do not think that I have come to abolish the law or the prophets. I have come not to abolish but to fulfil.

Jesus also believed that some people were destined for heaven and others would be left out:

Matthew 22:14—*(Jesus teaching)* For many are invited, but few are chosen.

Matthew 7:13–14—*(Jesus teaching)* Enter through the narrow gate, for the gate is wide and the road broad that leads to destruction, and those who enter through it are many. How narrow the gate and constricted the road that leads to life. And those who find it are few.

Paul believed that he and his followers were chosen by Jesus:

Ephesians 1:3, 5–6—Blessed be the God and Father of our Lord Jesus Christ . . . In love he destined us for adoption to himself through Jesus Christ, in accord with the favor of his will, for the praise of the glory of his grace that he granted us in the beloved.

Ephesians 1:11–12—In him we were also chosen, destined in accord with the purpose of the One who accomplishes all things according to the intention of his will, so that we might exist for the praise of his glory, we (*the early Jewish Christians*) who first hoped in Christ. (*This passage formed the basis of the "Doctrine of Predestination" promulgated by John Calvin, Swiss theologian and founder of the Presbyterian denomination.*)

Romans 8:28–30—We know that all things work for good for those who love God, who are called according to his purpose. For those he foreknew, he also predestined to be conformed to the image of his Son, so that he might be the firstborn among many brothers. And those he predestined he also called; and those he called he also justified; and those he justified he also glorified. (*To be "justified" means to be accepted by God as if one had not sinned.*)

John is even more definite:

Revelation 13:1–10—(*John describes a beast coming up out of the sea, the beast being the personification of the Roman Empire.*) All the inhabitants of the earth will worship it, all whose names were not written from the foundation of the world in the book of life, which belongs to the Lamb who was slain (*Jesus*) . . . Anyone destined for captivity goes into captivity. Anyone destined to be slain by the sword shall be slain by the sword.

7

God Guides Whomever He Chooses

In the Name of God the Compassionate the Merciful

We have just seen in the previous chapter that the Koran stresses God's total control over the fate of every individual on earth. He has predestined some believers for Paradise, some believers and all unbelievers for Hell. We shall now take a look at some of the many passages in the Koran that show that God has the power to withhold his blessing and his guidance from whomever he chooses.

Six distinct themes emerge.

1) God confounds the unbelievers:

Koran 17:97–98—Those whom God guides are rightly guided; but those whom He confounds shall find no friend besides Him. We shall gather them all on the Day of Resurrection, prostrate upon their faces, blind, dumb, and deaf. Hell shall be their home: whenever its flames die down We will rekindle them into a greater fire. Thus shall they be rewarded.

Koran 48:11—Say: "Who can intervene on your behalf with God if it be His will to do you harm or good?"

Koran 63:4—Regarding the hypocrites: *They* are the enemy. God will not forgive them. God does not guide the evil-doers.

There are two passages in the Old Testament that seem to indicate that God does not attempt to confound the believers.

Psalm 22:4–5—In you (*God*) our ancestors trusted; they trusted and you rescued them. To you they cried out and they escaped; in you they trusted and were not confounded.

Isaiah 50:7—The Lord God is my help, therefore I am not confounded. I have set my face like flint, knowing that I shall not be put to shame.

There is one instance in the New Testament where Jesus berates his listeners for trying to confound their fellow Jews.

Matthew 23:13–14, 27—(*Jesus speaking*) Woe to you, scribes and Pharisees, you hypocrites. You lock the kingdom of heaven before human beings. You do not enter yourselves, nor do you allow entrance to those trying to enter . . . You are like whitewashed tombs, which appear beautiful on the outside, but inside are full of dead men's bones and every kind of filth.

And there are numerous instances in the Old Testament where God is asked to confound the writer's enemies. Two examples:

Psalm 35:4—Let those who seek my life be put to shame and disgrace, let those who plot evil against me be turned back and confounded. (See also Psalms 40:15 and 70:1–2.)

Jeremiah 17:18—(*Jeremiah praying*) Let my persecutors, not me, be confounded; let them, not me, be broken. Bring upon them the day of misfortune, crush them with repeated destruction. (See also Jeremiah 22:21–22.)

But there are no passages in either Testament that indicate that God purposely singles out unbelievers in order to confound them, to lead them astray, to allow them to continue to sin.

2) God could have united all mankind into one community:

Koran 16:93—Had God pleased, He would have united you into one community. But He confounds whom He will and gives guidance to whom He pleases.

Koran 10:19—There was a time when mankind were but one community (*Rodwell's translation: one religion*). Then they disagreed among themselves: and but for a Word from your Lord, long since decreed, their differences would have been firmly resolved.

The following passage in the Old Testament shows God purposely confusing the people's languages:

Genesis 11:1–9—(Summary) The whole world spoke the same language. The people decided to build a city and a tower, the Tower of Babel. This made God worry that they were getting *too* strong.

So he scattered them all over the earth and gave them many languages so they couldn't understand each other.

3) God does not guide the unbelievers:

Koran 27:4–5—As for those that deny the life to come, We make their foul deeds seem fair to them, so they blunder about in their folly.

Koran 14:4—Each apostle We have sent has spoken in the language of his own people so that he might make his meaning clear to them. But God leaves in error whom He will and guides whom He pleases. He is the Mighty, the Wise One.

Koran 14:28—God will strengthen the faithful with His steadfast Word, both in this life and in the hereafter. He leads the wrongdoers astray. (See also 18:57, 6:110, and 13:31, 33.)

There are two passages, one in the Old Testament and one in the New, that might be construed to agree with the words we have just read in the Koran.

Psalm 125:4–5—Do good, Lord, to the good, to those who are upright of heart. But those who turn aside to crooked ways may the Lord send down with the wicked. Peace upon Israel!

Revelation 21:10—Then (*Jesus said to John*), "Do not seal up the prophetic words of this book, for the appointed time is near. Let the wicked still act wickedly, and the filthy still be filthy. The righteous must still do right, and the holy still be holy."

But there are others that disagree with the Koran:

Psalm 25:8–9—Good and upright is the Lord, who shows sinners the way, guides the humble rightly, and teaches the humble the way.

Romans 11:28–30—In respect to the gospel, they (*the Jews*) are enemies on your account; but in respect to election, they are beloved because of the patriarchs. For the gifts and the call of God are irrevocable.

4) The fate of unbelievers:

We read in the Koran that not only does God allow unbelievers to "blunder in their wrongdoing" or "even lead them astray," but dire punishment awaits them:

Koran 30:43–45—Therefore stand firm in your devotion to the true Faith before that day arrives which none may put off against the will of God. For then He will of His bounty reward those who have embraced the Faith and done good works. He does not love the unbelievers.

Matthew 25:31–34—(*Jesus speaking*) When the Son of Man comes in his glory, and all the angels with him, he will sit upon his glorious throne and all the nations will be assembled before him. And he will separate them one from another, as a shepherd separates the sheep from the goats. He will place the sheep on his right and the goats on his left. (*The sheep will inherit the kingdom prepared for them. The goats will go to the eternal fire prepared for the devil and his angels.*)

Koran 11:19—God's curse is on the wrongdoers, who debar others from the path of God and seek to make it crooked, and who deny the life to come.

Koran 3:128—Let not the unbelievers think that We prolong their days for their own good. We give them respite only so that they may commit more grievous sins. Shameful punishment awaits them. (See also 6:42–43, 3:26, and 57:29.)

Paul in writing to the Romans, disagrees with this attitude:

Romans 5:17–19—(*Paul writing*) For if, by the transgression of one person (*Adam*), death came to reign through that one, how much more will those who receive the abundance of grace and of the gift of justification through the one person Jesus Christ.

5) God can withhold his favors—such as light and rain—from the unbelievers:

Koran 24:43—Do you not see how God drives the clouds, then gathers and piles them up in masses which pour down torrents of rain? From heaven's mountains He sends down the hail, pelting with it whom He will and turning it away from whom He pleases.

Jesus disagrees with that attitude:

Matthew 5:43–45—(*Jesus speaking*) "I say to you, love your enemies, and pray for those who persecute you, that you may be children of your heavenly Father, for he makes his sun rise on the bad and the good, and causes rain to fall on the just and the unjust."

6) God chooses whom he will allow to understand his words:

Koran 6:25—But We have cast veils over their (*unbelievers'*) hearts and made them hard of hearing lest they understand your words.

Koran 5:13—With those who said they were Christians We made a covenant also, but they too have forgotten much of what they were enjoined. Therefore We stirred among them enmity and hatred, which shall endure till the Day of Resurrection, when God will declare to them all that they have done.

In the eighth century BCE, God decided to punish the Israelites by using Tiglath-Pileser of Assyria to take them captive. Isaiah's mission is to prevent repentance so that God's plan will succeed.

Isaiah 6:8–12—Then I heard the voice of the Lord saying, "Whom shall I send? Who will go for us?" "Here I am," I said, "send me!" And he replied: Go and say to this people (*the Israelites*): Listen carefully, but you shall not understand! Look intently, but you shall know nothing! You are to make the heart of this people sluggish, to dull their ears and close their eyes; else their eyes will see, their ears hear, their heart understand, and they will turn and be healed. "How long, O Lord?" I asked. And he replied: Until the cities are desolate, without inhabitants, houses without a man, and the earth is a desolate waste. Until the Lord removes men far away, and the land is abandoned more and more.

Jesus quotes Isaiah in seeming agreement with the Koran and clearly with Isaiah:

Mark 4:11–12—He answered them, "The mystery of the kingdom of God has been granted to you. But to those outside, everything comes in parables, so that 'they may look and see but not perceive, and hear and listen but not understand, in order that they may not be converted and be forgiven.' " (See also Isaiah 64:15–17.)

8

Tolerance of Unbelievers

In the Name of God the Compassionate the Merciful

Despite the seeming harshness with which God deals with unbelievers, as we read in the preceding chapter, there are many passages in the Koran that advocate tolerance of unbelievers, often including Christians and Jews.

There is also considerable ambiguity in the New Testament concerning the Christians' tolerance of unbelievers. There is *no* ambiguity in the Old Testament. However, the Old Testament never uses the words "believer" or "unbeliever." Instead, it uses phrases like "He sinned against the Lord." Or, "He did not follow the Lord's commands." This I consider to be unbelief and shall quote examples of the Lord's reaction to such unbelief. We shall look at the Koran first, then the New Testament, and then the Old.

From the Koran:

Koran 3:63—Say: "People of the Book (*Christians and Jews*), let us come to an agreement: that we will worship none but God, that we will associate none with Him, and that none of us shall set up mortals as deities besides God."

Koran 109:1–6—Say: "Unbelievers, I do not worship what you worship, nor do you worship what I worship. I shall never worship what you worship, nor will you ever worship what I worship. You have your own religion, and I have mine."

Koran 16:125—Call men to the path of your Lord with wisdom and kindly exhortation. Reason with them in the most courteous manner.

Koran 29:46—Say, "We believe in that which is revealed to us and which was revealed to you. Our God and your God is one. To Him we surrender ourselves."

Koran 42:16—We have our own works and you have yours; let there be no argument between us. God will bring us all together, for to Him we shall return.

Koran 2:40—Children of Israel, have faith in My revelations (*the Koran*), which confirm your Scriptures.

Koran 2:62—Believers, Jews, Christians, and Sabaeans, whoever believes in God and the Last Day and does what is right—shall be rewarded by their Lord; they have nothing to fear or regret. (*The Sabaeans in Mohammed's time were the "Christians of St. John" who lived at the mouth of the Euphrates River. They were a gnostic sect, believed that Jesus was only a prophet, and claimed descendancy from John the Baptist. There are still 20,000 of them in modern Iraq, but call themselves Mandeans. They were not the same people found in Job 1:15, Joel 3:8, Isaiah 45:14, and Ezekiel 23:42. Those were from Sheba [now Yemen] in southern Arabia.*)

Koran 2:109—Many among the People of the Book wish, through envy, to lead you back to unbelief, now that you have embraced the Faith and the truth has been made plain to them. Forgive them and bear with them until God makes known His will.

Koran 3:113—Yet they (*people of the Book*) are not all alike. There are among them some upright men; whatever good they do, its reward shall not be denied them.

Koran 5:14—You will ever find them (*the unbelievers*) deceitful, except for a few of them. But pardon them and bear with them. God loves those who do good.

From the New Testament:

In contrast, we read a parable told by Jesus:
Luke 12:37, 45–47—"Blessed are those servants whom the master finds vigilant on his arrival" . . . "But if that servant says to himself, 'My master is delayed in coming,' and begins to beat the menservants and the maidservants, and to eat and drink and get drunk, then that servant's master will come on an unexpected day and at an unknown hour and will punish him severely."

In another passage in Matthew, we see Jesus rebuffing those who reject his teaching:

Matthew 13:54–58—(Summary) Jesus returned to Nazareth, claimed to be the Messiah whom Isaiah prophesied. The people took offense and threatened to throw him over the cliff. For this treatment, Jesus did no healings or other "mighty deeds."

In a letter to the Corinthians and one to Titus, Paul agrees with this latter assessment:

2 Cor. 6:14a, 15b—(*Paul writing*) Do not be yoked with those who are different, with unbelievers. For what partnership do righteousness and lawlessness have . . . Or what has a believer in common with an unbeliever?

Titus 1:13–14, 16—(*Probably Paul writing*) Therefore, admonish them (*the false prophets amongst the Jewish Christians on Crete*) sharply, so that they may be sound in the faith, instead of paying attention to Jewish myths and regulations of people who have repudiated the truth . . . They are vile and disobedient and unqualified for any good deed.

But in Matthew and the other two synoptic gospels, we see another side of the coin:

Matthew 9:10–12, 13b—While he was at table in (Matthew's) house, many tax collectors and sinners came and sat with Jesus and his disciples. The Pharisees saw this and said to his disciples, "Why does your teacher eat with tax collectors and sinners?" Jesus heard this and said, "Those who are well do not need a physician, but the sick do . . . I did not come to call the righteous but sinners."

Paul agrees with this latter passage in his letter to the Romans:

Romans 11:1–24—(Summary) Paul uses an extended metaphor to show that Jews who did not accept Jesus as the Messiah may still be returned to God. He says that they were branches broken off because of their unbelief so that new wild olive shoots (*the Gentiles*) might be grafted in their place because they *did* believe. But then he says that they may be grafted back again by God's grace.

From the Old Testament:

The Lord shows his displeasure when his people disobey his commandments and show open disbelief. There are many, many stories that tell of his punishment. I shall recount just a few:

Genesis 6–9—Except for Noah and family, the whole world is flooded and everyone drowns.

Genesis 19—God rains fire and brimstone on Sodom and Gomorrah, killing everybody except Lot and his two daughters.

Exodus 32—God orders the Israelites to slay all those who had worshiped the golden calf while Moses was up on Mt. Sinai. Three thousand died.

Numbers 14—God tells Moses that he is going to punish all the men over twenty for having spurned him and for testing him ten times in the desert; they will all die before the crossing into Canaan.

Joshua 6—God orders the Israelites under Joshua to kill every living thing in Jericho.

2 Kings 18:10b–12—Shalmaneser (Sargon II), king of Assyria, attacked Samaria, laid siege to it, and after three years captured it. The king of Assyria then deported the Israelites to Assyria and to the cities of the Medes. This came about because they had not heeded the warning of the Lord, their God.

Psalm 78:21–22, 31–32—The Lord heard (*that the Israelites had rebelled against Moses*) and grew angry; fire blazed up against Jacob; anger flared up against Israel . . . God's anger attacked them, killed their best warriors, laid low the youth of Israel. In spite of all this they went on sinning, they did not believe in his wonders.

9

Regarding Jews and Christians

In the Name of God the Compassionate the Merciful

We have seen in the previous chapters what the Koran and the Bible teaches us about both tolerance and intolerance of unbelievers. Let us now record the teachings of the Koran regarding Jews and Christians. Obviously we won't find any passages in the Bible regarding Muslims or the Koran because both the Old and the New Testaments had been closed to further additions long before the Koran was written. However, there are occasional verses in the Koran that echo or are at variance with verses in the Bible and we will introduce them in the proper places.

    Koran 4:45b, 46a, 46c—Consider those to whom a portion of the Scriptures was given (*the Jews*). They purchase error for themselves and wish to see you go astray . . . Some Jews take words out of their context and say: "We hear, but disobey." . . . God has cursed them in their unbelief. They have no faith, except a few of them. You to whom the Scriptures were given! Believe in that which We have revealed, confirming your own scriptures, before We obliterate your faces and turn them backward, or lay Our curse on you.

    Koran 15:18–20—The Jews and Christians say: "We are the children of God and His loved ones." Say: "Why then does He punish you for your sins?"

    Koran 5:67—Say: "People of the Book, you will attain nothing until you observe the Torah and the Gospel and that which is revealed (*the Koran*) to you from your Lord."

    Koran 5:104—The unbelievers invent falsehoods about God. Most of them are lacking in judgement. When they are told: "Come to that which God has revealed (*the Koran*), and to the Apostle (*Mohammed*)," they reply: "Sufficient for us is the faith we inherited from our fathers," even though their fathers knew nothing and were not rightly guided.

Koran 52:5a, 6a—Those to whom the burden of the Torah was entrusted and yet refused to bear it are like a donkey laden with books . . . Say to the Jews: "If you claim that of all men you alone are God's friends, then you should wish for death, if what you say be true!"

Koran 108:3—He (*unbeliever, Christian and Jew*) that hates you (*Mohammed*) shall remain childless.

Koran 6:21—Who is more wicked than the man who invents a falsehood about God or denies His revelations? The wrongdoers (*Christians and Jews*) shall never prosper. (*This particular denunciation is found in eleven other passages in the Koran.*)

Koran 2:75a, 78—Do you (*believers*) then hope that they (*unbelievers*) will believe in you, when some of them have already heard the Word of God and knowingly perverted it, although they understood its meaning? . . . There are illiterate men among them, who, ignorant of the Scriptures, know of nothing but wishful fancies and vague conjecture. Woe to those that write the scriptures with their own hands and then declare: "This is from God," in order to gain some paltry end.

Koran 2:87—To Moses We gave the Scriptures and after him We sent other apostles. We gave Jesus the son of Mary veritable signs and strengthened him with the Holy Spirit. Will you then scorn each apostle whose message does not suit your fancies, charging some with imposture and slaying others? (*Muslims equate Gabriel with the Holy Spirit, so this passage is a bit obscure even to scholars. That is, Mohammed either knowingly rejected the divinity of the Holy Spirit, or confounded Gabriel's announcement to Mary that the Holy Spirit would overshadow her and cause her to conceive. J. M. Rodwell: "It is probable that Mohammed's ideas of the Holy Spirit were at first indefinite, but that the two expressions ultimately became synonymous."*)

**John 14:16–17—(*Jesus speaking to his disciples*) And I will ask the Father, and he will give you another Advocate to be with you always, the Spirit of truth (*the holy Spirit*), which the world cannot accept, because it neither sees nor knows it. But you know it, because it remains with you, and will be in you. (*Although the book of John was written in Greek, in this passage Jesus would have used the* word *"Ruah'"* which is Aramaic for *"the Spirit,"* a word of female gender in Hebrew and Arabic to this day. The holy Spirit is a concept that emerged from the Jewish notion of Sophia, the Wisdom spirit of Ecclesiastes, and the Wisdom of Solomon. The early Christian church eliminated all traces of *"her"* through the words and writings of Jerome, Augustine, and Ambrose.)

Koran 2:88b–91—And now that a Book (*the Koran*) confirming their own has come to them from God, they deny it. They have incurred God's most inexorable wrath. An ignominious punishment awaits the unbelievers.

Koran 2:91b—Say: "Why did you kill the prophets of God if you are true believers?"

Matthew 23:37—(*Jesus speaking to the crowds and the disciples*): "Jerusalem, Jerusalem, you who kill the prophets and stone those sent to you, how many times I yearned to gather your children together, as a hen gathers her young under her wings, but you were unwilling!"

Koran 2:92, 96—Say: "Moses came to you (*the Israelites*) with veritable signs, but in his absence you worshiped the golden calf and committed evil." For their unbelief they were made to drink the calf into their very hearts.

This last sentence will be enigmatic unless the reader is aware of the following passage from Exodus:

Exodus 32:19–20—(*Moses has just received Ten Commandments on Mt. Sinai and is coming down*) As he drew near the camp, he saw the calf and the dancing. With that, Moses' wrath flared up, so that he threw the tablets down and broke them on the base of the mountain. Taking the calf they had made, he fused it in the fire and then ground it down to powder, which he scattered on the water and made the Israelites drink.

Koran 5:78, 80, 82–83—Those of the Israelites who disbelieved were cursed by David and Jesus, the son of Mary, because they rebelled and committed evil . . . You see many among them making friends with unbelievers. Evil is that to which their souls prompt them . . . You will find that the most implacable of men in their enmity to the faithful are the Jews and the pagans, and that the nearest in affection to them (*the Muslim faithful*) are those who say: "We are Christians." That is because there are priests and monks among them; and because they are free from pride.

1 Timothy 3:6—(*Paul instructing Timothy in the qualifications of a good Christian minister*) He should not be a recent convert, so that he may not become conceited (*have exaggerated pride*) and thus incur the devil's punishment.

*   *   *

Throughout the Koran, Gabriel makes much of the fact that God made many covenants with the Israelites and they broke those covenants many times. One example:

Koran 3:77—Those that sell the covenant of God and their own oaths for a paltry price shall have no share in the world to come. God will neither speak to them, nor look at them, nor purify them on the Day of Resurrection. Woeful punishment awaits them.

Some of those covenants:

1) With Noah, before the Flood, Genesis 6:17–19.

2) With Abram, giving his descendants the Promised Land, Genesis 15:18.

3) With Abram when God changes his name to Abraham and promises "to make nations of you," Genesis 17:9.

4) With Abraham, promising a son from Sarah, Genesis 17:19.

5) With Jeremiah, in 31:31: The days are coming, says the Lord, when I will make a new covenant with the house of Israel and the house of Judah. (*Christians consider this to be a prophecy concerning Jesus as the Messiah.*)

6) With Jesus in Matthew 26: (*Jesus in the Upper Room, at the Last Supper with his disciples*) Then he took the cup, gave thanks, and gave it to them, saying, "Drink from it, all of you, for this is my blood of the covenant, which will be shed on behalf of many for the forgiveness of sins." (*The KJV reads, "blood of the new covenant."*)

*   *   *

Sura 5, THE TABLE, is the very last revelation that Mohammed received before he died. This is what Gabriel told Mohammed to recite at the end of his life.

Koran 5:58—Say: "People of the Book, is it not that you hate us only because we believe in God and in what has been revealed to us and to others before, and because most of you are evil-doers?"

61

Koran 5:64a, 64c—The Jews say: "God's hand is chained." May their own hands be chained! (*Muslims believe that on the day of judgment all the Jews will appear with the right hand tied to the neck. That is, God has ceased to be bounteous.*). May they be cursed for what they say! . . . We have stirred among them enmity and hatred, which will endure till the Day of Resurrection. They spread evil in the land, but God does not love the evil-doers.

Psalms 116:5–8—(*David, a Jew, praying*) Gracious is the Lord and just; yes, our God is merciful. The Lord protects the simple; I was helpless, but God saved me. Return, my soul, to your rest; the Lord has been bountiful to you. For my soul has been freed from death, my eyes from tears, my feet from stumbling.

10

Repentance and Forgiveness

In the Name of God the Compassionate the Merciful

Repentance and forgiveness is a major recurring theme in Islam's Koran, Judaism's Hebrew Bible, and Christianity's New Testament. To record all of the references would make a small book of its own. Therefore I have selected just a few from each of the three sources to illustrate the parallels and subtle differences. The brevity of this chapter should in no way diminish the importance of the concept of repentance and forgiveness to the practitioners of the three religions.

Koran 73:27–28—Attend to your prayers, render the alms levy, and give God a generous loan. Whatever good you do you shall surely find it with God, ennobled and richly rewarded by Him. Implore God to forgive you; God is forgiving and merciful.

Colossians 1:13–14—(*Paul writing*) **For he has rescued us from the dominion of darkness and brought us into the kingdom of the Son he loves, in whom we have redemption and the forgiveness of sins.**

Ezekiel 18:21–23—(*God speaking through Ezekiel*) **But if the wicked man turns away from all the sins he committed, if he keeps all my statutes and does what is right and just, he shall surely live, he shall not die. None of the crimes he committed shall be remembered.**

Koran 40:7—Those who bear the Throne and those who stand around give glory to their Lord and believe in Him.

Isaiah 6:2—Seraphim were stationed above (*the throne.*)

Ezekiel 1:26—Four living creatures hovered beneath the throne.

Revelation 4:4—(*John's vision*) **Surrounding the throne I saw twenty-four other thrones on which twenty-four elders sat.**

All give praise to God for his willingness to forgive a repentant sinner.

Koran 40:8, 10—Forgive those that repent and follow Your path . . . Admit them, O Lord, to the gardens of Eden which You have promised them. (*Muslims recognize two gardens of Eden, Bostan and Gulistan. In Salman Rushdies's* The Satanic Verses *Gabreel flies from India to England in an airliner called Bostan, and back to India in Gulistan.*)

Acts 3:19–20—(***Peter preaching in the temple in Jerusalem***) **Repent, therefore, and be converted, that your sins may be wiped away, and that the Lord may grant you times of refreshment and send you the Messiah already appointed for you, Jesus.**

Koran 16:106, 120—Those that are forced to recant (*deny God*) while their hearts remain loyal to the Faith shall be absolved; but those who deny God after professing Islam and open their bosoms to unbelief shall incur the wrath of God . . . To those who commit evil through ignorance, and then repent and mend their ways, your Lord is forgiving and merciful.

Luke 15:7—(*Jesus preaching to tax collectors, sinners, scribes and Pharisees*) "I tell you . . . there will be more joy in heaven over one sinner who repents than over ninety-nine righteous people who have no need of repentance."

2 Chronicles 7:15—(*God speaking to Solomon*) . . . and if my people, upon whom my name has been pronounced, humble themselves and pray, and seek my presence and turn from their evil ways, I will hear them from heaven and pardon their sins and revive their land.

Koran 39:53—Say: "Servants of God, you that have sinned against your souls (*by becoming apostates to Islam*), do not despair of God's mercy, for God forgives all sins."

Matthew 3:1–2—In those days John the Baptist appeared, preaching in the desert of Judea and saying, "Repent, for the kingdom of heaven is at hand!" (*Implying that there was no time to lose in repenting in order to be forgiven of their sins. Jesus repeats these exact words in Matthew 4:17, after his baptism by John, at the beginning of his Galilean ministry.*)

Acts 2:36–39—(*Peter at Pentecost has been berating the Jews for having crucified Jesus*) They asked Peter and the other apostles, "What are we to do, my brothers?" Peter said to them, "Repent and be baptized, every one of you, in the name of Jesus Christ for the forgiveness of your sins; and you will receive the gift of the holy Spirit."

Acts 26:17–18—(*Saul, later called Paul, is actively persecuting Christians. He has a vision of Jesus on the road to Damascus and hears the following words*): I shall deliver you from this people and from the Gentiles to whom I send you, to open their eyes that they may turn from darkness to light and from the power of Satan to God, so that they may obtain forgiveness of sins and an inheritance among those who have been consecrated by faith in me.

Koran 5:65—If the People of the Book accept the true faith and keep from evil, We will pardon them their sins and admit them to the gardens of delight. If they observe the Torah and the Gospel and what is revealed to them (*the Koran*) from their Lord they shall enjoy abundance from above and from beneath. (*The Jew should retain faith in the Torah, the Christian retain faith in the Gospel, and then receive the Koran as the complement of both.*)

2 Peter 3:9—(*Peter writing to Christian communities located in five provinces of Asia Minor—modern-day Turkey*) But do not ignore this one fact, beloved, that with the Lord one day is like a thousand years and a thousand years like one day (*i.e., since time is meaningless to God*). The Lord does not delay his promise, as some regard "delay," but he is patient with you, not wishing that any should perish but that all should come to repentance. But the day of the Lord will come like a thief, and then the heavens will pass away with a mighty roar and the elements will be dissolved by fire, and the earth and everything done on it will be found out.

Luke 24:46–48—(*Jesus speaking to his disciples after his resurrection*) And he said to them, "Thus it is written that the Messiah would suffer and rise from the dead on the third day, and that repentance, for the forgiveness of sins, would be preached in his name to all the nations, beginning from Jerusalem."

Koran 2:54—Moses said to his people: "You have wronged yourselves, my people, in worshiping the calf. Turn in repentance to your Creator and slay the culprits among you. That will be best for you in your Creator's sight." And He relented toward you. He is the Forgiving One, the Merciful.

Exodus 32:26–35—(Summary) Moses comes down from Mt. Sinai with the Ten Commandments. He finds the Israelites worshiping a golden calf. The Lord instructs him to order the priestly tribe of Levites to put to the sword everyone who had participated. Three thousand fell. The rest were doomed to die before crossing the Jordan into the Promised Land.

Koran 38:24—David realized that We were only testing him. He sought forgiveness of his Lord and fell down penitently on his knees. We forgave him his sin (*lying with Bathsheba, sending Uriah to his death*), and in the world to come he shall be honored and well received.

2 Samuel 12:13–14—Then David said to (*his prophet*) Nathan, "I have sinned against the Lord." Nathan answered David: "The Lord on his part has forgiven your sin: you shall not die. But since you have utterly spurned the Lord by this deed, the child born to you must surely die." (*This incident is described in detail in Chapter 18.*)

Koran 4:99—As for the helpless men, women, and children who have neither the strength nor the means to escape, God may pardon them: God pardons and forgives.

1 Kings 8:50–52—(*Solomon praying to God*) Forgive your people their sins and all the offenses they have committed against you, and grant them mercy before their captors, so that these will be merciful to them. For they are your people and your inheritance, whom you brought out of Egypt, from the midst of an iron furnace.

Some Muslim commentators consider the following passage, also quoted in Chapter 9, to be an unforgivable *sin:*

Koran 4:47–48—You to whom the Scriptures (*the Torah*) were given! Believe in that which We have revealed (*the Koran*), confirming your own scriptures, before We obliterate your faces and turn them backward, or lay Our curse on you.

Most Christians also believe that there is an unforgivable sin:

Matthew 12:32—(*Jesus speaking*) Whoever speaks a word against the Son of Man will be forgiven; but whoever speaks against the holy Spirit will not be forgiven, either in this age or in the age to come. (*However, Charlie Ryrie claims that once Christ no longer existed in human form on earth, there is no unpardonable sin. It required the visible and personal presence of Christ on earth.*)

11

Angels

In the Name of God the Compassionate the Merciful

The Koran and the Bible are filled with references to angels. Except for the "fallen angel" and his attendant angels, with whom we will deal in Chapter 16, angels in both Books are good.

The Koran also refers to "djinn" (sometimes spelled "jinn," or "jinee"). They are spirits, both good and bad, that hover mostly unseen over the actions of humans. They are capable, however, of assuming various forms, visible and invisible, and exercising supernatural power. According to Arab legend, they were created out of fire 2,000 years before the creation of Adam and Eve. I mention the djinn only to dissociate them from angels. They are *not* considered by Muslims to be angels. The Bible does not mention djinn or spirits like them.

Before we look at the part angels play in the lives of humans—according to the Bible and Koran—let us look at what the Koran and the Bible say about the sex of angels. Are they male, female, or neuter?

The Koran is quite clear:
Koran 53:25, 28–29—Numerous are the angels in the heavens . . . Those that disbelieve in the hereafter call the angels by the names of females. Yet of this they have no knowledge: they follow mere conjecture, and conjecture is no substitute for truth.

Koran 17:40—What! Has your Lord blessed you (*unbelievers*) with sons and Himself adopted daughters from among the angels? A monstrous blasphemy is that which you utter. (See also 37:149–157 and 43:19.)

All the references to angels in the Old Testament indicate that they are either males or their sex is not expressed. Examples:

Genesis 18:1a, 2a—The Lord appeared to Abraham by the terebinth of Mamre . . . Looking up, he saw three men standing nearby. (*These soon proved to be the Lord and two angels, clearly males, coming to announce that Sarah was to have a child.*)

Deuteronomy 32:43—Exult with him, you heavens, glorify him, all you angels of God. (*Their sex is not expressed.*)

Most of the references to angels in the New Testament make it clear that they are male:

Luke 24:2–4—(*The women came to Jesus' tomb on Easter Sunday morning*) Behold, two men in dazzling garments appeared to them. (*Although they were not called angels, it is clear from the context that they were.*)

Revelation 8:3–8—(Summary) The seventh seal has just been opened. Seven angels are given trumpets to sound to announce seven catastrophes. All are male.

However, there are several passages in the New Testament where there is a good possibility that angels are both male and female:

Matthew 18:2–3, 10—He (*Jesus*) called a child over, placed it in their midst and said, "Amen, I say to you, unless you turn and become like children, you will not enter the kingdom of heaven." . . . "See that you do not despise one of these little ones, for I say to you that their angels in heaven always look upon the face of my heavenly Father." (*"Their angels in heaven" could very well be either males or females.*)

Mark 12:24, 25—(*Jesus has just been asked, "To whom will a woman be married in heaven if she has been married to seven different men on earth?"*) Jesus said to them, "Are you not misled because you do not know the scriptures or the power of God? When they rise from the dead, they neither marry nor are given in marriage, but they are like the angels in heaven." (*I think this implies that angels are both male and female.*)

*   *   *

Later in this chapter I shall spend some time with the archangel Gabriel, but first let's look at what angels do:

68

1) As consorts and helpers of God:

Koran 2:30—He (God) taught Adam the names of all things and then set them before the angels, saying: "Tell Me the names of these."

Genesis 1:26—Then God said, "Let us make man in our image."

Is this the royal "us," or is God talking to his angels, to Jesus, to the heavenly host, or all of the above? Perhaps the following extra-biblical passage answers that question:

Midrash Rabbah, on Numbers 4; par. 19—When the Holy One, Blessed be He, would create man, He took counsel with the Angels and said to them, "We will make man in our image."

Further passages from the Bible that show angels as helpers and/ or consorts:

Exodus 14:19—(*The Israelites have just fled Egypt and are approaching the Red [Reed] Sea.*) The angel of God, who had been leading Israel's camp, now moved and went around behind them.

1 Kings 19:5–6—(*Elijah is fleeing from the wrath of Ahab and Jezebel*) He lay down and fell asleep under the broom tree, but then an angel touched him and ordered him to get up and eat. He looked and there at his head was a hearth cake and a jug of water.

Matthew 4:11—(*Jesus has just successfully resisted the devil's temptation in the wilderness*) Then the devil left him and, behold, angels came and ministered to him.

Luke 22:42–43—(*Jesus is on the Mount of Olives on the night he was betrayed*) He prayed, saying, "Father, if you are willing, take this cup away from me; still, not my will but yours be done." And to strengthen him an angel from heaven appeared to him.

Acts 5:19—(*Peter and other apostles have been thrown in jail.*) But during the night, the angel of the Lord opened the doors of the prison.

2) As messengers:

Koran 15:7—We shall send down the angels only with the truth. Then they shall never be reprieved.

Koran 97:1–5—We revealed this (*the Koran*) on the Night of Qadr (*Dawood: Night of Glory; Rodwell: Night of Power*). On that night the angels and the Spirit by their Lord's leave come down with each decree. That night is peace, till break of dawn. (*Qadr occurs seven nights before the end of Ramadan.*)

Koran 35:1—Praise be to God, Creator of the heavens and the earth! He sends forth the angels as His messengers, with two, three or four pairs of wings.

Genesis 16:7–11a—(*Hagar has run away from Sarai* (Sarah) *to escape Sarai's abusive treatment.*) The Lord's messenger found her by a spring in the wilderness, the spring on the road to Shur, and he asked, "Hagar, maid of Sarai, where have you come from and where are you going?" She answered, "I am running away from my mistress, Sarai."

Exodus 3:1–2a—Meanwhile Moses was tending the flock of his father-in-law Jethro, the priest of Midian. Leading the flock across the desert, he came to Horeb (*Sinai*), the mountain of God. There an angel of the Lord appeared to him in fire flaming out of a bush.

Matthew 1:19–20—(*Mary has become pregnant through the holy Spirit.*) Joseph her husband, since he was a righteous man, yet unwilling to expose her to shame, decided to divorce her quietly. Such was his intention when, behold, the angel of the Lord appeared to him in a dream and said, "Joseph, son of David, do not be afraid to take Mary your wife into your home."

Matthew 28:1–3, 5—After the sabbath, as the first day of the week was dawning, Mary Magdalene and the other Mary came to see the tomb (*of Jesus*) and behold, there was a great earthquake; for an angel of the Lord descended from heaven, approached, rolled back the stone, and sat upon it . . . Then the angel said to the women in reply, "Do not be afraid."

3) As escorts to Hell:

Koran 8:50–51—If you could see the angels when they carry off the souls of the unbelievers! They shall strike them on their faces and their backs, saying: "Taste the torment of the Conflagration! This is the punishment for what your hands committed."

Matthew 13:41—(*Jesus speaking to his disciples*) The Son of Man will send his angels and they will collect out of his kingdom all who cause others to sin and all evildoers. They will throw them into the fiery furnace, where there will be wailing and grinding of teeth.

4) As escorts to Heaven:

Koran 32:11—Say: "The angel of death in charge of you will reclaim your souls. Then to your Lord you shall return." (See also 6:62–63.)

Koran 6:62–63—He reigns supreme over His servants. He sends forth guardians (*angels*) who watch over you and carry away your souls without fail when death overtakes you. Then all are men restored to God, their true Lord. His is the Judgment, and most swift is His reckoning.

Matthew 16:25, 27—(*Jesus speaking to his disciples*) "For whoever wishes to save his life will lose it, but whoever loses his life for my sake will find it . . . For the Son of Man will come with his angels in his Father's glory, and then he will repay everyone according to his conduct."

5) Giving glory to God:

Koran 42:5—The heavens above well-nigh break apart as the angels give glory to their Lord and beg forgiveness for those on earth. Surely God is the Forgiving One, the Merciful.

Koran 39:75—You shall see the angels circling round the Throne, giving glory to their Lord. They shall be judged with fairness, and all shall say; "Praise be to God, Lord of the Universe!"

Deuteronomy 32:43—Exult with him, you heavens, glorify him, all you angels of God.

Psalm 148:1–2—Praise the Lord from the heavens; give praise in the heights. Praise him, all you angels; give praise, all you hosts.

Luke 2:9—(*On the night of Jesus' birth*) The angel of the Lord appeared to them (*the shepherds*) and the glory of the Lord shone around them and they were struck with great fear.

6) As guardians of individuals:

Koran 41:30–33—As for those who say: "Our Lord is God," and take the straight path to Him, the angels will descend to them, saying: "Let nothing alarm or grieve you. Rejoice in the Paradise you have been promised. We are your guardians in this world and in the hereafter."

Koran 13:10—It is the same whether you speak in secret or aloud, whether you hide under the cloak of night or walk about in the light of day. Each has guardian angels before him and behind him, who watch him by God's command.

Exodus 23:20–23a—(*The Lord to Moses*) I am sending an angel before you, to guard you on the way and bring you to the place I have prepared. Be attentive to him and heed his voice.

Psalm 91:10–12—God commands the angels to guard you in all your ways. With their hands they shall support you.

Matthew 2:13—(*The magi have just left gifts for the new-born Jesus, in Bethlehem.*) When they had departed, behold, the angel of the Lord appeared to Joseph in a dream and said, "Rise, take the child and his mother, flee to Egypt, and stay there until I tell you. Herod is going to search for the child to destroy him." (See also Matthew 26:52–54.)

7) As guardians of the Fire of Hell:

Koran 66:6–7—Believers, guard yourselves and guard your kindred against a Fire fueled with men and stones, in the charge of fierce and mighty angels who never disobey God's command and who promptly do His bidding. (See also 74:30–31.)

Nowhere in either Old or New Testaments are there any references to angels—or anyone or anything else—guarding the Fire of Hell.

8) As helpers in war:

Koran 3:123, 125—God had already given you victory at Badr when you were helpless. (*A major victory by the Medina Muslims over the Meccan idolators.*) Yes! If you have patience and guard yourselves against evil, God will send to your aid five thousand angels splendidly accoutered, if they suddenly attack you.

2 Kings 19:35–36—(*In 701* BCE, *Sennacherib, King of Assyria, has laid siege to Judean King Hezekiah's Jerusalem***) That night the angel of the Lord went forth and struck down one hundred and eighty-five thousand men in the Assyrian camp. Early the next morning, there they were, all the corpses of the dead. So Sennacherib, the King of Assyria, broke camp, and went back home to Nineveh.**

9) Duties on the Day of Doom:

Koran 69:11–18—When the Trumpet sounds a single blast; when earth with all its mountains is raised high and with one mighty crash is shattered into dust—on that day the Dread Event will come to pass. Frail and tottering, the sky will be rent asunder on that day, and the angels will stand on all its sides with eight of them carrying the throne of your Lord above their heads.

Matthew 25:31—(*Jesus speaking***) When the Son of Man comes in his glory, and all the angels with him, he will sit upon his glorious throne and all the nations will be assembled before him.**

Revelation 20:1–3a—Then I (*John***) saw an angel come down from heaven, holding in his hand the key to the abyss (***Hell***) and a heavy chain. He seized the dragon, the ancient serpent, which is the Devil or Satan, and tied it up for a thousand years.**

10) Givers of blessings:

Koran 51:1–5—By the dust-scattering winds and the heavily laden clouds; by the swiftly gliding ships, and by the angels who deal out blessings to all men; that which you are promised shall be fulfilled, and the Last Judgment shall surely come to pass!

Revelation 19:9a—Then the angel said to me (*John***), "Write this: blessed are those who have been called to the wedding feast of the Lamb." (***Jesus is the sacrificial Lamb of God.***)**

*   *   *

The archangel Gabriel ("God is great"):

As important as Gabriel is, he is mentioned by name only twice in the Koran. It should be remembered, however, that the entire Koran is in Gabriel's words as dictated to Mohammed and written down by Mohammed's followers. In six other places he isn't mentioned by name, though Muslims are certain that it is Gabriel being referred to. Even in the "annunciation of Mary," and in the promise to Zachariah that Elizabeth would have a child (John the Baptist), the angel is not named.

Here are a few references to Gabriel in the Koran:

Koran 2:98—Say: "Whoever is an enemy of God, His angels, or His apostles, or of Gabriel or Michael, will surely find that God is the enemy of the unbelievers."

Koran 16:102—Say: "The Holy Spirit (*Gabriel*) brought it (*the Koran*) down from your Lord in truth to reassure the faithful, and to give guidance and good news to those that surrender themselves."

Koran 81:22—No, your compatriot (*Mohammed*) is not mad. He saw him (*Gabriel*) on the clear horizon.

There are only four direct references to Gabriel in the Bible:

Daniel 8:15–19—While I, Daniel, sought the meaning of the vision I had seen, a manlike figure stood before me, and on the Ulai (*River*) I heard a human voice that cried out, "Gabriel, explain the vision to this man." When he came near where I was standing, I fell prostrate in terror. (*There follows, in poetic, vivid words, the fate of the Medes, Persians, and the Greeks.*) (See also Daniel 9:21.)

Luke 1:26–27—In the sixth month, the angel Gabriel was sent from God to a town of Galilee called Nazareth, to a virgin betrothed to a man named Joseph, of the house of David, and the virgin's name was Mary. (*There follows the annunciation of Mary as the mother of Jesus the Messiah.*) (See also Luke 1:10–13.)

But Gabriel could be the archangel in the following passage:

1 Thessalonians 4:16—(*Paul writing*) For the Lord himself with a word of command, with the voice of an archangel, and with the trumpet of God, will come down from heaven and the dead in Christ will rise first.

74

12

Attitudes Towards Females

In the Name of God the Compassionate the Merciful

The Koran has many references to how men should treat women as well as advice to women regarding their conduct. In fact, one whole Sura—entitled "Women"—is mostly devoted to this subject. Although found as the fourth Sura in the classic Koran, it is generally agreed that chronologically it is the 100th Sura, revealed in the fourth or fifth year after the flight from Mecca to Medina, ten years before Mohammed's death and three years after Khadijah's death.

In pre-Islamic times most women in Arabia were on a par with slaves. There were exceptions. For example, Khadijah was the wealthy owner of a caravanserai. But the status of women in Seventh Century Arabia—as well as in most other parts of the world—was generally abysmal. But now, as we shall see in this chapter, Mohammed was actually *upgrading* the status of women from having almost no rights to having some.

✻   ✻   ✻

The number of wives a man may take lawfully:

There are only two references in the Koran to the number of wives a man can have. One of them was quoted in Chapter 5, granting Mohammed the right to take as many wives as he wanted. The other one:

Koran 4:2–4—If you fear that you cannot treat orphan girls with fairness, then you may marry other women who seem good to you: two, three, or four of them. But if you fear that you cannot maintain equality among them, marry one only or any slave-girls you may own. This will make it easier for you to avoid injustice.

Almost all of the Old Testament men had more than one wife, apparently as many as they could afford and support. Some examples:

Genesis 25:1—Abraham married another wife whose name was Keturah.

Genesis 29:24, 28—At nightfall (*Laban*) took his daughter Leah and brought her to Jacob, and Jacob consummated the marriage with her. Jacob . . . finished the bridal week for Leah and then Laban gave him Rachel in marriage.

1 Kings 11:1–3—King Solomon loved many foreign women besides the daughter of Pharaoh . . . from nations with which the Lord had forbidden the Israelites to intermarry, "Because," he (*God*) said, "they will turn your heart to their gods." But Solomon fell in love with them. He had seven hundred wives of princely rank and three hundred concubines.

This all changed for the followers of Jesus:

Matthew 5:31—(*Jesus preaching*) It was also said, "Whoever divorces his wife must give her a bill of divorce." But I say to you, whoever divorces his wife (unless the marriage is unlawful) causes her to commit adultery, and whoever marries a divorced woman commits adultery.

1 Timothy 3:12—(*Paul instructing the young Timothy*)—Deacons (*ministers*) may be married only once and must manage their children and their households well.

1 Corinthians 7:3, 8–9—(*Paul writing*) Because of cases of immorality every man should have his own wife, and every woman her own husband . . . Now to the unmarried and to widows I say: it is a good thing for them to remain as they are, as I do, but if they cannot exercise self-control they should marry, for it is better to marry than to be on fire.

Laws regarding marriageable women:

Koran 5:5b—Lawful to you are the believing women and the free women from among those who were given the Book before you (*the Jews, but not the Christians*).

Koran 2:221—You shall not wed pagan women, unless they embrace the Faith.

Koran 4:19a, 20—Believers, it is unlawful for you to inherit the women of your deceased kinsmen against their will, or to bar them from re-marrying . . . If you wish to replace a wife with another, do not take from her the dowry . . . for how can you take back when you have lain with each other and entered into a firm contract?

The Old Testament takes a different stance, prescribing what is called a "levirate" marriage:

Deuteronomy 25:5–6—When brothers live together and one of them dies without a son, the widow of the deceased shall not marry anyone outside the family; but her husband's brother shall go to her and perform the duty of a brother-in-law by marrying her. (See also Deuteronomy 25:9–10.) (*The New Testament does not comment on this situation.*)

A list of ineligible women:

Koran 4:21–25—You shall not marry the women whom your father married: all previous such marriages excepted. That was an evil practice, indecent and abominable. Forbidden to you are your mothers, daughters, sisters, paternal and maternal aunts, the daughters of your brothers and sisters, your foster-mothers, your foster-sisters, the mothers of your wives, your step-daughters, the wives of your own begotten sons, two sisters at the same time. Such is the decree of God.

All women other than these are lawful to you.

If any one of you cannot afford to marry a free believing woman, let him marry a slave-girl who is a believer. Marry them with the permission of their masters.

Koran 33:54—You (*believers*) must not speak ill of God's apostle, nor shall you ever wed his wives after him; this would be a grave offence in the sight of God.

The Old Testament strictures are very similar:

Leviticus 18:7–18—(Excerpts) You shall not . . . have intercourse with your mother . . . your father's wife . . . your sister, your father's daughter or your mother's daughter . . . with your daughter's daughter . . . your father's sister . . . your mother's sister . . . your father's brother's wife . . . your daughter-in-law . . . your brother's wife . . . a woman and also with her daughter . . . nor her son's daughter

or her daughter's daughter . . . while your wife is still living you shall not marry her sister as her rival . . .

The New Testament has no comparable list of unmarriageable women.

The Old Testament also has instructions about marrying slave girls:

Deuteronomy 21:10–13—If you see a comely woman among the captives and wish to have her as wife, you may take her home to your house. After she has mourned her father and mother for a full month, you may have relations with her, and you shall be her husband and she shall be your wife.

Laws of inheritance:

Koran 4:8—Men shall have a share in what their parents and kinsmen leave; and women shall have a share in what their parents and kinsmen leave: whether it be little or much, they shall be legally entitled to a share.

However:

Koran 4:10b–11a, 12a—A male shall inherit twice as much as a female. If there be more than two girls, they shall have two-thirds of the inheritance; but if there be one only, she shall inherit the half. (*One-half of what the male gets.*) Parents shall inherit a sixth each, if the deceased have (*sic*) a child; but if he leave (*sic*) no child and his parents be his heirs, his mother shall have a third. If he have (*sic*) brothers, his mother shall have a sixth after payment of any legacy he may have bequeathed or any debt he may have owed. Your wives shall inherit one quarter of your estate if you die childless. If you leave children, they shall inherit one-eighth, after payment of any legacy you may have bequeathed or any debt you may have owed . . . Such are the bounds set by God.

And:

Koran 4:177—If a man die (*sic*) childless and he have (*sic*) a sister, she shall inherit half of his estate. If a woman die (*sic*) childless, her brother shall be her sole heir. If a childless man has two sisters, they shall inherit two-thirds of his estate; but if he has both brothers and sisters, the share of each male shall be that of two females. Thus God makes plain His precepts so that you may not err.

There are no references in the New Testament to laws of inheritance. There are several hundred references in the Old Testament to laws of inheritance, almost all of them having to do with land. There is only one reference to a woman's right to inherit:

Numbers 27:1–9—(Summary) Zelophehad had five daughters who, when he died without leaving sons, appealed to Moses for the property that would have gone to sons . . . When Moses laid their case before the Lord, the Lord said to him, "The plea of Zelophehad's daughters is just; you shall give them hereditary property."

This was later amended in Numbers 36:1–6 to make the heiress marry within the clan.

Laws regarding sexual conduct:

Koran 4:14—If any of your women commit fornication, call in four witnesses from among yourselves against them; if they testify to their guilt, confine them to their houses till death overtakes them or till God finds another way for them.

In the early years of Islam, a woman found guilty of adultery or fornication was literally imprisoned in a sealed room. This later was changed, by the Shari'a, in the case of a maiden, to one year's banishment and one hundred stripes, and in the case of a married woman, stoning to death. In Saudi Arabia today, the woman is stoned and the man beheaded.

The laws of Moses regarding adultery were equally severe:

Exodus 20:14, Deuteronomy 5:18—(*The seventh of Moses' Ten Commandments*) You shall not commit adultery.

Leviticus 20:10–12—(Summary) The death sentence was passed on a man who commits adultery with a neighbor's wife, his father's wife, his daughter-in-law (the woman is killed, too). 20:14–21 (Excerpts) If a man commits adultery with his neighbor's wife, both . . . shall be put to death. If a man disgraces his father by lying with his father's wife, both . . . shall be put to death . . . If a man lies with his daughter-in-law, both of them shall be put to death . . . If a man marries a woman and her mother also, they shall all be burned to death . . . If a man consummates marriage with his sister or his half-sister, they shall be publicly cut off from their people . . . You shall not have intercourse with your mother's sister or your father's sister . . . If a man disgraces his uncle by having intercourse with his uncle's wife, (*both*) shall pay the penalty by dying childless.

The Old Testament laws revealed by God through Moses never prescribed the manner of death for a married person, just that the adulterer and/or adulteress should be put to death—see the previously quoted passages from Leviticus 20. However, Moses did prescribe stoning for both man and woman if the woman was betrothed but unmarried and was consenting. If she was not *betrothed, the man must marry her and give her father fifty silver shekels and promise never to divorce her [Deuteronomy 22:23]. If she was raped, only the man was stoned.*

Proof of adultery or fornication is a complicated process in both the Koran and the Old Testament. For the interested reader, the process is described in the Koran in Sura 24:3–6, and in the Bible in Numbers 5:11–28.

The New Testament is somewhat ambiguous. Consider the following:

Romans 7:2–3—(*Paul writing*) Thus a married woman is bound by law to her living husband; but if her husband dies she is free from that law, and she is not an adulteress if she consorts with another man.

Matthew 5:27–30—(*Jesus speaking*) "You have heard that it was said, 'You shall not commit adultery.' But I say to you, everyone who looks at a woman with lust has already committed adultery with her in his heart."

But Jesus pardoned a woman caught in adultery:

John 8:3–5, 9, 10–11—Then the scribes and Pharisees brought a woman who had been caught in adultery and made her stand in the middle. They said to him, "Teacher, this woman was caught in the very act of committing adultery. Now in the law, Moses commanded us to stone such women. So what do you say?" . . . "Let the one among you who is without sin be the first to throw a stone at her." . . They went away one by one, beginning with the elders . . . "Woman, where are they? Has no one condemned you?" She replied, "No one, sir." Then Jesus said, "Neither do I condemn you. Go and from now on do not sin any more."

Male authority over women:

Koran 2:223—Women are your fields; go, then, into your fields whence (*sic*) you please.

Koran 4:34–35—Men have authority over women because God has made the one superior to the other and because they spend their wealth to maintain them . . . They guard their unseen parts because God has guarded them . . . As for those from whom you expect disobedience, admonish them and send them to beds apart (*from yours*) and beat them. Then if they obey you, take no further action against them. Surely God is high, supreme. (*Mohammed Asadi interprets these two verses as a three-step process in quelling a rebellion by a wife: 1) talk to her, 2) make her sleep apart, 3) give her a single symbolic hit, not in anger as in a beating.*)

Koran 4:127—If a woman fears ill-treatment or desertion on the part of her husband, it shall be no offence for them to seek a mutual agreement. Man is prone to avarice.

Ephesians 5:22–23, 28—(*Paul writing*) As the church is subordinate to Christ, so wives should be subordinate to their husbands in everything . . . So also husbands should love their wives as their own bodies.

But:

1 Corinthians 11:11–12—(*Paul writing*) Woman is not independent of man or man of woman in the Lord.

1 Corinthians 14:33b, 35—(*Excerpts—Paul writing*) As in all the churches of the holy ones, women should keep silent in the churches . . . But if they want to learn anything, they should ask their husbands at home.

1 Timothy 2:9–12—(*Paul's instructions to the young Timothy*) Women should adorn themselves with proper conduct, with modesty and self-control, not with braided hairstyles and gold ornaments, or pearls, or expensive clothes, but rather, as befits women who profess reverence for God, with good deeds. A woman must receive instruction silently and under complete control. I do not permit a woman to teach or to have authority over a man.

But:

Romans 16:1–3—(*Paul writing*) I commend to you Phoebe, our sister, who is also a minister of the church at Cenchrae (*a suburb of Corinth*) that you may receive her in the Lord in a manner worthy of the holy ones, and help her in whatever she may need from you, for she has been a benefactor to many and to me as well. Greet Priscilla and Aquila, my co-workers in Christ Jesus, who risked their necks for my life. (*There is no good explanation for the apparent contradiction.*)

Advice to the wives of Mohammed:

Koran 33:28—Prophet, say to your wives: "If you seek this nether life and all its finery, come, I will make provision for you and release you honorably." *(This passage was introduced because Mohammed's wives had been annoying him by asking for rich dresses, etc. He gave them the choice of staying with him and dressing conservatively, or being divorced. They all chose to stay.)*

Koran 33:30a, 31b, 33, 35—Wives of the Prophet! Those of you who commit a proven sin shall be doubly punished . . . Wives of the Prophet, you are not like other women . . . Stay in your homes and do not display your finery as women used to do in the days of ignorance (*pre-Islamic days*). Attend to your prayers, give alms and obey God and His apostle.

Women of the Household (*Mohammed's*), those who surrender themselves to God and accept the true Faith, who are devout, sincere, patient, humble, charitable, and chaste; who fast and are ever mindful of God—on these, both men and women, God will bestow forgiveness and a rich reward.

There are, of course, no parallels to these verses in the Bible, but in a letter to Titus on Crete, Paul does give advice to women on how to live:

Titus 2:3–5—Similarly, older women should be reverent in their behavior, not slanderers, not addicted to drink, teaching what is good, so that they may train younger women to love their husbands and children, to be self-controlled, chaste, good homemakers, under the control of their husbands, so that the word of God may not be discredited.

Women in Paradise:

Koran 4:124—The believers who do good works, both men and women, shall enter paradise.

Galatians 3:26–29—(*Paul writing*) For through faith you are all children of God in Christ Jesus. For all of you who were baptized into Christ have clothed yourselves with Christ. There is neither Jew nor Greek, there is neither slave nor free person, there is not male and female; for you are all one in Christ Jesus. And if you belong to Christ, then you are Abraham's descendant, heirs (*of heaven*) according to the promise.

Veils—there are only three references in the Koran:

Koran 33:55—It shall be no offence for the Prophet's wives to be seen unveiled by their fathers, their sons, their brothers, their brothers' sons, their sisters' sons, their women, or their slave-girls.

Koran 33:59—Prophet, enjoin your wives, your daughters, and the wives of true believers to draw their veils close round them. That is more proper, so that they may be recognized and not be molested. (*The head-to-toe "veil" [burka or chador] is not sanctioned by the Koran.*)

1 Corinthians 11:5–6, 9–10—(*Paul writing*) But any woman who prays or prophesies with her head unveiled brings shame upon her head, for it is one and the same thing as if she had her head shaved. (***This injunction applied only to religious services.***)

Koran 24:30b, 31b—Enjoin believing women to turn their eyes away from temptation and to preserve their chastity; to cover their adornments . . . And let them not stamp their feet when walking so as to reveal their hidden trinkets.

Isaiah 3:16—The Lord said: Because the daughters of Zion are haughty, and walk with their necks outstretched, ogling and mincing as they go, their anklets tinkling with every step, the Lord shall cover the scalps of Zion's daughters with scabs, and the Lord shall bare their heads. And for the coiffure, baldness; for the rich gown, a sackcloth skirt.

Female infanticide. There are numerous references to the practice in the Koran. One will suffice to show Mohammed's feelings in the matter:

Koran 16:57–59—They (*pagans*) foist daughters upon God (glory be to Him!), but for themselves they choose what they desire.

When a new-born girl in announced to one of them, his countenance darkens and he is filled with gloom. On account of the bad news he hides himself from men: should he put up with the shame or bury her in the earth? How ill they judge! (*The idolatrous Arabs regarded some angels as females and daughters of God. But their own preference was for male offspring. And it is apparent that the Koran's teachings did not eliminate the practice of female infanticide even among Muslims, because it is said that the only occasion on which the third caliph, Uthman (644–656), ever shed a tear was when his little daughter, whom he was burying alive, wiped the dust of the grave-earth from his beard.*)

There are no references in the Bible to burying children alive, but there are many concerning infanticide by burning:
Leviticus 18:21—(*God to Moses*) You shall not offer any of your offspring to be immolated to Molech, thus profaning the name of your God. (*In Judah the furnaces for burning children in sacrifice to Molech, a Canaanite god, were in the valley of Hinnom—Gehinnom in Hebrew, eventually Gehenna. By the time of Jesus, the Jews felt such horror at the practice that went on at Topheth in Gehinnom that both Topheth and Gehenna became synonymous with Hell.*)
Leviticus 20:1–5—The Lord said to Moses, "Tell the Israelites: anyone, whether an Israelite or an alien residing in Israel, who gives any of his offspring to Molech, shall be put to death. Let his fellow citizens stone him."
2 Kings 23:10—The king (*Josiah*) also defiled Topheth in the Valley of Ben-hinnom, so that there would no longer be any immolation of sons or daughters by fire in honor of Molech. (*See also 1 Kings 11:7–9 and Jeremiah 33:35.*)

13

Divorce

In the Name of God the Compassionate the Merciful

The instructions regarding divorce for male Muslims, Jews and Christians are not only quite different but quite explicit. Jews draw their instructions from Moses, Christians from Jesus and Paul, and Muslims from Mohammed's revelations. The procedure for a woman to institute divorce proceedings is not given in either the Old or the New Testament, but there is a procedure in the Koran for women to obtain a divorce, as we shall see.

For the Muslim:

Koran 2:228—Divorced women must wait, keeping themselves from men, three menstrual courses. It is unlawful for them, if they believe in God and the Last Day, to hide what God has created in their wombs; in which case their husbands would do well to take them back, should they desire reconciliation.

Koran 65:2–7—(During those three months) you shall not expel them from their homes, nor shall they go away, unless they have committed a proven sinful act.

When their waiting term is ended, either keep them honorably or part with them in honor. Call to witness two honest men among you and give your testimony before God.

As for pregnant women, their term shall end with their confinement . . . Lodge them in your own homes, according to your means. You shall not harass them so as to make life intolerable for them. If, after that, they give suck to the infants they bore, give them their pay and consult together in all reasonableness. But if you cannot bear each other, let other women suckle for you. (*A "wet nurse" is hired, the woman is divorced and leaves the baby in the husband's household.*)

Koran 33:3—God has never put two hearts within one man's body. He does not regard the wives whom you divorce as your mothers. (*The pagan custom in Arabia at the time was for a man to divorce his wife by saying, "Be to me as my mother's back."*)

Koran 2:228c—Women shall with justice have rights similar to those exercised against them, although men have a status above women. God is mighty and wise.

Koran 2:229a—Divorce may be pronounced twice, and then a woman must be retained in honor or allowed to go with kindness. (*A man divorces his wife by pronouncing the formula "I divorce you" three times. The interval between the three pronouncements can vary enormously. The man can say it three times in rapid succession, divorcing her on the spot. Or he can say it once as a warning "to shape up," and not repeat it again for months or years. The second utterance can also be considered a warning and either never be repeated or be repeated for the third time months or years later, in which case the divorce then becomes final.*)

Koran 2:229b—It is unlawful for husbands to take from them anything they have given them, unless both fear that they may not be able to keep within the bounds set by God; in which case it shall be no offence for either of them if the wife ransoms herself. (*This means that **she** institutes divorce proceedings by returning the property given her at their marriage.*)

Koran 2:230—If a man divorces his wife he cannot remarry her until she has wedded another man and been divorced by him; in which case it shall be no offence for either of them to return to the other, if they think that they can keep within the bounds set by God.

Koran 33:37–38—And when Zayd (*Mohammed's adopted son*) divorced his wife, We gave her to you (*Mohammed*) in marriage, so that it should become legitimate for true believers to wed the wives of their adopted sons if they divorced them.

Koran 2:236–238—It shall be no offence for you to divorce your wives before the marriage is consummated or the dowry settled. Provide for them with fairness, the rich man according to his means, and the poor man according to his. If you divorce them before the marriage is consummated, but after their dowry has been settled, give them the half of their dowry, unless they or the husband agree to waive it. But it is more proper that the husband should waive it. Do not forget to show kindness to each other. God observes your actions.

Koran 2:240—You shall bequeath your widows a year's maintenance without causing them to leave their homes. Reasonable provision shall also be made for divorced women. That is incumbent on righteous men.

*   *   *

The laws of divorce in the Old and New Testaments are quite different from each other.

For the Jew:

Malachi 2:15–16—Did he (*God*) not make one being, with flesh and spirit: and what does that one require but godly offspring? You must . . . not break faith with the wife of your youth. For I hate divorce, says the Lord, the God of Israel.

But divorce did become possible by common consent of the priests. The man merely had to hand his wife a "bill of divorce." There were some restrictions, however, as seen in the following passages:

Deuteronomy 24:1–4a—(Summary) If a woman is divorced by a man, marries again, and is again divorced, she cannot marry the first man again. "That would be an abomination before the Lord."

Deuteronomy 22:13–21—(Summary) If a man tries to divorce his wife by claiming that she was not a virgin when he married her, he must prove it before the elders. If he cannot, he shall be flogged, and must remain married to the woman, and never divorce her. If he does prove it, the woman shall be stoned to death in the entrance to her father's house.

Leviticus 21:13–15—The priest shall marry a virgin.

For the Christian:

Mark 10:2a, 3a, 6–9—The Pharisees approached (*Jesus*) and asked, "Is it lawful for a husband to divorce his wife?" . . . Jesus told

87

them . . . "From the beginning of creation, 'God made them male and female. For this reason a man shall leave his father and mother and be joined to his wife, and the two shall become one flesh' (*Genesis 2:24*). So they are no longer two but one flesh. Therefore what God has joined together, no human being must separate."

1 Corinthians 7:10–16—(*Paul writing*) To the married, however, I give this instruction (not I, but the Lord): a wife should not separate from her husband—and if she does separate she must either remain single or become reconciled to her husband—and a husband should not divorce his wife.

14

Retaliation and War

In the Name of God the Compassionate the Merciful

The very first thing to emphasize is that *jihad* does *not* mean "holy war." It means "struggle" or "strive." The term *can* be applied to a struggle or fight against one's enemies, but it is not called a holy struggle. A *jihad* can also be a struggle to get an education, to win an election, to get a good job, and so forth. In other words, a struggle for anything one wants badly.

But most Muslims will quickly point out that the *primary* meaning of *jihad* is a struggle within oneself to follow the tenets of Islam as laid down by Mohammed in the Koran, a warfare against the passions. They will use *jihad* in a phrase such as this: "Jihad li tajdid al-ruh al-Islami," which means, "A struggle for the soul of Islam."

What is the Arabic for "holy war"? It is *harbun Muqaddasatun,* not *jihad.* Furthermore, Mohammed in the Koran never describes war against the infidels or idolaters as being holy.

It should be noted that when Mohammed talks about the "infidel" and the "unbeliever," he almost always is referring to his own countrymen, the idolatrous Arabs, especially his own tribe.

*   *   *

Koran 2:178, 180—Believers, retaliation is decreed for you in bloodshed: a free man for a free man, a slave for a slave, and a female for a female . . . In retaliation you have a safeguard for your lives.

Koran 17:32—You shall not kill any man whom God has forbidden you to kill, except for a just cause. If a man is slain unjustly, his heir shall be entitled to satisfaction. But let him not carry his vengeance too far, for his victim will in turn be assisted and avenged.

89

Koran 22:39—Permission to take up arms is hereby given to those who are attacked, because they have been wronged. God has power to grant them victory: those who have been unjustly driven from their homes, only because they said: "Our Lord is God."

The Old Testament takes different stances for fellow countrymen and for other nations:
Leviticus 19:18—Take no revenge and cherish no grudge against your countrymen.
Isaiah 1:24—Now, therefore, says the Lord, the Lord of hosts, the Mighty One of Israel: Ah! I will take vengeance on my foes and fully repay my enemies! (See also Ezekiel 25:15–17)

Jesus and Paul take still a different stance on retaliation:
Luke 6:29, 31—(*Jesus teaching*) To the person who strikes you on one cheek, offer the other one as well, and from the person who takes your cloak, do not withhold even your tunic . . . Do to others as you would have them do to you.
Ephesians 4:31–32—(*Paul writing*) All bitterness, fury, anger, shouting, and reviling must be removed from you, along with all malice. And be kind to one another, compassionate, forgiving one another as God has forgiven you in Christ.
Koran 5:46—Unbelievers are those who do not judge according to God's revelations. We decreed for them a life for a life, an eye for an eye, a nose for a nose, an ear for an ear, a tooth for a tooth, and a wound for a wound.
Exodus 21:23–25—If an injury ensues, you shall give life for life, eye for eye, tooth for tooth, hand for hand, foot for foot, burn for burn, wound for wound, stripe for stripe.
To the Christian and Jew, the quote from Koran 5:46 seems to indicate that Mohammed had a rather detailed knowledge of the Old Testament. Indeed, this Sura [THE TABLE] was chronologically the last one to be revealed, near the end of Mohammed's life. But Muslims contend that it was not Mohammed but God who had that knowledge and passed it on to Mohammed through Gabriel.
Koran 2:190–194a—Fight for the sake of God those that fight against you, but do not attack them first. God does not love the aggressors. Slay them wherever you find them. Drive them out of the places from which they drove you. Idolatry is more grievous than

bloodshed. But do not fight them within the precincts of the Holy Mosque unless they attack you there; if they attack you put them to the sword. A sacred month for a sacred month; sacred things too are subject to retaliation. (*Rodwell explains this difficult passage: in wars fought for the cause of religion, the sacred month [Ramadhan] may be the time, and the temple in Mecca the scene, of contests which normally would be prohibited.*)

Koran 2:194b—If anyone attacks you, attack him as he attacked you. Have fear of God and know that God is with the righteous.

Koran 8:15–17—Believers, when you encounter the infidels on the march, do not turn your backs to them in flight. If anyone on that day turns his back to them, except for tactical reasons, or to join another band, he shall incur the wrath of God and Hell shall be his home: an evil fate. It was not you, but God, who slew them . . . God smote them so that He might richly reward the faithful. (*In Sura 8[THE SPOILS], from which the previous passage was taken, God recalls for Mohammed the battle at Bedr in 624, when 319 Muslims defeated 1,000 Meccans with the help of 1,000 of God's angels. The literal translation of "smote them" is "cast at them," a reference to the sand and gravestones that God's angels cast into the eyes of the Meccans so that the numerically inferior Muslims could defeat them.*)

Leviticus 26:6–9—(God speaking to Moses) I will establish peace in the land, that you may lie down to rest without anxiety. You will rout your enemies and lay them low with your sword. Five of you will put a hundred of your foes to flight, and a hundred of you will chase ten thousand of them.

Koran 2:216—Fighting is obligatory for you, much as you dislike it. But you may hate a thing although it is good for you, and love a thing although it is bad for you. God knows, but you know not.

Koran 2:155—Do not say that those slain in the cause of God (*war with the infidels*) are dead. They are alive, but you are not aware of them.

Koran 3:156–158—Believers, do not follow the example of the infidels, who say of their brothers when they meet death abroad or in battle: "Had they stayed with us they would not have died, nor would they have been killed." God will cause them to regret their words. It is God who ordains life and death.

Joshua 8:1–2—(*The Israelites under Joshua's leadership have crossed the Jordan into Canaan from the east after living in the*

desert for forty years. This is just one example out of many when the Lord came to the military aid of his Chosen People.) The Lord then said to Joshua, "Do not be afraid or dismayed. Take all the army with you and prepare to attack Ai. I have delivered the king of Ai into your power, with his people, city and land. Do to Ai and its king what you did to Jericho and its king (*every living thing was killed*); except that you may take its spoil and livestock as booty."

Joshua 23:10—One of you puts to flight a thousand, because it is the Lord, your God, himself who fights for you.

Koran 8:40–41, 65—Make war on them (*unbelievers*) until idolatry shall cease and God's religion shall reign supreme. Know that one-fifth of your spoils shall belong to God, the Apostle (*Mohammed*), the Apostle's kinsfolk, the orphans, the destitute, and those that travel the road . . . Prophet, rouse the faithful to arms. If there are twenty steadfast among you, they shall vanquish two hundred, and if there are a hundred, they shall rout a thousand unbelievers, for they are devoid of understanding.

Koran 47:7—As for those who are slain in the cause of God, He will not allow their works to perish. He will vouchsafe them guidance and ennoble their state: He will admit them to the Paradise He has made known to them. (*This promise is repeated in almost exactly the same words many, many times throughout the Koran. See Chapter 22 for the description of Paradise.*)

Koran 47:35, 39—Do not falter or sue for peace when you have gained the upper hand. God is on your side and will not grudge you the reward for your labors . . . If you pay no heed (*to the Prophet and the Koran*) God will replace you by others who shall bear no resemblance to yourselves.

Koran 3:158, 195—If you die or be slain in the cause of God, His forgiveness and His mercy would surely be better than all the riches they amass . . . I shall forgive them their sins and admit them to gardens watered by running streams.

Koran 4:74, 76—Let those who would exchange the life of this world for the hereafter, fight for the cause of God; whoever fights for the cause of God, whether he dies or triumphs, We shall richly reward him . . . The true believers fight for the cause of God but the infidels fight for the devil. Fight then against the friends of Satan.

Matthew 5:11—(*Jesus speaking*): Blessed are you when they insult you and persecute you and utter every kind of evil against you

92

falsely because of me. **Rejoice and be glad, for your reward will be great in heaven.**

Koran 5:34—Those that make war against God and His apostle and spread disorder in the land shall be put to death or crucified or have their hands and feet cut off on alternate sides, or be banished from the land. They shall be held up to shame in this world and sternly punished in the hereafter: except those that repent before you reduce them. For you must know that God is forgiving and merciful.

Koran 9:28—Fight against such of those to whom the Scriptures were given (*Jews*) as believe neither in God nor the Last Day, who do not forbid what God and His apostle have forbidden, and do not embrace the true Faith, until they pay tribute out of hand and are utterly subdued. (*This is one of the few references to fighting the Jews, and refers only to the Jews who do not believe in God and the Last Day. See also 19:1–6, and 33:25–27. It is the 113th Sura chronologically, next to the last, and was revealed shortly before Mohammed's death.*)

Koran 9:12–14—If they (*idolaters*) repent and take to prayer and render the alms levy, they shall become your brothers in the Faith. Thus do We make plain Our revelations for men of knowledge. But if, after coming to terms with you, they break their oaths, and revile your faith, make war on the leaders of unbelief. They were the first to attack you. Do you fear them? Surely God is more deserving of your fear, if you are true believers.

15

The Creation Stories

In the Name of God the Compassionate the Merciful

We come now to the creation stories in the Koran and the Bible. We shall see that the stories of the creation of the universe and of woman are strikingly similar in both Books, whereas there are major differences in the stories of the creation of man.

But before we get to those stories, there is an important point to be made. Because of Mohammed's belief that Jesus was not the Son of God, and therefore not divine, there are no verses in the Koran corresponding to the following passages from John's gospel and Paul's letter to the Colossians, which clearly indicate to the Christian that Jesus was the agent of God's creation:

John 1:1–4—In the beginning was the Word, and the Word was with God, and the Word was God. He was with God in the beginning. Through him all things were made: without him nothing was made that has been made.

Colossians 1:15–17—He (*Jesus*) is the image of the invisible God, the firstborn of all creation. For in him were created all things in heaven and on earth, the visible and the invisible, whether thrones or dominions or principalities or powers; all things were created through him and for him. He is before all things and in him all things hold together.

Creation of the earth and heaven:

Koran 39:63—God is the Creator of all things. His are the keys of the heavens and the earth.

Koran 79:27–33—He raised it high and fashioned it, giving darkness to its night and brightness to its day. After that he spread the earth, and, drawing water from its depth, brought forth its pastures. He set down the mountains, for you and for your cattle to delight in. (*In both the Koran and the Bible, "cattle" usually includes cows, camels, sheep, and goats.*)

Isaiah 42:5—(It was God) who created the heavens and stretched them out, who spread out the earth and all that comes out of it, who gives breath to its people, and life to those who walk on it.

Genesis 1:1–19—(Excerpts) In the beginning, when God created the heavens and the earth, the earth was a formless wasteland, and darkness covered the abyss, while a mighty wind swept over the waters. Then God said, "Let there be light." "Let there be a dome in the middle of the waters." "Let the water under the sky be gathered into a single basin so that the dry land may appear." "Let the earth bring forth vegetation." "Let there be lights in the dome of the sky to separate day from night. Let them mark the fixed times, the days and the years."

Psalm 24:1–2—The earth is the Lord's, and everything in it, the world, and all who live in it; for he founded it upon the seas and established it upon the waters.

*   *   *

In Sura 55 and Psalm 136 we find Mohammed's revelation and the psalmist's writings to be in a very similar style, differing mainly in the interjectory phrase. We need not record the entire Sura and psalm but the following verses are a sample of the technique.

Koran 55:2, 5, 10–13, 14–15, 17–18—The sun and the moon pursue their ordered course . . . He raised the heaven on high . . . He laid the earth for His creatures, with all its fruits and blossom-bearing palm, chaff-covered grain and scented herbs. Which of your Lord's blessings would you deny?

He created man from potter's clay, and the jinn from smokeless fire. Which of your Lord's blessings would you deny?

The Lord of the two easts is He, and the Lord of the two wests. Which of your Lord's blessings would you deny? (*Two easts: where the sun rises in summer and winter; two wests: where it sets.*)

(*There are twenty-three more like these.*)

Psalm 136:1, 5, 6, 8—Praise the Lord, who is so good; God's love endures forever;

95

Who skillfully made the heavens, God's love endures forever;
Who spread the earth upon the waters, God's love endures
forever; The sun to rule the day, God's love endures forever:
(*There are twenty-two more like these.*)

The creation of the first man:

*Scattered throughout the Koran are different versions of the
creation of man by God:*
Koran 96:1—Recite in the name of your Lord who created—created man from clots of blood.

Koran 86:5–6—(Man was) created from an ejaculated fluid that
issues from between the loins and the ribs.

Koran 80:17–18—From what did God create him? From a little germ.

Koran 66:56—It was He who created man from water.

Koran 23:12–15—We first created man from an essence of clay;
then placed him, a living germ, in a secure enclosure (*the womb
according to Rodwell, but if so, I must ask, "whose?"*). The germ
We made (*into*) a clot of blood, and the clot (*into*) a lump of flesh.
This We fashioned into bones, then clothed the bones with flesh.

*There are two versions of the creation of man in Genesis. In the
first, man was created after the earth and the entire universe:*
Genesis 1:27–28—God created man in his image, in the divine
image he created him; male and female he created them. God blessed
them, saying: "Be fruitful and multiply, fill the earth and subdue it.
Have dominion over the fish of the sea, the birds of the air, and all
the living things that move on the earth."

*In the second version, when man was created the earth had been
formed but was barren of life:*
Genesis 2:4–5a, 7—At the time when the Lord God made the
earth and the heavens—while as yet there was no field shrub on earth
and no grass of the field had sprouted . . . the Lord God formed man
out of the clay of the ground and blew into his nostrils the breath
of life, and so man became a living being.

*There are many other references in the Bible to the creation of
man. One example:*

Isaiah 139:13, 15—For you created my inmost being; you knit me together in my mother's womb. When I was woven together in the depths of the earth, your eyes saw my unformed body.

Creation of the first woman:

We have similar stories in the Bible and the Koran about the creation of woman, although the Koran is not quite as specific as the Bible about the actual means:

Koran 39:5a–6—He created you (*man*) from a single being, then from that being He created its mate. He molds you in your mothers' wombs by stages in threefold darkness.

Genesis 2:21—So the Lord God cast a deep sleep on the man, and while he was asleep, he took out one of his ribs and closed up its place with flesh. The Lord God then built up into a woman the rib that he had taken from the man. When he brought her to the man, the man said, "This one, at last, is bone of my bones and flesh of my flesh; this one shall be called 'woman,' for out of 'her man' this one has been taken."

Creation of animals:

Koran 51:48—And all things we have made in pairs, so that you might give thought.

Koran 24:44—God created every beast from water. Some creep upon their bellies, others walk on two legs, and others yet on four. God creates what he pleases.

Koran 39:5b—He has given you four different pairs of cattle (*camels, cows, sheep, and goats*).

Genesis 1:20, 24—Then God said, "Let the water teem with an abundance of living creatures, and on the earth let birds fly beneath the dome of the sky." And so it happened.

Then God said, "Let the earth bring forth all kinds of living creatures: cattle, creeping things, and wild animals of all kinds." And so it happened.

97

Creation of vegetation, rain, and fire:

Koran 6:99—It is He who sends down water from the sky with which We bring forth the buds of every plant. From these We bring forth green foliage and close-growing grain, palm-trees laden with clusters of dates, vineyards and olive groves, and pomegranates alike and different

Genesis 1:11–12—Then God said, "Let the earth bring forth vegetation: every kind of plant that bears seeds and every kind of fruit tree on earth that bears fruit with its seed in it." And so it happened. God saw how good it was.

Koran 56:67–69—Consider the water which you drink. Was it you that poured it from the cloud, or We?

Job 36:29—Lo! He spreads the clouds in layers as the carpeting of his tent.

Koran 56:70–73—Observe the fire which you light. Is it you that create its wood, or We?

Genesis 2:8–9a—Then the Lord God planted a garden in Eden, in the east, and he placed there the man whom he had formed. Out of the ground the Lord God made various trees grow that were delightful to look at (*and presumably good for firewood!*).

God finishes his creation:

Koran 50:38—In six days We created the heavens and the earth and all that lies between them; nor were We ever wearied.

Genesis 2:2—Since on the seventh day God was finished with the work he had been doing, he rested on the seventh day. (*A fifth grader once asked me, "Why did God rest? Was he tired?"*)

16

The People of the Book: Before the Egyptian Enslavement

In the Name of God the Compassionate the Merciful

We come now to the people who appear in both the Bible and the Koran. There are hundreds of stories. In the Koran, however, with the exception of the story of Joseph, son of Jacob, only a fragment of each character's story is found in any one Sura. For example, there are literally dozens of references to Moses scattered throughout the 500 pages of the Koran. So you get most of the story as told in the Bible, but not in any one Sura and not in chronological order. To illustrate the point, in Sura 44 we see Moses in Midian listening to a voice coming out of a fire, "Moses, I am your Lord. Take off your sandals for you are now in the scared valley of Ṭuwā." Later in that same Sura we find the story of the baby Moses being put into the river in a basket.

This presents a problem for the reader who would like to read in one place the entire story of Moses, or of Jesus, or any of the other people. So I have done just that. I have collected all the pertinent references to a given character, eliminated most repetitions, of which there are many, and arranged them in chronological order.

I shall deal with the People of the Book in chronological order. I have arbitrarily divided them into:

1) Those before the Egyptian enslavement
2) Moses
3) Those of the monarchy
4) Those of the post-monarchial era
5) Jesus
6) The three Christian apostles

People of the Book Before the Egyptian Enslavement

(1) Satan, Adam and Eve

As we shall see below in the first passage from the Koran, Satan was seen by Mohammed as an angel who disobeyed God and was banished from Heaven. The story of his involvement with Adam and Eve is told three times in the Koran. There are over twenty other references to Satan, some of which we will relate at the end of this section.

For the Jews of Old Testament times, the concept of a "Satan" was a post-exilic, sixth century BCE, notion. This can be seen by the curious reader by comparing 2 Samuel 24:1 (written before the exile) with 1 Chronicles 21:1 (written afterward). During the Babylonian captivity, Zarathustra in Persia influenced them to consider Satan as a supernatural power for evil. He appears in Zechariah 3:1–2 (circa 520 BCE) as the "prosecuting attorney" of the Jews in one of Zechariah's visions. Later, the concept of Satan as a fallen angel appeared and placed him in Eden first and then ruling all the forces of evil in the world.

Many Christians have also personified Satan, following the teachings of Jesus, as well as the letters of Paul and other New Testament writers.

Satan banished from heaven:

Koran 15:28—We created man from dry clay, from black molded loam, and before him Satan from smokeless fire.

Koran 7:11–18—Then We said to the angels, "Prostrate yourselves before Adam." They all prostrated themselves except Satan. "Why did you not prostrate yourself when I commanded you?" He (*God*) asked.

"I am nobler than he. You created me from fire, but You created him from clay."

He said: "Get you down hence! This is no place for your contemptuous pride. Away with you! Henceforth you shall be humble."

He replied, "Reprieve me until the Day of Resurrection."

"You are reprieved," said He.

"Because You have led me into sin," he declared, "I will waylay Your servants as they walk on Your straight path, then spring upon them from the front and from the rear, from their right and from their left. Then You will find the greater part of them ungrateful."

"Begone!" He said. "A despicable outcast you shall henceforth be. As for those that follow you, I shall fill Hell with you all."

There is no exact parallel to this story in the Bible, but there are several passages that come close. One of them:
Revelation 12:9, 12—The huge dragon, the ancient serpent, who is called the Devil and Satan, who deceived the whole world, was thrown down to earth, and its angels were thrown down with it . . . Therefore, rejoice, you heavens, and you who dwell in them. But woe to you, earth and sea, for the Devil has come down to you in great fury, for he knows he has but a short time." (See also 2 Peter 2:4, 9 and Revelation 20:7–10.)

Naming the animals:

Koran 2:31–32—He (*God*) taught Adam the names of all things and then set them before the angels, saying, "Tell Me the names of these, if what you say be true." "Glory to You," they replied, "we have no knowledge except that which You have given us. You alone are all-knowing and wise." Then said He: "Adam, tell them their names." And when Adam had named them, He (*God*) said, "Did I not tell you that I know the secrets of the heavens and earth, and all that you reveal and all that you conceal?"

Genesis 2:18–20—The Lord God said; "It is not good for the man (*Adam*) to be alone. I will make a suitable partner for him." So the Lord God formed out of the ground various wild animals and various birds of the air, and he brought them to the man to see what he would call them; whatever the man called each of them would be its name. The man gave names to all the cattle, all the birds of the air, and all the wild animals, but none proved to be the suitable partner for the man.

There is no account in the Bible of God asking angels to name the animals, but I did find an account in an extra-Biblical source. In the Midrash Rabbah on Genesis 1, paragraph 8, we read: **"God said to the Angels, 'His wisdom is greater than yours.' Then he brought** before them beasts, cattle, and birds, and asked for their names, but they knew them not."

The "fall" of man:

Koran 20:116–126—"Adam," We said, "Satan is an enemy to you and to your wife. Let him not turn you both out of Paradise and plunge you into affliction. Here you shall not hunger or be naked; you shall not thirst, or feel the scorching heat." But Satan whispered to him, saying: "Adam, shall I show you the Tree of Immortality and an everlasting kingdom?" They both ate of its fruit, so that they saw their nakedness and began to cover themselves with the leaves of the Garden. Thus did Adam disobey his Lord and go astray. Then his Lord had mercy on him; He relented towards him and rightly guided him. "Get you down, both," He said, "and may your offspring (*Cain and Abel*) be enemies to each other."
    (*For a slightly different Koranic version of the "fall" of man, see Sura 7:19–24.*)
    Genesis 3:1–7—Now the serpent was the most cunning of all the animals that the Lord God had made. The serpent asked the woman, "Did God really tell you not to eat from any of the trees in the garden?" The woman answered the serpent: "We may eat of the fruit of the trees in the garden; it is only about the fruit of the tree in the middle of the garden that God said, 'You shall not eat it or even touch it, lest you die.'" But the serpent said to the woman: "No, God knows well that the moment you eat of it your eyes will be opened and you will be like gods who know what is good and what is bad." The woman saw that the tree was good for food, pleasing to the eye and desirable for gaining wisdom. So she took some of its fruit and ate it; and she also gave some to her husband, who was with her, and he ate it. Then the eyes of both of them were opened, and they realized that they were naked; so they sewed fig leaves together and made loincloths for themselves.

*   *   *

Before going on to references to Satan's work outside of Eden, let's complete the story of the two sons of Adam, called Cain and Abel in the Bible, Habeel and Kabeel by Muslim Arabs, though never named in the Koran.

102

Koran 5:27–28, 30, 33—Recount to them in all truth the story of Adam's two sons; how they each made an offering, and how the offering of one was accepted while that of the other was not . . . One (*Habeel*) said: "I will surely kill you." His soul prompted him to slay his brother; he slew him and thus became one of the lost . . . Then God sent down a raven which dug the earth to show him how to bury the naked corpse of his brother. (*In Jewish tradition, the raven shows Adam, not Cain, the proper burial procedure, though the story is not in the Bible.*)

Genesis 4:3–5, 8–9, 15–16—In the course of time Cain brought an offering to the Lord from the fruit of the soil, while Abel for his part brought one of the best firstlings of his flock. The Lord looked with favor on Abel and his offering, but on Cain and his offering he did not. Cain greatly resented this and was crestfallen . . . Cain said to his brother Abel, "Let us go out into the field." When they were in the field, Cain attacked his brother Abel and killed him. Then the Lord asked Cain, "Where is your brother Abel?" He answered, "I do not know. Am I my brother's keeper?" . . . The Lord said to him, "If anyone kills Cain, Cain shall be avenged sevenfold." So the Lord put a mark on Cain, lest anyone should kill him at sight. Cain then left the Lord's presence and settled in the land of Nod, east of Eden.

* * *

Let's now consider some of the scattered references to Satan in the Koran along with Biblical passages that correspond, sometimes closely, sometimes not so close.

Satan as tempter:

Koran 22:50–55—Never have We sent a single prophet or apostle before you with whose wishes Satan did not tamper. But God abrogates the interjections of Satan and confirms His own revelations. God is all-knowing and wise.

Matthew 4:1–2—Then (*after his baptism by John in the Jordan*) Jesus was led by the Spirit into the desert to be tempted by the devil. He fasted for forty days and forty nights, and afterwards he was hungry. 4:3–11—(Summary) Satan tempted him to turn stones to bread to assuage his hunger, to leap off the temple parapet and summon God's angels to rescue him, to rule over all the world. Satan quoted scripture in each instance, and Jesus refuted each one with another quote from scripture. (*Hence the quote from Shakespeare: The Devil can cite scripture for his purpose [Merchant of Venice, I, iii, 99].*)

Acts 26:12–18—(Summary) Paul describes how he once persecuted the Christians under the influence of Satan, but had a vision on the road to Damascus in which Jesus spoke to him and said he would deliver him from the power of Satan.

Satan as a sower of discord:

Koran 17:53—Tell My servants to be courteous in their speech. Satan would sow discord among them; Satan is surely the sworn enemy of man.

Luke 22:31–32—(*Jesus speaking to Simon Peter at the Last Supper*) "Simon, Simon, behold Satan has demanded to sift you like wheat, but I have prayed that your own faith may not fail; and once you have turned back, you must strenghthen your brothers." (See also 1 Timothy 5:14–15)

Satan as a guide of human conduct:

Koran 14:21–24—The humble will say to those who thought themselves mighty: "We were your followers. Can you protect us from God's punishment?" They will reply: "Had God given us guidance, we would have guided you. Neither panic nor patience will help us now. There is no escape for us." And when Our judgment has been passed, Satan will say to them: "True was the promise which God made you. I too made you a promise, but did not keep it. Yet had I no power over you. I called you, and you answered me. Do not now blame me, but blame yourselves. I cannot help you, nor can you help me. I never thought, as you did, that I was God's equal."

2 Corinthians 2:10–11—(*Paul writing*) Whomever you forgive anything, so do I. For indeed what I have forgiven, if I have forgiven anything, has been for you in the presence of Christ, so that we might not be taken advantage of by Satan, for we are not unaware of his purposes.

Satan vanquished by belief in God:

Koran 16:97–100—When you recite the Koran, seek refuge in God from accursed Satan: no power has he over those who believe and who put their trust in their Lord. He has power only over those who befriend him and those who serve other gods besides God.

Romans 16:19–20—(*Paul writing*) For while your obedience is known to all, so that I rejoice over you, I want you to be wise as to what is good, and simple as to what is evil; then the God of peace will quickly crush Satan under your feet. (See also 1 Corinthians 7:5–6.)

Satan in wine, gambling, idols, and drawing lots:

Koran 5:90, 91—Believers, wine and games of chance, idols and divining arrows, are abominations devised by Satan. (*To portion out the cuts of meat of a camel, it was the custom to draw lots with arrows, some feathered and others unfeathered, kept for this purpose in the Ka'bah in Mecca.*) Avoid them, so that you may prosper. Satan seeks to stir up enmity and hatred among you by means of wine and gambling, and to keep you from the remembrance of God and from your prayers. Will you not abstain from them? (*Strict observers of the Koran also extend this proscription to the game of chess.*)

There are many references in the Old Testament to the use of wine as the preferred drink:
1 Samuel 16:20—Then Jesse took five loaves of bread, a skin of wine, and a kid, and sent them to Saul by his son David.
Genesis 27:28—(*Jacob blessing Isaac*) "Ah, the fragrance of my son is like the fragrance of a field that the Lord has blessed! May God give to you of the dew of the heavens and of the fertility of the earth abundance of grain and wine."
But:
Numbers 6:1–2—The Lord said to Moses: "Speak to the Israelites and tell them: When a man (or a woman) solemnly takes the nazarite vow to dedicate himself to the Lord, he shall abstain from wine and strong drink."

There are also many references in the New Testament to the use of wine. John in his gospel records a wedding at Cana where the wine ran out:

John 3:7–9a—Jesus told them, "Fill the jars with water." So they filled them to the brim. Then he told them, "Draw some out now and take it to the headwaiter." So they took it. And when the headwaiter tasted the water that had become wine . . .

Matthew 26:27–29—Then he (*Jesus*) took a cup (*of wine*), gave thanks and gave it to them, saying, "Drink from it, all of you, for this is my blood of the covenant, which will be shed on behalf of many for the forgiveness of sins."

1 Timothy 5:23—(*Paul writing to Timothy*) Stop drinking only water, but have a little wine for the sake of your stomach and your frequent illnesses.

*　　*　　*

There are many references in both Old and New Testament to casting lots to decide what course to take. In fact, the Lord's will was often sought by use of the Urim and Thummim. The exact nature of the Urim and Thummin is uncertain. But they were clearly lots of some kind which were drawn or cast by the priest to ascertain God's decision in doubtful matters. Both "Urim" and "Thummim" are plural words, so there must have been more than one of each. We see that clearly in the passage from Deuteronomy below, where Thummim takes a plural verb.

Exodus 28:29–30—(*God's instructions to Aaron through Moses*) Whenever Aaron enters the sanctuary he will thus bear the names of the sons of Israel (*Jacob*) on the breastpiece of decision over his heart as a constant reminder before the Lord. In this breastpiece of decision you shall put the Urim and Thummim . . . thus he shall always bear the decisions for the Israelites over his heart in the Lord's presence.

Proverbs 18:18—The lot puts an end to disputes, and is decisive in a controversy between the mighty.

Deuteronomy 33:8—(*The blessings of the dying Moses on each of the twelve tribes of Israel*) Of Levi he said, "To Levi belong your Thummim, to the man of your favor your Urim." (See also Ezra 2:62 and Joshua 18:8.)

In the New Testament, the most riveting instance of lot-casting occurred after the crucifixion of Jesus by Roman soldiers:

Matthew 27:35—After they crucified him, they divided his garments by casting lots.

After the death, resurrection, and ascension of Jesus, the disciples chose a twelfth apostle to take the place of Judas Iscariot:

Acts 1:23, 26—So they proposed two, Joseph called Barsabbas . . . and Matthias. Then they prayed, "You, Lord, who knows the hearts of all, show which one of these two you have chosen" . . . Then they gave lots to them, and the lot fell upon Matthias, and he was counted with the eleven apostles.

There are no passages in the Bible that deal with games of chance.

The concern over worshiping idols is dealt with in Chapter 4, DUTIES OF BELIEVERS.

(2) Noah

I have "patched together" the story of Noah and the flood from fifteen different passages, comparing it with the Bible as the story proceeds.

Koran 54:1, 9–10—The hour of Doom is drawing near, and the moon is cleft in two. Yet . . . the people of Noah disbelieved. They disbelieved Our servant and called him madman. Rejected and condemned, he cried out, saying: "Help me, Lord, I am overcome!"

Koran 23:23–26—We sent Noah forth to his people. "Serve God, my people," he said, "for you have no god but Him. Will you not take heed?" The unbelieving elders of his people said: "This man is but a mortal like you, feigning himself your superior. He is surely possessed. Keep an eye on him awhile."

Koran 37:78–81—Noah prayed to Us and his prayers were graciously answered. We delivered him and all his tribe from the mighty scourge, and made his descendants the sole survivors. The others We peremptorily drowned.

Koran 71:21–26a, 27–29—And Noah said: "Lord, my people disobey me, and follow those whose wealth and offspring will only hasten their perdition . . . They say, 'Do not forsake Wadd and Suwā or Yaghūth or Ya'ūq or Naṣr (*names of idols*).' . . . Lord, do not leave a single unbeliever on the earth. If You spare them, they will mislead Your servants and beget none but sinners and unbelievers. Forgive me, Lord, and forgive my parents and every true believer who seeks refuge in my house.

In the biblical story of the Flood, Noah does not ask the Lord to destroy the people and animals on earth. Rather, God speaks to Noah:

Genesis 6:5a, 6–8—When the Lord saw how great was man's wickedness on earth . . . he regretted that he had made man on the earth, and his heart was grieved. So the Lord said: "I will wipe out from the earth the men whom I have created, and not only the men, but also the beasts and the creeping things and the birds of the air, for I am sorry that I made them." But Noah found favor with the Lord.

Koran 23:27–30—We revealed Our will to him, saying: "Build an ark under Our watchful eye, according to Our instructions. Take aboard a pair of every species and the members of your household, except those of them already doomed. Do not plead with Me for those who have done wrong; they shall be drowned. And when you and all your followers have gone aboard, say: 'Praise be to God who has delivered us from a sinful nation.' "

Koran 11:38–39—So he built the ark. And whenever the elders of his people passed by him they jeered at him. He said, "If you mock us, we shall mock you just as you mock us. You shall know who will be seized by a scourge that shall disgrace him, and be smitten by a scourge everlasting."

There is no record in the Bible of the people harassing Noah. But the Jewish writing Sanhedr. 108 reports that "They scorned him and said, 'Old man! For what purpose is this ark?' "

This writing also claims that Job 12:4 refers to Noah: (Job speaking) I have become the sport of my neighbors: "The one whom God answers when he calls upon him, the just, the perfect man," is a laughingstock.

Genesis 6:14–15—(*God speaking to Noah*) "Make yourself an ark of gopherwood and put various compartments in it, and cover it inside with pitch. This is how you shall build it: the length of the ark shall be three hundred cubits, its width fifty cubits, and its height thirty cubits." (*This would be approximately 440 × 73 × 44 feet. Picture a field half again as long as a football field and half its width. Now place a five-story building on it to cover the entire field and you have the size of the ark.*)

Genesis 6:18–7:1—"But with you I will establish my covenant; you and your sons, your wife and your sons' wives, shall go into the ark. Of all other living creatures you shall bring two into the ark, one male and one female, that you may keep them alive with you. Of all kinds of birds, of all kinds of beasts, and of all kinds of creeping things, two of each shall come into the ark with you, to stay alive. Moreover, you are to provide yourself with all the food that is to be eaten, and store it away, that it may serve as provisions for you and for them." This Noah did; he carried out all the commands that God gave him. Then the Lord said to Noah: "Go into the ark, you and your household, for you alone in this age have I found to be truly just."

Koran 54:11–16—We opened the gates of heaven with pouring rain and caused the earth to burst with gushing springs, so that the waters met for a predestined end. We carried him in a vessel built with planks and nails, which drifted on under Our eyes: a recompense for him who had been disbelieved.

Genesis 7:11–12—In the six hundredth year of Noah's life, in the second month, on the seventeenth day of the month: it was on that day that all the fountains of the great abyss (*subterranean ocean*) burst forth and the floodgates of the sky were opened.

Koran 11:41b–42, 44a—And as the ark moved on with them amidst the mountainous waves, Noah cried out to his son, who stood apart, "Embark with us, my child. Do not remain with the unbelievers!" He replied, "I shall seek refuge in a mountain which will protect me from the flood.". . . And thereupon the billows rolled between them and Noah's son was drowned.

(*The son is not named, but Rodwell thinks it was probably Ham, and the incident was derived from a story in Genesis 9:20–25. In the Biblical account, all three of Noah's sons survive:*

Genesis 9:18–19—The sons of Noah who came out of the ark were Shem, Ham, and Japheth . . . These three were the sons of Noah, and from them the whole earth was peopled.)

Koran 69:10—When the Flood rose high We carried you (*your forefathers*) in the floating ark, making the event a warning, so that all attentive ears might heed it.

Genesis 7:17a, 19–21—The flood continued upon the earth for forty days . . . until all the highest mountains everywhere were submerged, the crest rising fifteen cubits (*twenty-two and a half feet*) higher than the submerged mountains. All creatures that stirred on earth perished: birds, cattle, wild animals, and all that swarmed on the earth, as well as all mankind . . . Only Noah and those with him in the ark were left.

Koran 11:44–48—A voice cried out: "Earth, swallow up your waters. Heaven, cease your rain!" The floods abated, and His will was done. The ark came to rest upon Al-Jūdï, and a voice declared: "Gone are the evil-doers." . . . The Lord (said), "Go ashore in peace. Our blessings are upon you and on some of the descendants of those that are with you."

Genesis 7:24–8:5, 15—(Excerpts) The waters maintained their crest over the earth for one hundred and fifty days, and then God remembered Noah and all the animals, wild and tame, that were with him in the ark. So God made a wind sweep over the earth and the waters began to subside . . . Gradually the waters receded from the earth . . . The ark came to rest on the mountains of Ararat . . . The water began to dry up on the earth . . . In the second month, on the twenty-seventh day of the month, the earth was dry. Then God said to Noah: "Go out of the ark, together with your wife and your sons and your sons' wives. Bring out with you every thing that is with you . . . ."

Genesis 9:1–2—God blessed Noah and his sons and said to them: "Be fertile and multiply and fill the earth. Dread fear of you shall come upon all the animals of the earth and all the birds of the air, upon all the creatures that move about on the ground and all the fishes of the sea: into your power they are delivered."

Koran 23:32–33, 43–44—Thus did we put mankind to the proof. Then We raised a new generation and sent forth to them an apostle of their own . . . After them we raised other generations—no people can delay their doom or go before it—and sent Our apostles in succession.

Genesis 9:8–13—(Excerpts) God said to Noah and to his sons with him: . . . "Never again shall all bodily creatures be destroyed by waters of a flood . . ." God added: . . . "I set my (*rain*) bow in the clouds to serve as a sign of the covenant between me and the earth."

Koran 11:50—That which We have now revealed to you (*the story of Noah*) is secret history. It was unknown to you and to your people. Have patience; the righteous shall have a joyful end. (*The Hebrew Bible, later called the Old Testament by Christians, was extant long before the Koran was revealed. The following dates are accepted by most scholars: The J source, 950–850 BCE; the E source, 750 BCE; the D source, 750–675 BCE; the P source, 450 BCE.)*

(3) Abraham

In the Bible, the story of Abraham is recounted in Genesis from his birth at the end of Chapter 11 to his death in Chapter 25, fourteen chapters and over fourteen pages. In the Koran, parts of Abraham's story are found in almost fifty different places, with much repetition. So again I have gathered them into a continuous story. I have recorded only those parts of the Biblical account that have counterparts in the Koran.

First, from the Koran, Abraham's call from God:

Koran 6:74–79—Tell of Abraham, who said to Azar, his father, "Will you worship idols as your gods? Surely you and all your people are in palpable error." (*In the Bible, Abraham's father is called Terah. Mohammed may have borrowed the name "Azar" from Eusebius, bishop of Caesarea Maritime, writing in the fourth century CE, who called Abraham's father "Athar.")* Thus did We show Abraham the kingdom of the heavens and the earth, so that he might be a firm believer. When night drew its shadow over him, he saw a star. "That," he said, "is surely my God." But when it faded in the morning light, he said: "I will not worship gods that fade." When he beheld the rising moon, he said: "That is my God." But when it set, he said: "If my Lord does not guide me, I shall surely go astray." Then, when he beheld the sun shining, he said: "That must be my God: it is the largest." But when it set, he said to his people: "I disown your idols. I will turn my face to Him who has created the heavens and the earth and will live a righteous life. I am no idolater."

Koran 6:85–86—We gave him Isaac and Jacob. Among his descendants were David and Solomon, Job and Joseph and Moses and Aaron (thus do We reward the righteous); Zacharias and John, Jesus and Elias (*Elijah*) (all were upright men); and Ishmael, Elisha, Jonah and Lot. (*The Bible records that Jacob was Isaac's son, not Abraham's, and Lot was Abraham's nephew.*)

111

Koran 19:42–44—He said to his father: "Why do you serve a worthless idol, a thing that can neither hear nor see? Father, things you know nothing of have come to my knowledge: therefore follow me that I may guise you along an even path. Father, do not worship Satan."

(*Although the concept of a Satan didn't enter Jewish thinking until the sixth century* BCE, *Abraham could have been aware of the concept because he came from Mesopotamia, close by Persia where the concept arose.*)

Koran 19:46–47—He (*Azar*) replied: "Do you dare renounce my gods, Abraham? Desist, or I will stone you. Begone from my house this instant!"

"Peace be with you," said Abraham. "I shall implore my Lord to forgive you: for to me He has been gracious. But I will not live with you or with your idols."

Koran 37:91–92, 94–95—He stole away to their idols and said to them: "Will you not eat your offerings? Why do you not speak?" With that he fell upon them, striking them down with his right hand. The people came running to the scene . . . They (said): "Build up a pyre and cast him into the blazing flames." Thus did they scheme against him: but We abused them all.

The Koran does not name any of the places where Abraham lived after he received his call from God to worship Him alone. And though the Koran has many references to the Israelites, and to the Jews, it never uses the place names Ur, Haran, Israel or Canaan, which we find in the Bible narrative.

Genesis 11:27–31—This is the record of the descendants of Terah. Terah became the father of Abram, Nahor and Haran, and Haran became the father of Lot. (*God later changed Abram's name to Abraham, and his wife Sarai's to Sarah.*) Haran died before his father Terah, in his native land, in Ur of the Chaldeans (*in the far south of modern Iraq*). Terah took his son Abram, his grandson Lot, son of Haran, and his daughter-in-law Sarai, the wife of his son Abram, and brought them out of Ur of the Chaldeans to go to the land of Canaan. But when they reached Haran they settled there. (*Haran lay in the southeastern part of what is now Turkey, and in fact is still there, though spelled with two r's. It is a coincidence that Lot's father had the same name.*)

112

Genesis 12:1–2a, 4, 5b–6a—The Lord said to Abram (*probably about fifty years later*): "Go forth from the land of your kinsfolk and from your father's house to a land that I will show you. I will make of you a great nation, and I will bless you." . . . Abram went as the Lord directed him, and Lot went with him. Abram was seventy-five years old when he left Haran . . . When they came to the land of Canaan, Abram passed through the land as far as the sacred place at Shechem, by the terebinth of Moreh. (*Shechem lay in the northern part of what is now Israel, probably just to the southwest of the Sea of Galilee.*)

Genesis 15:1–2a, 4–5—Some time after these events (*the war with the four kings and the meeting with Melchizedek*) this word of the Lord came to Abram in a vision: "Fear not, Abram! I am your shield; I will make your reward very great." But Abram said, "O Lord God, what good will your gifts be, if I keep on being childless?" . . . Then the word of the Lord came to him: "Your own issue shall be your heir." He took him outside and said, "Look up at the sky and count the stars, if you can. Just so," he added, "shall your descendants be."

Both the Koran and the Bible take pains to show that Abram was a righteous man:

Koran 16:121–124—Abraham was a paragon of piety, an upright man obedient to God. He was no idolater . . . and in the world to come he shall dwell among the righteous.

Koran 3:67—He was an upright man, one who surrendered himself to God.

Genesis 15:6—Abram put his faith in the Lord, who credited it to him as an act of righteousness.

The story of the birth of Abraham's son Ishmael, from the Bible:

Genesis 16:1–4a—Abram's wife Sarai had borne him no children. She had, however, an Egyptian maidservant named Hagar. Sarai said to Abram: "The Lord has kept me from bearing children. Have intercourse, then, with my maid; perhaps I shall have sons through her." Abram heeded Sarai's request. Thus, after Abram had lived ten years in the land of Canaan, his wife Sarai took her maid,

Hagar the Egyptian, and gave her to her husband to be his concubine. He had intercourse with her and she became pregnant.

Genesis 16:15–16—Hagar bore Abram a son, and Abram named the son whom Hagar bore him Ishmael. Abram was eighty-six years old when Hagar bore him Ishmael.

Nowhere in the Koran is there a story about Ishmael being born to Sarah's Egyptian slave girl, Hagar. Ishmael is listed with other prophets five times, but there are only two references to his being Abram's son. One is in Sura 14:39—"Praise be to God who has given me Ishmael and Isaac in my old age." The other is in Sura 47:98–114, recounted below after the birth stories of Isaac. But Muslim tradition identifies a burial place of Hagar and Ishmael opposite the north wall of the Ka'bah.

The birth story of Abraham's son Isaac in the Koran:

Koran 11:69–74—Our messengers came to Abraham with good news. They said, "Peace!" "Peace!" he answered and hastened to bring them a roasted calf. But when he saw their hands being withheld from it, he mistrusted them and was afraid of them (*because they were angels and did not eat?*). They said: "Have no fear. We are sent forth to the people of Lot." His wife, who was standing by, laughed. We bade her to rejoice in Isaac and in Jacob after Isaac. They told him that he was to have a son. "Alas!" she replied. "How shall I bear a child when I am old and my husband is well-advanced in years? This is indeed a strange thing." They replied, "Do you marvel at the ways of the God? May God's mercy and blessings be upon you, dear hosts! Worthy of praise is He and glorious."

The phrase "rejoice in Isaac and in Jacob after Isaac" implies that they were brothers, which differs from the biblical story. The Bible story has Isaac being born to Abraham and Sarah fifteen years after the birth of Ishmael. Jacob was Isaac's son, not his brother. According to the Bible, Sarah was long dead by the time Jacob was born. Abraham was probably dead, too, because in Genesis 25 we read that the birth of the twins Jacob and Esau to Isaac and Rebecca follows the account of Abraham's death.

The birth story of Isaac from the Bible:

Genesis 18:1—The Lord appeared to Abraham by the terebinth of Mamre, as he sat in the entrance of his tent, while the day was growing hot. (*The terebinth is a sumac-like tree which yields turpentine. Mamre later became the site of Hebron, which was David's first capital before he conquered Jerusalem and made that his capital. Modern-day Hebron lies about fifteen miles south of Jerusalem.*) 18:2–14a—(Summary) There were three "men." Abraham killed a steer while Sarah made bread. The three ate. Then they told Abraham that Sarah would have a son, Isaac, and Sarah laughed at the idea of having a child at the age of ninety. ("Isaac" means "laughter" in Hebrew.) 21:2—Sarah became pregnant and bore Abraham a son in his old age at the set time that God had stated.

This following story of the testing of Abraham is one of two major references to Ishmael in the Koran. The other story will be told shortly.

Koran 37:98–114—We gave him news of a gentle son. And when he (*Ishmael*) reached the age when he could work with him, his father said to him: "My son, I dreamt that I was sacrificing you. Tell me what you think." Ishmael replied, "Father, do as you are bidden. God willing, you shall find me steadfast." And when they had both submitted to God's will, and Abraham had laid down his son prostrate upon his face, We called out to him, "Abraham, you have fulfilled your vision." Thus do We reward the righteous. That indeed was a bitter test. We ransomed his son with a noble sacrifice (*brought from Paradise by an angel*) and bestowed on him the praise of later generations.

(*Note in the previous passage that Ishmael is called "a gentle son." In the Bible, the angels tells Hagar that she is to name her son Ishmael and adds, "He shall be a wild ass of a man, his hand against everyone, and everyone's hand against him."*)

The following story from the Bible, Abraham's testing by the Lord, is very similar to the Koran's version, except that in the Bible it is Isaac *who is the potential sacrifice:*

Genesis 22:1b–2—God put Abraham to the test. He called to him, "Abraham!" "Ready!" he replied. Then God said: "Take your son Isaac, your only one, and go to the land of Moriah. There you shall offer him up as a holocaust on a height that I will point out to you." (*In 2 Chronicles 3:1, we read that 1700 years later Solomon built his temple on the threshing floor of Ornan on Mt. Moriah, perhaps the present day Temple Mount in Jerusalem where Muslims have built a magnificent mosque called "The Dome of the Rock."*)

Genesis 22:3–9—(Summary) Abraham left the next morning with Isaac, two servants, and a load of wood on a donkey. When they arrived at the mountain, Isaac carried the wood to the top, where Abraham built an altar and laid Isaac on it.

Genesis 22:10–13—Then he reached out and took the knife to slaughter his son. But the Lord's messenger called to him from heaven, "Abraham, Abraham!" "Yes, Lord," he answered. "Do not lay your hand on the boy," said the messenger. "Do not do the least thing to him. I know now how devoted you are to God, since you did not withhold from me your beloved son." As Abraham looked about, he spied a ram caught by its horns in the thicket. So he went and took the ram and offered it up as a holocaust in place of his son.

The stoned devil:

Koran 15:17–18—We have decked the heavens with the signs of the Zodiac and made them lovely to behold. We have guarded them from every stoned devil. Eavesdroppers are pursued by fiery comets. (*Rodwell explains this enigmatic passage: The stoned devil is Satan. According to a Muslim tradition not found in the Bible or the Koran, Abraham drove Satan away with stones when Satan would have hindered him from sacrificing Ishmael. Today the place where Abraham saw the apparition of Satan is marked by three small pillars in the valley of Mina, near Mecca. Hence the present-day custom during the Hajj of throwing stones at the pillars as if at Satan. The demons are said to learn the secrets of the future by listening [eavesdropping] behind a veil.*)

The construction of the Ka'bah:

Salman Rushdie in The Satanic Verses *describes the very first Ka'bah: "Adam came here and saw a miracle: four emerald pillars bearing aloft a giant glowing ruby, and beneath this canopy a huge white stone, also glowing with its own light, like a vision of his soul.*

He built strong walls around the vision to bind it forever to the earth. This was the first House. It was rebuilt many times . . ."

As we shall see in this next passage, the above story is not based on the Koran, although tradition holds that the Ka'bah was built on the spot where Adam built a temple that was later destroyed by the Flood.

Koran 3:96—The first temple ever to be built for mankind was that at Mecca, a blessed site, a beacon for the nations. In it there are veritable signs and the spot where Abraham stood. Whoever enters it is safe. Pilgrimage to the House (*the Ka'bah*) is a duty to God for all who can make the journey. As for the unbelievers, God can surely do without them.

Koran 2:127–128, 130—Abraham and Ishmael built the House and dedicated it, saying: "Accept this from us, Lord. You are the One that hears all and knows all. Lord, make us submissive to You; make of our descendants a nation that will submit to you . . . Who but a foolish man would renounce the faith of Abraham?"

There is a small building near the Ka'bah which contains a stone which Muslims claim was used by Abraham to stand on when building the Ka'bah with Ishmael. The Ka'bah is a massive structure, 55 by 45 feet and 60 feet high, not quite a perfect cube, although the name means "the cube" in Arabic. It stands in an open parallelogram about 500 to 530 feet, surrounded by 554 pillars in a quadruple row on the east, a triple row on the other sides. It is constructed of grey stone and marble. The interior contains nothing but the three pillars that support the roof and a number of suspended silver and gold lamps. It is covered with an enormous cloth of black brocade embroidered in gold threads with quotes from the Koran. On Hajj, the pilgrim walks around it seven times, kisses and touches the Black Stone of Mecca which was given to Adam on his expulsion from Eden to obtain forgiveness of his sins. The Black Stone has been built into the eastern wall of the Ka'bah. It now consists of three large pieces and some fragments held together by a silver band and surrounded by a stone ring. Legend has it that it was originally white, now has become black by absorbing the sins of the pilgrims who have touched and kissed it.

There is no biblical counterpart to these stories. Nowhere in the Bible does it say that Abraham and/or Ishmael went to Arabia.

Nor is there mention of the Ka'bah. Despite this silence, it is interesting to note that after several hours of research on the Ka'bah, I found absolutely nothing that refutes the story as found in the Koran.

God shows Abraham how to restore life to the dead:

Koran 2:260–261—When Abraham said: "Show me, Lord, how You will raise the dead," God said, "Have you no faith?" "Yes," said Abraham, "but just to reassure my heart." "Take four birds," said He, "draw them to you and cut their bodies to pieces. Scatter them over the mountain tops, then call them back. They will come swiftly to you. Know that God is mighty and wise."

There is a similar story in the Bible, but with a different end in mind. God uses slaughtered animals to ratify his covenant with Abraham:
Genesis 15:7–10, 17–18a—He (God) said to him (Abraham), "I am the Lord who brought you out from Ur of the Chaldeans to give you this land as a possession." "O Lord God," he asked, "How am I to know that I shall possess it?" He answered him, "Bring me a three-year-old heifer, a three-year-old she-goat, a three-year-old ram, a turtledove, and a young pigeon." He brought him all these, split them in two and placed each half opposite the other but the birds he did not cut up . . . When the sun had set and it was dark, there appeared a smoking brazier and a flaming torch (*representing God's presence*) which passed between those pieces. It was on that occasion that the Lord made a covenant with Abram, saying: "To your descendants I give this land . . ." (*In the Bible, e.g. Jeremiah 34:19–20, and also on contemporary inscriptions, agreements were sometimes ratified by walking between the divided pieces of animals, while the parties invoked on themselves a fate similar to that of the slaughtered animals if they should fail to keep their word.*)

There is one other interesting reference to Abraham in the Koran that does not seem to tie in with the biblical narrative of Abraham's life:
Koran 2:258—Have you not heard of him (*Nimrod*) who argued with Abraham about his Lord because God had bestowed sovereignty upon him? Abraham said: "My Lord is He who has power to give life and to cause death."

118

"I, too," replied the other (*Nimrod*), "have power to give life and to cause death."

"God brings up the sun from the east," said Abraham. "Bring it up yourself from the west."

The unbeliever was confounded. God does not guide the evil-doers.

In Genesis 10:8ff we read that Nimrod was the great-grandson of Noah. He was "a mighty hunter," and the "first potentate," ruling all of what is now the southern half of Iraq, including Babylon, Erech, and Akkad. According to the Bible, his appearance with Abraham is an anachronism of many centuries.

(4) Lot

The story of Abraham's nephew Lot, Sodom and Gomorrah, in the Koran:

Koran 11:75–79—(*Abraham and Sarah have just been informed by two angel-messengers that Sarah will bear a child within a year.*) And when fear left him as he pondered the good news, Abraham pleaded with Us for the people of Lot. Abraham was gracious, tender-hearted, and devout. We said: "Abraham, plead no more. Your Lord's will must needs be done. Irrevocable is the scourge which shall smite them."

And when Our messengers came to Lot, he grew anxious about them, for he was powerless to offer them protection from the men who wanted to have homosexual relations with the strangers. "My people," he said, "here are my daughters: surely they are more wholesome to you. Fear God, and do not humiliate me by insulting my guests. Is there not one good man among you?" They replied: "You know we have no need of your daughters."

Koran 11:80–85—They (*the messengers*) said: "Lot, we are the messengers of your Lord: they (*the people*) shall not touch you. Depart with your kinsfolk in the dead of night and let none of you turn back, except your wife. She shall suffer the fate of the others. In the morning their hour will come. Is not the morning near?" And when Our judgment came to pass, We turned their city upside down and let loose upon it a shower of claystones bearing the tokens of your

Lord. (*The "tokens" were the names of the persons that each burning piece of brimstone should strike.*)

Koran 26:168–173—We delivered Lot and all his kinsfolk, save for one old woman (*Lot's wife*) who stayed behind, and the rest We utterly destroyed. (See also Sura 29:28–35 for a slightly different version of this same story.)

The story as found in the Bible:

The Biblical story of Lot, Sodom and Gomorrah, takes two full chapters to tell, Genesis 18 and 19, so I shall summarize the story:

Three angels appearing to be men tell Abraham and Sarah that Sarah is to bear Isaac. Abraham accompanies the three angels as they walk toward Sodom. One of the "men" is God himself. God muses to himself, wondering if he should tell Abraham that he is going to destroy Sodom and Gomorrah. He decides to do so, and does. The other two angels continue on toward Sodom. Abraham turns back, only to find God standing in front of him. Abraham argues with God about destroying the innocent along with the guilty. He asks God if he will spare the entire city if there are fifty innocent people there. God says, "Yes." Abraham asks if he will spare the city if there are forty-five, then forty, then thirty, then ten, with the answer from God each time, "Yes." Then God disappears and Abraham returns home.

The two angels go to Lot's house in Sodom and accept his invitation to stay overnight. A mob of townspeople come and order Lot to turn over the men to them for their sexual pleasure. Lot offers his daughters, which the mob refuses. They attack Lot but the angels pull Lot into the house and strike the men at the entrance with a blinding light, paralyzing them.

Lot and his family leave Sodom early the next morning, led by the hand by the two angels. The angels warn them not to look back or to stop anywhere until they come to the town of Zoar (*about five miles from Sodom, near the southern tip of the Dead Sea, in an area that later became Moab*). Ignoring the angels' warning, Lot's wife looks back and is turned into a pillar of salt. As Lot and his two daughters arrive in Zoar, the Lord rains down sulphurous fire upon both Sodom and Gomorrah "and the whole Plain." (*In the biblical book of Wisdom, written in the first century BCE, the author states in 10:6 that "She [Wisdom] delivered the just man [Lot] from among*

the wicked who were being destroyed, when he fled as fire descended upon Pentapolis." The Pentapolis consisted of five cities, which were the Cities of the Plain, listed in Genesis 14:2: Sodom, Gomorrah, Admah, Zeboiim, and Zoar. The differing accounts of the cities destroyed cannot be reconciled.)

(5) Joseph, Son of Jacob

In telling the story of Joseph, Jacob's son, Mohammed departs from his usual method of distributing the various components throughout the Koran. Except for a very brief reference in Sura 6:85, where Joseph is identified only as one of the descendants of Abraham, and in Sura 40:33, where Joseph is briefly portrayed as having come to Pharaoh in Egypt with "veritable signs," the entire story of Joseph is told in Sura 12. It is, in fact, the only subject so treated by Mohammed.

It was recited to the first eight of his *ansars* (converts to Islam in Mecca, who later accompanied him to Medina), and is considered by non-Muslim commentators as a strong indication that Mohammed was in contact with learned Jews. Mohammed seems to deny this near the end of the twelfth Sura, where in verse 102 he quotes Gabriel as saying to him, "That which We have now revealed to you is a tale of the unknown." But then, only ten verses later, Gabriel ends the Sura with the following words: "This is no invented tale, but a confirmation of previous scriptures, an explanation of all things, a guide and a blessing to true believers."

It's a long story in the Koran, covering fully ten pages in both translations used in this study and cannot reasonably be quoted in its entirety. The biblical story is also very long, filling thirteen chapters in fourteen pages with great detail. So I, like Mohammed, shall also depart from my usual method of presentation. I shall summarize the biblical account, episode by episode, followed immediately by the corresponding episode in the Koran.

The biblical story that follows the Koran is taken from Genesis, Chapters 37, 39–47:1–12. The Koranic story is taken from Sura 12, entitled JOSEPH. It should be noted that nowhere in the Koran is anyone identified by name except for Jacob and Joseph. For example,

Reuben is always just called "the eldest brother," Benjamin "the youngest brother," and Potiphar "the Egyptian," or "the Prince."

Bible—When Joseph was 17, his father made him a long tunic (a "coat of many colors" in the KJV) which made his eleven brothers jealous and caused them to hate him.

Koran—There is no mention of the brothers' envy of Joseph's fine tunic. Their reason for hating Joseph was merely jealousy of him as his father's favorite.

Bible—Joseph had two dreams, one in which eleven sheaves of wheat bowed down to a twelfth one, and another in which the sun and moon and eleven stars bowed to Joseph himself. He told his brothers the dreams and this angered them. He told his father, Jacob, too, who sarcastically asked if this meant that father and mother and brothers would all have to bow to him.

Koran—Joseph's dream of the sheaves bowing to him is not recorded. He dreamt about the sun, moon, and eleven stars bowing down to him. He told his dream to his father, Jacob, who advised him not to tell his brothers of the dream lest they act as Satan and do him evil. (He did, of course, and this precipitated his kidnaping.)

Bible—While the twelve brothers were tending their flocks, Reuben, the eldest, prevented the others from killing Joseph but helped them throw him into a dry cistern. The brothers killed a goat, dipped Joseph's tunic in its blood, showed it to Jacob and told him that a wild beast had killed Joseph. There is no indication at this time as to whether or not Jacob believed them.

Koran—"The eldest" convinced the others not to kill Joseph, but to throw him into a deep pit. They returned to Jacob with their story and showed him "their brother's shirt, stained with false blood." Jacob clearly knew what had happened because he reprimanded them and said their souls had been tempted to do evil. The pit into which they had cast him had water in it; Joseph was found by a water boy dropping his bucket into the pit.

Bible—Later the brothers agreed not to let Joseph die in the pit and sold him for twenty pieces of silver to a caravan of Ishmaelites who took him to Egypt and sold him to Potiphar, the chief steward of Pharaoh.

Koran—Joseph was sold to a passing caravan but it was not identified as Ishmaelites.

Bible—Potiphar soon recognized Joseph's potential and made him steward of his entire personal household and possessions.

Koran—"The Egyptian" who bought Joseph for a few pieces of silver was told by his wife to be kind to him because he might prove useful, might even be adopted as their son.

Bible—Potiphar's wife (*never named*) tried to seduce Joseph, but he resisted. As he ran away, she tore off his cloak and accused him of rape before Potiphar.

Koran—Potiphar's wife tried to seduce Joseph, but he ran off. She tore off his cloak. She told Potiphar that Joseph had tried to seduce her.

Bible—Potiphar threw Joseph into jail, which was part of Potiphar's compound, where he became the steward of two other prisoners, the king's cupbearer and baker. They both had dreams, which Joseph correctly interpreted. Joseph did not try to convert them to his religion.

Koran—Potiphar recognized the significance of the shirt ripped from behind—that Joseph was fleeing from her—and accused his wife of tricking Joseph. She admitted this, but despite the evidence "they thought it right to jail him for a time." Two unidentified young men entered prison with Joseph. They each had a dream, which Joseph properly interpreted. Joseph tried to convert his fellow prisoners to his God.

Bible—Two years later, while Joseph was still in prison, Pharaoh had a dream in which seven gaunt cows ate seven fat cows. Then he had another dream in which seven thin ears of grain consumed seven fat ears (*not identified, but probably wheat or barley*). None of Pharaoh's sorcerers, magicians, or sages could interpret the dreams. The cupbearer, now attending Pharaoh again, told him of Joseph's prowess. Joseph was sent for and interpreted the dreams to be a prediction of seven years of abundance followed by seven years of famine.

Koran—the king had a dream of "seven fatted cows which seven lean ones devoured; also seven green ears of corn and seven others dry." (*"Corn" in the Koran is used as a term for all kinds of cereal grains, and in this case probably means wheat or barley. What we call corn did not reach the "Old World" until the "New World" was discovered.*) After his people could not interpret the dream, Joseph was sent for and interpreted it to mean seven good crop years and seven lean ones.

Bible—Pharaoh was so impressed that he released Joseph from prison and made him second in command of the entire land of Egypt.

Koran—Joseph asked Pharaoh to set him over the granaries of the land, not the entire land. Pharoah agreed.

Bible—Egypt did have seven years of plenty and Joseph ordered huge granaries to be built to store the surplus grain.

Koran—Does not tell whether or not the prediction of seven fat years came true.

Bible—During these years Joseph married Asenath and had two sons, Manasseh, and Ephraim.

Koran—There is no mention of Joseph marrying or having sons.

Bible—The seven years of famine arrived and Egypt was the only country in the area to have grain.

Koran—Does not tell whether or not the prediction of seven lean years came true.

Bible—Back in Canaan, famine there also drove Jacob to send ten of his sons, all except Benjamin, to Egypt to buy grain.

Koran—The brothers of Joseph arrived in Egypt but there is no explanation at this point as to why they came. Later, however, it is clear that they came for grain.

Bible—Joseph was in charge of grain distribution. He recognized his brothers but they didn't recognize him. Speaking through an interpreter so as not to give himself away, he accused them of being spies and locked them up in the guardhouse for three days, then told them that only one brother—Simeon—would be jailed, while the others would return home with the grain. He directed them to bring Benjamin back with them to ransom Simeon.

Koran—Joseph told the brothers that they must bring "the other brother" (presumed to be Benjamin) or they would not "come near me again." No mention is made of Simeon being held as a hostage.

Bible—While still in Joseph's presence, they spoke amongst themselves about how they were now being punished for selling Joseph, not knowing that Joseph understood them. He turned aside and wept.

Koran—This episode is not recorded.

Bible—Joseph sent them on their way with the grain and also returned their payment in the sacks, which they discovered at the first encampment.

124

Koran—Joseph sent them on their way with the grain and also returned their payment, hoping that when they discovered that their payment had been returned to them, they would come back to Egypt.

Bible—**On their arrival back in Canaan, Jacob refused at first to allow them to return with Benjamin but the famine became so bad that he had to allow it. He sent rich gifts and double the money needed.**

Koran—After a long argument, Jacob agreed to send "the youngest" but only when the brothers pledged to bring him back safely. He also insisted that they enter the city by different gates. The reason for the ruse is not explained.

Bible—**The brothers were told by Joseph's head steward to join Joseph at dinner, which they did. Again Joseph decided not to tell them about their kinship even after seeing Benjamin. Again he turned aside and wept.**

Koran—Joseph embraced his brother (presumably Benjamin) and told him that they were brothers, but apparently did not tell the others. They all started back to Canaan. It is not explained why Benjamin didn't tell the others that Joseph was their brother.

Bible—**Then for the second time Joseph sent them back to Jacob with grain and with their payment returned in the sacks. He also had a silver goblet slipped into Benjamin's personal clothes bag. Joseph sent a steward after them, to accuse them of the theft of the goblet. They denied this vehemently, saying that if one of them was found with the goblet he would die and the rest would be the Egyptians' slaves.**

Koran—Joseph himself hid the king's drinking-cup in Benjamin's bag, then he himself set out after the party. He told them the cup was missing and accused them of stealing it. They denied it vehemently but agreed to the search. They promised that if it were found in someone's bag, that person would become Joseph's bondman forever.

Bible—**Their bags were searched and the goblet found in Benjamin's sack. The brothers tore their garments in anguish and returned to Joseph's house where they told him the entire story of Joseph's abduction and their ruse to fool Jacob into thinking he had been destroyed by a wild beast. They pleaded with him to remember the anguish Jacob would suffer if still another son was killed because of a false accusation. He would probably die of grief.**

Koran—Joseph himself searched the bags of the party returning to Canaan with their second portion of grain. Joseph searched all the others' bags first, then Benjamin's, from which he produced the cup. The other brothers implored Joseph to take one of them instead of Benjamin. He refused. He allowed them to return to Canaan without Benjamin but with the admonition that they must inform Jacob of Benjamin's thievery. They did, but Jacob merely broke down in a fit of crying for his lost Joseph and became blind. "His eyes went white with grief."

Bible—Joseph could no longer control himself, sent his attendants out of the room, and admitted that he was their brother. He explained that he had been sent on ahead of them by God to ensure that a remnant of the family would remain on earth. He implored them to return to Canaan and bring Jacob and the rest of the family down to Egypt.

Koran—They returned a third time from Canaan to Egypt and again implored Joseph to give them grain. This time the brothers recognized Joseph and Joseph revealed himself as their brother. He took off his shirt and told them to throw it over their father's face so that he would recover his sight. They returned to Canaan, threw Joseph's shirt over Jacob's face and his sight was restored.

Bible—Pharaoh was greatly pleased, too, and offered Jacob's family land in Goshen, in the fertile and well-watered northeast part of the country, the best land in Egypt. The brothers returned to Canaan and amazed Jacob with their news. So Jacob, his sons and daughters with their spouses and their children, all migrated to Egypt, sixty-six in all, and joined Joseph, Asenath, and their two sons.

Koran—Joseph welcomed his parents when the extended family of Jacob returned to Egypt. They all fell prostrate before him, fulfilling the dream of sun, moon and eleven stars bowing before him. (*Muslim commentators say that it was Bilhah meant here as Joseph's surrogate mother, because Joseph's and Benjamin's natural mother, Rachel, had died many years before after giving birth to Benjamin.*)

Except for a short prayer by Joseph thanking the Lord for what He had done for him and his family, the story of Joseph ends here in the Koran. However, I find it fitting to round out the Biblical story of Joseph:

126

Genesis 47:27–31, Chapters 48–50—When Jacob's health began to fail, he adopted Manasseh and Ephraim so that their heritage should be the same as the ten other brothers, but eliminating Joseph from inheritance. (*This is the origin of the twelve eponymous ancestors of the twelve tribes of Israel.*)

As he lay dying, Jacob gathered his sons around him and foretold what would happen to each of them and their descendants.

When Jacob died, the brothers were afraid that Joseph would now take his revenge and implored him to let them live and become his slaves. They told him that before he died, Jacob had begged the brothers to ask Joseph for forgiveness, indicating that Jacob did indeed know that they had sold Joseph into slavery. Joseph did forgive them and reassured them that they should not fear reprisal.

Joseph lived to be 110. As he was dying he promised the family that God would surely lead them out of Egypt back to Canaan, the land He had promised Abraham, Isaac, and Jacob. He also placed the brothers under oath to take his bones with them when they left Egypt. He died, was embalmed and placed in a coffin. (According to Exodus 12:40, the Israelites had to wait 430 years before Moses led them back to Canaan. And, according to Exodus 13:19, they did take Joseph's bones with them.)

17

People of the Book: Moses

In the Name of God the Compassionate the Merciful

By far the lengthiest and most numerous passages in the Koran are devoted to the story of Moses. All told, there are seventy-five passages telling part of his story. Many are several pages long, and of course many are repetitious, often with variations that are interesting or that even differ significantly from each other. And, as usual, they are scattered throughout the Book. So I have collated these stories into a reasonably continuous narrative.

In the Bible's Old Testament, Moses dominates the Torah, that is, the first five books. He appears on stage (actually, in a reed basket in the Nile!) in the first chapter of the second book, Exodus, and doesn't make his exit until the last chapter of the fifth book, Deuteronomy. In my Bible, that's four books, 137 chapters, and 152 pages later. Therefore, in this work we can only touch lightly on his story, his life, his law-giving, and that only where there is correlation or disagreement with the Koranic treatment of Moses. Several interesting stories in the Koran have no counterpart in the Bible and therefore are not related in this work. I strongly urge the reader to read Exodus, Leviticus, Numbers, and Deuteronomy. Only then can he fully appreciate the Moses of the Koran.

*　　*　　*

Koran 28:1–5—These are the verses of the Glorious Book. In all truth We shall recount to you the tale of Moses and Pharaoh for the instruction of the faithful. Now Pharaoh made himself a tyrant in the land. He divided his people into castes, one group of which he persecuted (*the Israelites*), putting their sons to death and sparing only their daughters. Truly, he was an evil-doer. But it was Our will to favor those who were oppressed in the land and to make them leaders among men, to bestow on them a noble heritage and to give them power in the land; and to inflict on Pharaoh, Haman, and their warriors the very scourge they dreaded. (*The only Haman in the Bible appears as the evil Prime Minister of the sixth century* BCE *Persian King Ahasuerus [Xerxes] in the Book of Esther.*)

Exodus 1:6–8—Now Joseph and all his brothers and that whole generation died. But the Israelites were fruitful and prolific. They became so numerous and strong that the land was filled with them. Then a new king, who knew nothing of Joseph, came to power in Egypt.

The story of Moses begins over 400 years after the death of Joseph (Genesis 12:40). The Egyptians were unlikely to have kept any records of the Hebrew people, so Pharaoh would not have known—or cared to know—about Joseph.

Biblical scholars do not agree on who this Pharaoh was. Many think that it may have been Ramses II who ruled about that time for 67 years (1304–1237 BCE*).*

Exodus 1:9–10—He (*Pharaoh*) said to his subjects, "Look how numerous and powerful the Israelite people are growing, more so than we ourselves! Come, let us deal shrewdly with them to stop their increase; otherwise, in time of war they too may join our enemies to fight against us, and so leave our country."

Exodus 1:11–21—(Summary) First, Pharaoh tried to curb the Israelites by oppressive forced labor, but they just became stronger. Then he ordered the midwives to kill all boy babies, but they refused.

Exodus 1:22—Pharaoh then commanded all his subjects, "Throw into the river every boy that is born to the Hebrews, but you may let all the girls live."

Koran 28:6–13—We revealed Our will to Moses' mother, saying: "Give him suck, but if you are concerned about his safety, then put him down the river. Have no fear, nor be dismayed; for We shall restore him to you and shall invest him with a mission." Pharaoh's household picked him up, so that he might become their adversary and their scourge. For Pharaoh, Haman, and their warriors were sinners all.

Moses' mother's heart was sorely troubled. She said to his sister (*Miriam in the Bible, not named in the Koran*): "Go, and follow him." She watched him from a distance unseen by others. His sister said to them: "Shall I direct you to a family who will bring him up for you and take good care of him?" Thus did We restore him to his mother.

Exodus 2:1–10—Now a certain man of the house of Levi married a Levite woman, who conceived and bore a son. Seeing that he was a goodly child, she hid him for three months (*because Pharaoh had ordered all boy babies drowned*). When she could hide him no longer, she took a papyrus basket, daubed it with bitumen and pitch, and putting the child in it, placed it among the reeds on the river bank. His sister (*Miriam*) stationed herself at a distance to find out what would happen to him. Pharaoh's daughter came down to the river to bathe, while her maids walked along the river bank. (*If the Pharaoh was Ramses II, it could have been any of his fifty daughters.*) Noticing the basket among the reeds she sent her handmaid to fetch it. On opening it, she looked and lo, there was a baby boy crying. She was moved with pity for him and said, "It is one of the Hebrews' children." There his sister asked Pharaoh's daughter, "Shall I go and call one of the Hebrew women to nurse the child for you?" "Yes, do so," she answered. (*Moses was therefore returned to his mother till he was weaned, then adopted by Pharaoh's daughter, and taken into the royal household.*)

Koran 28:14–17—And when he had reached maturity and grown to manhood. We bestowed on him wisdom and knowledge. Thus do We reward the righteous. He entered the town unnoticed by its people (*because it was the mid-day siesta time*), and found two men at each other's throats, the one of his own race, the other an enemy. The Israelite appealed for Moses' help against his enemy, so that Moses struck him (*the Egyptian*) with his fist and slew him. "This is the work of Satan," said Moses. "He is the sworn enemy of man and seeks to lead him astray. Forgive me, Lord, for I have sinned against my soul." And God forgave him, for He is the Forgiving One, the Merciful.

Exodus 2:11–12—On one occasion, after Moses had grown up, when he visited his kinsmen and witnessed their forced labor, he saw an Egyptian striking a Hebrew, one of his own kinsmen. Looking about and seeing no one, he slew the Egyptian and hid him in the sand.

Koran 28:18–22—(Summary) Moses soon learned that his act was known in town and fled to Midian. (*This was the land surrounding the northern tip of what is now known as the Gulf of*

Aqaba, the long tongue of the Red Sea that separates the Sinai Penin-
sula from Saudi Arabia. I lived there for two years, in Tabuk, Saudi
Arabia.) When he came to the well of Midian, he found around it a
multitude of men watering their flocks, and beside them two women
who were keeping back their sheep.

Exodus 2:15–17—Pharaoh, too, heard of the affair and sought
to put him to death. But Moses fled from him and stayed in the land
of Midian. As he was seated there by a well, seven daughters of a
priest of Midian came to draw water and fill the troughs to water
their father's flock. But some shepherds came and drove them away.
Then Moses got up and defended them and watered their flock.

Koran 28:23b–28—"What is it that troubles you?" Moses asked
the girls. They replied: "We cannot water them until the shepherds
have driven away their flocks. Our father is an aged man." Moses
watered for them their sheep and then retired to the shade, saying,
"Lord, I surely stand in need of the blessing which You have sent
me (*that is, in need of a wife*)." One of the girls came bashfully
towards him and said: "My father calls you. He wishes to reward
you for watering our flock." And when Moses went and recounted
to him his story, the old man said: "Fear nothing. You are now safe
from those wicked people." One of the girls said: "Father, take this
man into your service. Men who are strong and honest are the best
that you can hire." The old man said; "I will give you one of these
two daughters of mine in marriage if you stay eight years in my
service, but if you wish it, you may stay ten."

Exodus 2:18–20—(Summary) The girls returned to Jethro and
told him of Moses' bravery.

Exodus 2:21–22—"Where is the man?" he asked his daughters.
"Why did you leave him there? Invite him to have something to eat."
Moses agreed to live with him, and the man gave him his daughter
Zipporah in marriage.

Koran 28:29–32—Moses descried a fire on the mountain-side.
He said to his people: "Stay here, for I can see a fire. Perhaps I can
bring you news, or a lighted torch to warm yourselves with." When
he came near, a voice called out to him from a bush in a blessed spot
on the right side of the valley, saying: "Moses, I am God, Lord of
the Universe. Throw down your staff." And when he saw it writhing
like a serpent, he turned his back and fled, running on and on. "Moses," said the voice, "approach and have no fear. You are safe. Put

your hand in your pocket: it will come out white, although un-harmed. Now draw back your arm, and do not stretch it out in terror. These are two signs from your Lord for Pharaoh and his people. Truly, they are sinful men."

There are multiple versions of this part of the story in the Koran. See also Sura 20:10–23 for another one.

Exodus 3:1–2, 4b–8—Meanwhile, Moses was tending the flock of his father-in-law Jethro, the priest of Midian. Leading the flock across the desert, he came to Horeb, the mountain of God. There an angel of the Lord appeared to him in fire flaming out of a bush. As he looked on, he was surprised to see that the bush, though on fire, was not consumed . . . God called out to him from the bush, "Moses! Moses!" He answered, "Here I am." God said, "Come no nearer! Remove the sandals from your feet, for the place where you stand is holy ground. I am the God of your father," he continued, "the God of Abraham, the God of Isaac, the God of Jacob." Moses hid his face for he was afraid to look at God. (*Because it was believed that no one could see God and live.*)

But the Lord said, "I have witnessed the affliction of my people in Egypt and have heard their cry of complaint against their slave drivers, so I know well what they are suffering. Therefore I have come down to rescue them from the hands of the Egyptians and lead them out of that land into a good and spacious land, a land flowing with milk and honey . . ."

Koran 28:33–34—"Lord," said Moses, "I have killed one of their number and fear that they will slay me. Aaron my brother is more fluent of tongue than I; send him with me that he may help me and confirm my words, for I fear they will reject me." He replied, "We will strengthen your arm with your brother, and will bestow such power on you both, that none shall harm you."

There are multiple versions of this incident. See also Suras 20:23b–32, and 27:8–11.

Exodus 4:1–7—(Summary) Moses argues with God. God shows him how to change a staff into a snake and back again, then how to make his hand leprous and then clean again.

Exodus 4:10–16—(Summary) Moses argues again that he is not a good speaker. God says he will send the eloquent Aaron to do the talking.

Exodus 4:18, 20, 27—After this, Moses returned to his father-in-law Jethro and said to him, "Let me go back, please, to my kinsmen in Egypt, to see whether they are still living." Jethro replied, "Go in peace." . . . So Moses took his wife and his sons, and started back to the land of Egypt, with them riding the ass. The staff of God he carried with him . . . The Lord said to Aaron, "Go into the desert to meet Moses." So he went, and when they met at the mountain of God, Aaron kissed him. Moses informed him of all the Lord had said in sending him, and of the various signs he had enjoined upon him. Then Moses and Aaron went and assembled all the elders of the Israelites (*in Egypt*). Aaron told them everything the Lord had said to Moses.

Koran 43:46–56—We sent forth Moses with Our signs to Pharaoh and his nobles. He said: "I am the apostle of the Lord of the Universe." But when he showed them Our signs they laughed at them, yet each fresh sign We revealed to them was mightier than the one that came before it. Pharaoh said, "Am I not better than this despicable wretch, who can scarcely make his meaning plain? Why have no bracelets of gold been given him, or angels sent down to accompany him?" (*The "gold bracelets" is probably a reference to the gold ring and gold chain given to Joseph by the Pharaoh of 400 years before, in Genesis 41:42.*) Thus did he incite his people. They obeyed him, for they were degenerate men.

Koran 7:133–135—So We plagued them with floods and locusts, with lice and frogs and blood; clear miracles, yet they scorned them all, for they were a wicked nation. And when each plague smote them, they said: "Moses, pray to your Lord for us: invoke the promise He has made you. If you lift the plague from us, we will believe in you and let the Israelites go with you." But when We had lifted the plague from them, they broke their promise.

Exodus Chapters 7–11—(Summary) The Lord visited ten plagues upon the Egyptians because of the hardness of heart of the Pharaoh. They were: turning to blood all the waters of Egypt, a swarming of frogs everywhere in the land, all of the dust turned into gnats, swarms of flies, a pestilence afflicting all domestic beasts, festering boils on every man and beast, hail that struck down every man and beast who were in the open, locusts that ate up all the vegetation, dense darkness for three days, and finally the death of every first-born. None of these plagues affected the Israelites.

Exodus 12:1–28—(Summary) The Passover. The Lord told Moses and Aaron how the people must sacrifice lambs and apply their blood to the door posts of their houses so that the Lord would "pass over" their houses when he came to kill the first-born of every Egyptian. He also told them to celebrate this Feast forever on the tenth day of the first month by eating unleavened bread and doing no work. Then the Lord did come.

Exodus 12:29—At midnight the Lord slew the first-born of Pharaoh on the throne to the first-born of the prisoner in the dungeon, as well as all the first-born of the animals.

Koran 20:77—Then We revealed Our will to Moses, saying, "Set forth with My servants in the night and strike for them a dry path across the sea. Have no fear of being overtaken, nor let anything dismay you." Pharaoh pursued them with his legions, but the waters overwhelmed them. For Pharaoh misled his people: he did not guide them.

Exodus 12:31–38—(Summary) Pharaoh let the Israelites go with their flocks and herds. The Egyptian people were eager to see them go and even gave them silver and gold. Six hundred thousand adults plus children set out from Rameses for Succoth. (*Rameses lay in the far northern part of Egypt, about half way between where the modern cities of Alexandria and Cairo lie. Succoth was about fifty miles to the southeast of Rameses, about twenty miles from the north end of the Red Sea. Counting the children would put the total number at about two million. Most commentators agree that this is an impossibly high number.*)

Exodus 13:20–22—Setting out from Succoth, they camped at Etham near the edge of the desert (*and just a few miles from the Red Sea*). The Lord preceded them, in the daytime by means of a column of cloud to show them the way, and at night by means of a column of fire to give them light.

Exodus 14:5–9b—When it was reported to the king of Egypt that the people had fled, Pharaoh and his servants changed their minds about them. So Pharaoh made his chariots ready and mustered his soldiers—six hundred first-class chariots and all the other chariots of Egypt, with warriors on them all. The Egyptians then pursued them; Pharaoh's whole army, his horses, chariots and charioteers, caught up with them as they lay encamped by the sea.

Exodus 14:21–29—(Summary) God told Moses to stretch his hand over the sea. He did so and the sea parted to allow them to cross on dry land. When they were across, the Egyptian chariots were on the sea floor. Moses stretched out his hand again and the sea flowed back and drowned all the Egyptians.

Koran 10:90–92—We led the Israelites across the sea, and Pharaoh and his legions pursued them with wickedness and spite. But as he was drowning, Pharaoh cried: "Now I believe no god exists except the God in whom the Israelites believe. To Him I give up myself."

(The Lord answers): "Only now! But before this you were a rebel and a wrongdoer. We shall save our body this day, so that you may become a sign to all posterity: for a great many of mankind do not heed Our signs."

There is no biblical record of a conversation between Pharaoh and God.

Koran 2:61–62a—(The Israelites are now in the desert of north Sinai.) "Moses," the Israelites said, "we will no longer put up with this monotonous diet. Call on your Lord to give us some of the varied produce of the earth, green herbs and cucumbers, corn and lentils and onions." "What!" he answered. "Would you exchange that which is good for what is worse? Go back to some city. There you will find all you have asked for."

Numbers 11:5—The Israelites lamented again, "Would that we had meat for food! We remember the fish we used to eat without cost in Egypt, and the cucumbers, the melons, the leeks, the onions, and the garlic."

Koran 2:56—We caused the clouds to draw their shadow over you and sent down for you manna and quails, saying: "Eat of the good things We have given you." Indeed, they did not wrong Us, but they wronged themselves (by gathering more than they needed for the day, in violation of God's command).

Exodus 16:4a—Then the Lord said to Moses, "I will now rain down bread from heaven for you. Each day the people are to go out and gather their daily portion."

Exodus 16:12b–14, 31, 19–20—(The Lord speaking to Moses) "Tell them: In the evening twilight you shall eat flesh, and in the morning you shall have your fill of bread, so that you may know that I, the Lord, am your God." In the evening quail came up and covered the camp. In the morning a dew lay all about the camp, and when the dew evaporated, there on the surface of the desert were fine flakes like hoarfrost on the ground . . . The Israelites called this food manna. It was like coriander seed, but white and it tasted like wafers made with honey . . . Moses also told them, "Let no one keep any of it over until tomorrow morning." But they would not listen to him. When some kept a part of it over until the following morning, it became wormy and rotten.

Koran 2:67—When Moses said to his people: "God commands you to sacrifice a cow," they replied: "Are you making game of us?" "God forbid that I should be so foolish!" he rejoined.

Koran 2:68–71—(Summary) They asked Moses to call on the Lord to make known what kind of cow: not too young and not too old; its color: a rich yellow; exact type of cow: a healthy cow not worn out with plowing.

Koran 2:72–73—"Now you have told us all," they answered. And they slaughtered a cow, after they had nearly declined. And when you slew a man and then fell out with one another concerning him, God made known what you concealed. We said: "Strike him with a part of it." Thus God restores the dead to life and shows you His signs, that you may grow in understanding. (*A piece of the meat was to be used to strike the corpse of the slain man so that the murderer would be discovered.*)

Numbers 19:1–2—The Lord said to Moses and Aaron: "This is the regulation which the law of the Lord prescribes. Tell the Israelites to procure for you a red heifer that is free from every blemish and defect and on which no yoke has ever been laid."

Numbers 19:3–22—(Summary) The heifer is to be burned completely along with cedar wood, hyssop and scarlet yarn. The ashes are to be gathered up to make lustral water which will be used to make ritually clean anyone who has touched a dead body, whether it be in a tent, or in open country, whether slain by the sword or died naturally. Then follows the intricate details of the rites of purification of their bodies, clothes, vessels, and tents.

Koran 7:159—We divided them into twelve tribes, each a whole community. And when his people demanded drink of him, We revealed our Will to Moses, saying: "Strike the rock with your staff." Thereupon twelve springs gushed from the rock and each tribe knew its drinking place.

Exodus 15:27—Then they came to Elim, where there were twelve springs of water and seventy palm trees, and they camped there near the water. (*Elim was probably half way down the west coast of the Sinai peninsula. There is no mention here of Moses striking the rock to procure water. In the Bible he procures water from the rock some time later, as seen in this next passage.*)

Exodus 17:1—From the desert of Sin the whole Israelite community journeyed in stages, as the Lord directed, and encamped at Rephidim (*far down the Sinai Peninsula, close to Mt. Sinai/Horeb*). Here there was no water for the people to drink. 17:2–6—(Summary) The people accused Moses of bringing them out of Egypt only to die of thirst in the desert. Moses was told by the Lord to strike a rock with his staff and water gushed out.

Koran 7:143, 145—And when Moses came (*to the mountain*) at the appointed time and His Lord communed with him, he said: "Lord, reveal Yourself to me, that I may look upon You." "You shall not see Me." He replied. "Moses, I have chosen you of all mankind to make known My messages and My commandments. Take therefore what I have given you, and be thankful." We inscribed for him upon the Tablets all manner of precepts and instructions concerning all things, and said to him: "Observe these steadfastly, and enjoin your people to observe what is best in them." (*It is not recorded which ones Moses received while on the Mountain.*)

Exodus 19:1, 5–6—In the third month after their departure from the land of Egypt, on its first day, the Israelites came to the desert of Sinai . . . (*The Lord called to Moses*), "Therefore, if you hearken to my voice and keep my covenant, you shall be my special possession, dearer to me that all other people, though all the earth is mine. You shall be to me a kingdom of priests, a holy nation. That is what you must tell the Israelites."

Exodus 19:9a, 16–20—The Lord also told him, "I am coming to you in a dense cloud so that when the people hear me speaking with you, they may always have faith in you also." . . . Mount Sinai was all wrapped in smoke, for the Lord came down upon it in fire. The smoke rose from it as though from a furnace, and the whole mountain trembled violently. The trumpet blast grew louder and louder, while Moses was speaking and God answering him with thunder. When the Lord came down to the top of Mount Sinai, he summoned Moses to the top of the mountain, and Moses went up to him.

Exodus 20:1–17—(*Excerpts*) Then God delivered all these commandments (*called by Christians and Jews "The Ten Commandments"*): (1) You shall not have other gods besides me . . . (2) You shall not carve idols for yourselves . . . nor bow down before them . . . (3) You shall not take the name of the Lord your God in vain . . . (4) Remember to keep holy the Sabbath day . . . (5) Honor your father and your mother . . . (6) You shall not kill . . . (7) You shall not commit adultery . . . (8) You shall not steal . . . (9) You shall not bear false witness against your neighbor . . . (10) You shall not covet your neighbor's house . . . wife . . . slaves . . . ox or ass nor anything that belongs to him. (*With the exception of a portion of Chapter 23 and all of Chapter 24, the rest of the book of Exodus—Chapters 21–40—contains the laws given to Moses by God on Mt. Sinai. In addition, all of the twenty-seven chapters in the book of Leviticus—with the exception of Chapter 10—contain the laws given Moses on Mt. Sinai, most of these being a repetition of the laws in Exodus.*)

Moses was instructed to build an Ark to house the stone tablets. But there are contradictory passages in the Bible about what else was put into the ark:

I Kings 8:9—There was nothing in the Ark but the two stone tablets which Moses had put there at Horeb (*Sinai*), when the Lord made a covenant with the Israelites at their departure from the land of Egypt.

And:

Deuteronomy 9:15–17, 10:1–5—(Summary) Moses and the Israelites have come to the Jordan River. Moses speaks to the entire nation and reminds them of their forty years in the wilderness. He relates how he came down from Mt. Sinai with the Ten Commandments written on two stone tablets, found Aaron and the Israelites worshiping the golden calf, broke the tablets in anger, and punished the Israelites. The Lord told him to cut two tablets, take them up to the mountain where the Lord would write on them again. He told Moses to make an Ark of acacia wood and place the tablets in it. (*The Israelites carried the ark with them for forty years in the desert, and carried it into the Promised Land of Canaan. It was passed down from priest to priest up to the time of Solomon (965–928 BCE,*

138

and then disappeared at the time of the schism between Judah and Israel which occurred shortly after Solomon died.)
But:

Hebrews 9:4b—In it (*the ark*) were the gold jar containing the manna, the staff of Aaron that had sprouted, and the tablets of the covenant.

And in a later chapter in Exodus it appears that all of the commandments were placed in the ark:

Exodus 25:10–16—(Summary) God gives Moses elaborate instructions for building the Ark: 4' by 4' by 2', plated with gold, rings for carrying it with poles. And then he says, "In the Ark you are to put the commandments which I will give you."

The story of the Golden Calf:

Koran 7:148–151—In his absence the people of Moses made a calf from their ornaments, an image with a hollow sound. Did they not see that it could neither speak to them nor give them guidance? Yet they worshiped it and thus committed evil. And when Moses returned to his people, angry and sorrowful, he said: "Evil is the thing you did in my absence!" He threw down the Tablets and, seizing his brother (*Aaron*) by the hair, dragged him closer. "Son of my mother," cried Aaron, "the people overpowered me and almost did me to death. Do not let my enemies gloat over me; do not number me among the wrongdoers." "Lord," said Moses, "forgive me and forgive my brother."

In Sura 7:156–157, God replies in a long speech, including:

"I will show mercy to those that keep from evil and give alms, and to those that follow the Apostle—the Unlettered Prophet—whom they shall find described in the Torah and the Gospel."

Exodus 32:1–28—(Summary) When Moses was up on the mountain, the people enjoined Aaron to make a golden calf from their ornaments. They worshiped it, calling it their God. Then they ate, drank, and reveled. Moses came down, threw down the tablets and broke them. He called the Levites (the tribe of priests) and ordered them to kill their own tribesmen. They did and 3,000 died that day.

God records prophecies in the Book he gave to the Israelites:

139

Koran 17:2–4—We gave Moses the Book and made it a guide for the Israelites, saying: "Take no other guardian than Myself. You are the descendants of those whom We carried in the Ark with Noah. He was truly a thankful servant." In the Book We solemnly declared to the Israelites: "Twice you shall commit evil in the land. You shall become great transgressors."

According to Muslim commentators, the first evil was the killing of Isaiah in the 8th century BCE *and the imprisoning of Jeremiah in the 7th century* BCE. *The second evil was the killing of Zachariah (John the Baptist's father), John the Baptist himself, and Jesus.*

Neither the Bible nor the Koran records the fate of Isaiah, nor is there any reliable extra-biblical source.

Jeremiah was imprisoned by the Jewish authorities because he prophesied that the Lord would punish the Israelites by having them taken into exile in Babylon: Jeremiah 37:7. Tradition has it that he was exiled to Egypt and killed there.

The fate of John's father is not recorded in the Bible. There was a Zechariah murdered in the Temple courtyard in the ninth century BCE: *2 Chronicles 24:20–21.*

According to the Bible, John was beheaded by Herod Antipas, an Idumean, not a Jew. Jesus was crucified by the Romans at the instigation of the Jews.

Koran 17:5—And when the prophecy of your first transgression came to be fulfilled. We sent against you a formidable army which ravaged your land and carried out the punishment with which you had been threatened. (*This was the invasion of Israel by the Assyrians under Sennacherib in 701* BCE *and the deportation of the ten "lost" tribes of Israel to Assyria. See 2 Kings 20:12–18.*)

Koran 17:7—And when the prophecy of your second transgression came to be fulfilled, We sent another army to afflict you and to enter the Temple as the former entered it before, utterly destroying all that they laid their hands on. (*This was the Romans, who ruled the entire known world, including Palestine, at the time of Jesus. When the Jews revolted in 68–72* CE, *Rome crushed them, including total destruction of the Temple in Jerusalem in 70* CE.)

Jesus also predicted the destruction of the Temple:

Mark 13:1–2—As he (*Jesus*) was making his way out of the temple area one of his disciples said to him, "Look, teacher, what stones and what buildings!" Jesus said to him, "Do you see these great buildings? There will not be one stone left upon another that will not be thrown down."

After only a few months in the desert, Moses decided to send scouts up into Canaan. Both the Koran and the Bible describe what happened:

Koran 5:22–26—(*Moses speaking*) "Enter, my people, the holy land which God has assigned to you. Do not turn back, and thus lose all."

"Moses," they replied, "a race of giants dwells in this land. We will not set foot in it till they are gone. As soon as they are gone we will enter."

Thereupon two God-fearing men (*Joshua and Caleb, not named*) whom God had favored said: Go in to them through the gates, and when you have entered you shall surely be victorious. In God put your trust, if you are true believers.

But they replied: "Moses, we will not go in so long as *they* are in it. Go, you and your Lord, and fight. Here we will stay."

"Lord," cried Moses, "I have none but myself and my brother. Keep us apart from these wicked people."

He replied, "They shall be forbidden this land for forty years, during which time they shall wander homeless on the earth. Do not grieve for these wicked people."

Numbers 13–14 (Summary) Twelve scouts (one from each tribe) were sent to reconnoiter the land of Canaan. They went as far as Hebron (fifteen miles south of modern Jerusalem) and found that the land did indeed flow with milk and honey. They brought back a cluster of grapes so large that it had to be carried on a pole between two men. But they reported that the people were fierce, the towns fortified and very strong, and besides, they found the descendants of a race of giants there, descendants of the Anakim (see Genesis 6:4). Only Caleb of the tribe of Judah and Joshua of the tribe of Ephraim recommended going on up to seize the land. The other ten scouts convinced the people that it would be too dangerous and threatened to stone Caleb and Joshua when they persisted. This angered the Lord and he threatened to wipe them out. Moses argued with the Lord, saying that if now the Lord destroyed the Israelites, the other nations of the world would say that they were slaughtered because the Lord was not strong enough to bring them into the land he had promised them. God relented but said, "None of these who have spurned me shall see it (the Promised Land) . . . Here in the desert shall your dead bodies fall . . . except Caleb, son of Jephunneh, and Joshua, son of Nun."

Koran 28:43–44, 46—After We had destroyed the first generations (*in the wilderness*) We gave the Book to Moses as a clear sign, a guide and a blessing for mankind. You (*Mohammed*) were not on the western side of the mountain when We charged Moses with his commission, nor did you witness the event . . . Yet have We sent you forth, a blessing from your Lord, to forewarn a nation to whom no one has been sent before."

Koran 2:57–58—"Enter this city," We said, "and eat where you will to your hearts' content. Make your way reverently through the gates, saying: 'We repent.' We shall forgive you your sins and bestow abundance on the righteous." But that which they were told, the wrongdoers replaced with other words; and We let loose on the wrongdoers a scourge from heaven as a punishment for their misdeeds. (*Rodwell believes that this rather obscure passage indicates that the Israelites entered Jericho after God "destroyed the first generations." The "other words" were actually one word, "habbat," meaning "corn," rather than what they were supposed to say, "hittat," meaning "forgiveness," but translated by both Dawood and Rodwell as "We repent."*)

Koran 10:93—We settled the Israelites in a secure land and provided them with good things.

At this point, the Koranic story of Moses ends. And from this point on, the biblical story of the settlement of Canaan is told in Numbers, Deuteronomy, and Joshua, far too long and complicated to be recounted here, especially since there is no counterpart in the Koran. Suffice it to say that the Lord committed the Israelites to another thirty-nine years in the desert, until all were dead who had opposed him and tested him. Joshua and Caleb, who had not opposed the Lord, led the Israelites across the Jordan. Moses traveled with them as far as the Jordan, but died before the crossing of the Jordan and the first battles with the native people in Jericho and Ai.

18

People of the Book: The Monarchial Period

In the Name of God the Compassionate the Merciful

Following the death of Moses and the conquest of Canaan under the leadership of Joshua, the Bible records that the Israelites were ruled by a series of judges for about two hundred years. There were undoubtedly many of them distributed around the country, but only twelve made it into the biblical history books. Among these mostly unremembered judges were Deborah, Gideon, and Samson, but neither they nor any other judges are recorded in the Koran.

In about 1025 BCE, the Israelites went to their chief priest and prophet Samuel and asked him to anoint a king for them. He did, and initiated the Monarchy by choosing Saul. The united monarchy ruling all twelve tribes of Israel lasted only until the death of the third king, Solomon. It then split into Israel with ten tribes, and Judah with two. The Bible records in great detail the succession of kings of Israel and Judah, in 1 and 2 Samuel, and in 1 and 2 Kings. But the Koran deals only with the first three kings: Saul, David, and Solomon. So this is where we pick up the story.

(1) Saul

In Sura Two there is a series of stories about Saul. They were revealed in the second year after the Hejira, in 623, at a time when Mohammed foresaw an open rupture with the idolatrous pagans of Medina in the near future. He felt it necessary to stimulate the zeal and courage of his people with examples from Jewish history. The story is told in THE COW and is the first of the Suras to be recited in Medina after the flight from Mecca.

The story of Saul in the Bible begins in 1 Samuel 8 and continues through twenty-three more chapters, far too many to even summarize here. Therefore I shall lift out only those passages that have a corollary in the Koran. As usual, I recommend strongly that the reader put these short passages into context by reading 1 Samuel in the Bible.

The Israelites ask for a king:

Koran 2:245—Have you not heard of what the leaders of the Israelites demanded of one of their prophets (*Samuel, never named in the Koran*) after the death of Moses? "Raise up for us a king," they said, "and we will fight for the cause of God."

1 Samuel 8:1–9—(Summary) As Samuel aged and his sons became corrupt, the Israelites went to Samuel and asked him to appoint a king. Samuel was not pleased but the Lord said to him, "Now grant their request; but at the same time, warn them solemnly and inform them of the rights of the king who will rule them."

Koran 2:246–247—He (*Samuel*) replied: "What if you refuse to fight, when ordered so to do?"

"Why should we refuse to fight for the cause of God," they said, "when we have been driven from our dwellings and our children?" But when at last they were ordered to fight, they all refused, except a few of them. God knows the evil-doers.

Their prophet said to them: "God has appointed Saul to be your king."

But they replied: "Should he be given the kingship when we are more deserving of it than he? Besides, he is not rich at all."

He said: "God has chosen him to rule over you and made him grow in wisdom and stature. God gives His sovereignty to whom He will. God is munificent and all-knowing."

1 Samuel, Chapters 9–13 (Summary)—The choosing of Saul as king is laboriously told in five chapters, with long passages chronologically out of order. In fact, there are two stories of Saul's anointing. In one, he is found by Samuel wandering far from home, looking for some lost donkeys. Samuel is told by God that this is his choice for king. So Samuel anoints him on the spot. In the other story, lots are cast (Urim and Thummim?) and Saul wins. Then Samuel says to the people, "Come, let us go to Gilgal to inaugurate the kingdom there." So all the people went to Gilgal, where, in the presence of

the Lord, they made Saul king. (*Gilgal was probably near Jericho, about 12–15 miles northeast of Jerusalem.*)

The ark of the covenant:

Koran 2:248a–249a—Their prophet (*Samuel*) also said to them. "The advent of the Ark shall be the portent of his (*Saul's*) reign. Therein shall be tranquility from your Lord and the relics which the House of Moses and the House of Aaron left behind. (*The Arabic word for tranquility is* sakinah, *which may well be related to the Hebrew word for Holy Presence,* shekhinah, *which was believed by the Israelites to be present within the Ark. The "relics" are not described in the Koran. Muslim tradition holds that they were the shoes and rod of Moses, the miter of Aaron, a vase of manna, and the fragments of the two tablets of the law given to—and broken by—Moses on Mt. Sinai.*

The biblical references to the Ark have been noted in Chapter 17, MOSES.

An army is chosen:

Koran 2:248b—And when Saul marched out with his army, he said: "God will put you to the proof at a certain river. He that drinks from it shall cease to be my soldier, but he that does not drink from it, or contents himself with a taste of it in the hollow of his hand, shall fight by my side." But they all drank from it, except a few of them.

This story is very similar to the story of Gideon, the fifth judge over Israel long before the people asked Samuel for a king. Gideon's story can be found in Judges, Chapters 6–9. The Bible passage pertinent to the Koran follows:

Judges 7:1–7—(Summary) Gideon was encamped near Mt. Gilboa near the Sea of Galilee, preparing to fight the Midianites. The Lord chose 300 men from 22,000 by a test: Those who knelt down to the river to drink were disqualified because they became vulnerable to attack. Those who raised the water in their hands and lapped it like a dog were chosen because they stayed on guard.

Goliath:

Koran 2:249b–250—And when Saul had crossed the river with those who shared his faith, they said: "We have no power this day against Goliath and his warriors." But those of them who believed that they would meet God replied: "Many a small band has, by God's grace, vanquished a mighty army. God is with those who endure with fortitude." When they met Goliath and his warriors, they cried, "Lord, fill our hearts with steadfastness. Make us firm of foot and help us against the unbelievers." By God's will they routed them.

In the accounts in both the Bible and the Koran, David slew Goliath. That story is told in the following passages dealing with David.

(2) David

There are two stories told of David in the Koran: his confrontation with Goliath, and a parable relating God's judgement after David took Bathsheba from Uriah. There are also several other brief references to David, which we will consider after the stories.

In the Bible, David's story takes forty-one chapters to tell: 1 Samuel, chapters 16–31, all twenty-four chapters of 2 Samuel, and the first one and a half chapters of 1 Kings. If the reader is unfamiliar with the biblical story, the vignettes in the Koran may not make much sense. However, in this study, we will compare only the stories told in the Koran and leave to the reader the task of fleshing out David's complete story in the Bible.

The first story, David and Goliath:

Koran 2:250–251—When they (*Saul's army*) met Goliath and his warriors, they cried: "Lord, fill our hearts with steadfastness. Make us firm of foot and help us against the unbelievers." By God's will they routed them. David slew Goliath and God bestowed on him sovereignty and wisdom and taught him what He pleased. Had God not defeated some by the might of others, the earth would have been utterly corrupted. But God is bountiful to mankind.

1 Samuel 17:3–59—(Summary) The Philistine champion Goliath wears a helmet, armor weighing 156 pounds, greaves, and scimitar, all of bronze. He carries a javelin with a fifteen-pound head. (My Bible says he was 6′ 6″ tall. The Masoretic Text says he was 9′ 9″ and the Septuagint says 6′ 9″.) He challenges Israel to send a man to fight him. Whoever loses, places his country in slavery to the other. The youth David has been sent by his father from his home to the Israelite army camp with provisions for his brothers. He hears the challenge and accepts it in King Saul's hearing. Saul outfits David with his own armor but David takes it all off because he has never worn armor and he can hardly walk in it. He selects five stones from a creek bed and goes to meet Goliath. The Philistine then moves to meet David at close quarters. David hurls a stone with the sling, and strikes the Philistine on the forehead. The stone embeds itself in his brow, and he falls prostrate on the ground. Then David runs and stands over him; with the Philistine's own sword he dispatches him and cuts off his head.

The second story, David and Bathsheba:

In most instances in this study I have quoted first from the Koran, then the Bible. However, this story in the Koran is very difficult to understand if you don't know the Bible's version. So I shall tell the story from the Bible first:
2 Samuel 11:1–12:18—(Summary) David saw Bathsheba bathing on the roof of her house. He sent for her and made her his mistress. He ordered his general Joab to place Bathsheba's husband Uriah in the first rank in the next battle with the Ammonites so that he was sure to be killed, and he was. David then married Bathsheba. Nathan, his prophet, confronted him and told him a story: A man with many flocks and herds takes from one of his tenants his only ewe lamb in order to prepare a meal for a visitor. David was angered and said to Nathan that the man merited death. Nathan answered, "You are the man." Then Nathan recounted all that the Lord had done for David. He told him that his punishment would be that the Lord would "strike down" the child of Bathsheba and David, and later the child did die.

The parable from the Koran:

147

Koran 38:21–27—Have you heard the story of the two litigants (*angels*) who entered his (*David's*) chamber by climbing over the wall? When they went in to David and saw that he was alarmed, they said: "Have no fear. We are two litigants, one of whom has wronged the other. Judge rightly between us and do not be unjust; guide us to the right path. My brother here has ninety-nine ewes, but I have only one ewe. He demanded that I should entrust it to him, and got the better of me in the dispute."

David replied: "He has certainly wronged you in seeking to add your ewe to his flock. Many partners are unjust to one another; but not so those that have faith and do good works, and they are few indeed."

David realized that We were only testing him. He sought forgiveness of his Lord and fell down penitently on his knees. We forgave him his sin, and in the world to come he shall be honored and well received.

We said, "David, We have made you master in the land. Rule with justice among men and do not yield to lust, lest it turn you away from God's path. Because they forget the Day of Reckoning, those that stray from God's path shall be sternly punished." (*In this parable the angels clearly represent Nathan, and the one ewe, Bathsheba.*)

The following are the other brief Koranic references to David.
Koran 38:30—We have revealed to you (*David*) this book (*Psalms*) with Our blessing, so that the wise might ponder its revelations and take warning. (*Mohammed apparently believed that all the Psalms were written by David. Old Testament scholars now believe that the collection was begun in David's time, but was not completed until ca. 400 BCE, six hundred years after David lived.*)

Koran 38:17–20—Bear with what they say (*those waiting for the Day of Doom*) and remember Our servant David, who was both a mighty and a penitent man. We made the mountains join with him in praise evening and morning, and the birds, too, in all their flocks; all were obedient to him. We made his kingdom strong, and gave him wisdom and discriminating judgment.

Psalm 148:9–10, 13—You mountains and all hills, fruit trees and all cedars; you animals wild and tame, you creatures that crawl

148

and fly . . . Let them all praise the Lord's name, for his name alone is exalted, majestic above earth and heaven.

Koran 21:79—We taught him (*David*) the armorer's craft, so that you might have protection in your wars. Will you then give thanks?

Koran 34:10—On David We bestowed Our bounty . . . We made hard iron pliant to him, saying: "Make coats of mail and measure their links with care."

1 Samuel 16:19–21—Thus David came to Saul and entered his service. Saul became very fond of him and made him his armor-bearer. (*Nowhere in the Bible is it recorded that David acted as a blacksmith to make armor or weapons. The numerous wars in which David fought may have given rise to the belief that he was an armorer, not merely an armor-bearer, and this story became known to Mohammed. Throughout Islam, therefore, the blacksmith has been respected because his artisanship is thought to have been passed down from David, "the father of his craft."*)

(3) Solomon

Though we do find biblical counterparts for most of the Koranic references, the story of Solomon as found in the Koran is rather sketchy and does not fully define the impact that his reign had on the Monarchy that Saul and David established. It is limited to his relationship with the Queen of Sheba, his building projects, his wisdom, and his horses. In order to understand the story as told by the Koran, I must occasionally turn to extra-Koranic sources, which I will do in the appropriate places.

The biblical account of Solomon's reign is found in 1 Kings 1:11–11:43, beginning with his mother Bathsheba's battle to have him crowned king, up to his death in 933 BCE.

*   *   *

Koran 38:30–33—We gave Solomon to David: and he was a good and faithful servant. When, one evening, his prancing steeds were ranged before him, he said: "My love for good things has distracted me from the remembrance of my Lord; for now the sun has

vanished behind the veil of darkness. Bring me back my chargers!"
And with this he fell to hacking their legs and necks. (*Solomon was
so intent on admiring his horses that he forgot the evening
prayer—"the sun has vanished"—and in penance slaughtered his
horses. There is no biblical counterpart to this act but there are
references to Solomon's horses.*):

1 Kings 10:26–29—Solomon collected chariots and drivers; he
had one thousand four hundred chariots and twelve thousand drivers. Solomon's horses were imported from Cilicia, where the king's
agents purchased them for 150 shekels. (*Cilicia was located in the
southeastern part of what is now Turkey, where a millennium later
Saul [Paul] of Tarsus would be born and raised.*)

Koran 27:15–16—Solomon succeeded David. He said, "Know,
my people, we have been taught the tongue of birds and endowed
with all good things. Surely this is the signal favor." His forces of
jinn and men and birds were called to Solomon's presence and ranged
in battle array. (*The legend of Solomon's power over the jinn origi-
nated in the early Arabic mistranslation of* **Ecclesiastes 2:8b**—"*I got
for myself male and female singers," not "jinn and men and birds."*)
. . . When they came to the Valley of the Ants, an ant said: "Go into
your dwellings, ants, lest Solomon and his warriors should unwit-
tingly crush you." He (*Solomon*) smiled at her words.

*It is recorded in 1 Kings 5:12 that Solomon wrote three thou-
sand proverbs, and since it is said that Mohammed also believed this,
he may very well have known this one:*

Proverbs 6:6–7—Go to the ant, O sluggard, study her ways and
learn wisdom. For though she has no chief, no commander or ruler,
she procures her food in the summer, stores up her provisions in
the harvest.

Koran 27:20–24—He (*Solomon*) inspected the birds and said,
"Where is the lapwing (*hoopoe*)? I cannot see him here. If he does not
offer me a good excuse, I shall sternly punish him or even slay him."

The bird, who was not long in coming, said: "I have just seen
what you know nothing of. With truthful news I come to you from
Sheba, where I found a woman reigning over the people. She is possessed of every virtue and has a splendid throne." (*Most Muslim
commentators place Balkis, or Bilqis, the Queen of Sheba, in Ethiopia. There is, in fact, a province in modern-day Ethiopia called*

150

Shewa. But Christian-Jewish tradition and some Muslims place Sheba in Yemen.)

Koran 27:25–42—(Summary) Then the lapwing told Solomon about the Queen of Sheba. She and her people had been seduced by Satan away from the right path. Solomon invited her to Jerusalem with the words, "In the name of God, the Compassionate, the Merciful. Do not exalt yourselves above me, but come to me in all submission." She was suspicious of Solomon's motives because of the reputation of many kings for ruining their conquered cities and enslaving their chieftains. So, instead of obeying him, she sent an envoy with much gold. Solomon was angered and threatened to march against her with overwhelming forces. So she came to him.

Koran 27:43–45—He (*Solomon*) said, "Before her we were endowed with knowledge and surrendered to the Lord. Her false gods have led her astray, for she comes from an unbelieving nation." She was bidden to enter the palace and when she saw it she thought it was a pool of water and bared her legs.

But Solomon said, "It is a palace paved with glass."

"Lord," she said, "I have sinned against my own soul. Now I submit with Solomon to God, Lord of the Universe."

Muslim tradition holds that one of King Solomon's demons feared that Solomon might be tempted into marriage with the Queen. The demon whispered to him that the Queen had hairy legs and the hooves of an ass. Solomon had a glass floor built before his throne so when Balkis raised her skirts, thinking to cross through water, she would—and did—reveal hairy legs and hooves. Solomon then ordered his demons to create a depilatory for her. (In 1 Kings 6:15, we read that the entire inside of his palace was made of wood, including the floor. Mohammed may have had access to Revelation 4:6, which reads, "In front of the throne [of God in heaven] was something that resembled a sea of glass like crystal.")

Muslim tradition also holds that the Queen had a child by Solomon named Menelik, ancestor to the line of ruling emperors that ended with Haile Selassie in 1974 CE. One of Selassie's many titles was "Lion of Judah," referring to his supposed Judean ancestry. However, there can be no claim to a direct blood line because Haile Selassie was the son-in-law of Menelik II who had ruled from 1889 to 1913.

1 Kings 10:1–6—The Queen of Sheba, having heard of Solomon's fame, came to test him with subtle questions. She arrived in Jerusalem with a very numerous retinue, and with camels bearing spices, a large amount of gold, and precious stones. She came to Solomon and questioned him on every subject in which she was interested. King Solomon explained everything she asked about, and there remained nothing hidden from him that he could not explain to her. When the Queen of Sheba witnessed Solomon's great wisdom, the palace he had built, the food at his table, the seating of his ministers, the attendance and garb of his waiters, his banquet service, and the holocaust he offered in the temple of the Lord, she was breathless. "The report I heard in my country about your deeds and your wisdom is true," she told the king.

1 Kings 10:9–13—(Summary) Then she gave him gold, spices, and precious stones. She ordered Hiram to bring wood in his fleet, which he did. Solomon used it for his temple, palace, and for harps and lyres. Then she returned home.

Koran 34:12–17—To Solomon We subdued the wind, traveling a month's journey morning and evening. We gave him a spring flowing with molten brass, and jinn who served him by leave of his Lord. They made for him whatever he pleased: shrines and statues, basins as large as watering-troughs, and built-in cauldrons. (*The Talmud tells of the worm Shameer, used by Solomon to cut the stones for the Temple. This legend may have resulted from a misinterpretation of 1 Kings 6:7, which states that all of the Temple building stones were dressed at the quarry so that no hammering need be done on the building site*, not *that the stones were miraculously dressed by spirits, which Mohammed would have called jinn, without any noise on the building site itself.*)

1 Kings 6:2, 14–15—The temple which King Solomon built for the Lord was ninety feet long and thirty feet high . . . When Solomon finished building the temple its walls were lined from floor to ceiling beams with cedar paneling and its floor was laid with fir planking. (*This is a relatively small temple compared to the one built by Nehemiah and the returned exiles from Babylon in the late sixth century* BCE, *and greatly enlarged by Herod the Great at the end of the first century* BCE. *Solomon's temple has never been found by archaeologists.*)

1 Kings 7:23–25, 26b—The sea (*a circular tank*) was then cast; it was made with a circular rim, and measured fifteen feet across, seven and a half feet high, and forty-five feet in circumference. Under the brim, gourds encircled it, ten for every eighteen inches all the way around; the gourds were in two rows and were cast in one mold with the sea. This rested on twelve oxen, (*three facing in each direction*) . . . Its capacity was 12,000 gallons.

Koran 21:77–79, 82—And tell of David and Solomon: how they passed judgement regarding the cornfield in which strayed lambs had grazed by night. We gave Solomon insight into the case and bore witness to both their judgements. (*This incident is not recorded in the Bible, though other examples of his wisdom are.*) We bestowed on them wisdom and knowledge, and caused the mountains and the birds to join with David in Our praise . . . We assigned him devils who dived for him into the sea and who performed other tasks besides. (*The divers may have been searching for Murex sea snails from which royal purple dye was made. The Bible does not record divers being employed by Solomon.*)

Koran 38:34–35, 37–39—We put Solomon to the proof and placed a counterfeit (*a djinn*) upon his throne, so that he at length repented. He said: "Forgive me, Lord, and bestow upon me such power as shall belong to none after me. You are the Bountiful Giver." . . . "All this We give you," We said. "It is for you to bestow or to withhold, without reckoning." In the world to come he shall be honored and well received.

The passage above may have been derived from the following biblical story of Solomon's last days as king:

1 Kings 11:3b–4, 11–13, 42–43—(Excerpts) King Solomon had seven hundred wives of princely rank and three hundred concubines . . . When Solomon was old, his wives had turned his heart to strange gods . . . So the Lord said to Solomon: "Since this is what you want . . . I will deprive you of the kingdom . . . I will not do this during your lifetime, however; it is your son whom I will deprive . . . I will not take away the whole kingdom. I will leave your son one tribe. (*Solomon was the last king to rule over all twelve tribes of Israel. Solomon's son Rehoboam did rule over only one tribe, Judah, and only for a very short time because of his oppressive regime.*)

(4) Elijah

In the Bible, Elijah plays a very important role in Israel in the 9th century BCE. He enters the picture when Ahab became king of the northern kingdom of Israel in 875 BCE. He remained the chief prophet until ç 841, during the reign of Ahaziah and Joram. He was one of three biblical characters who the Bible says were taken up bodily into heaven, the other two being Enoch (Genesis 5:24), and Jesus (Mark 16:19 and elsewhere). Elijah was carried off in a whirlwind after fiery horses pulling a fiery chariot passed between him and his successor Elisha.

Elijah is mentioned only twice in the Koran (where he is called Elias). In Sura 6:84, he is listed with a dozen other Old Testament men as a descendant of Abraham. The following is the other reference:

Koran 37:124–130—We also sent forth Elias, who said to his people: "Have you no fear? Would you invoke Baal and forsake the Most Gracious Creator? God is your Lord and the Lord of your forefathers." We bestowed on him the praise of later generations: "Peace on Elias!" Thus do We reward the righteous. He was one of Our believing servants.

The following episode in the Bible may be the basis for the above passage in the Koran:

1 Kings 18:1–37—(Summary) King Ahab's Queen Jezebel had ordered hundreds of "prophets of the Lord" murdered. Elijah was indignant and met with Ahab. He asked Ahab to summon Jezebel's 450 prophets of Baal and 400 prophets of Asherah to the top of Mt. Carmel. None of them could start the holocaust fire by calling on their gods. Elijah prayed to the Lord God of Abraham, Isaac, and Israel (*Jacob*).

1 Kings 18:38–40—The Lord's fire came down and consumed the holocaust, wood, stones, and dust, and it lapped up the water in the trench. Seeing this, all the people fell prostrate and said, "The Lord is God! The Lord is God!" Then Elijah said to them, "Seize the prophets of Baal. Let none of them escape!" They were seized, and Elijah had them brought down to the brook Kishon and there he slit their throats.

154

19

People of the Book: Post-Monarchial Era

In the Name of God the Compassionate the Merciful

In 721 BCE, Sargon II of Assyria destroyed Samaria and took all ten tribes of Israel into captivity. These were the so-called "Ten Lost Tribes of Israel." They were not lost at all; they were completely assimilated into the population of Assyria and its other conquered countries and in that way disappeared and were "lost."

In 597 and 586 BCE Nebuchadnezzar conquered the two tribes of Judah and Benjamin (including Jerusalem) and carried them off to Babylon.

Neither of these events is recorded in the Koran but the three characters to be discussed now lived in that era.

(1) Jonah

Jonah actually plays a very small part in the Koran, but Gabriel includes him six times in listing the important prophets. One example of that has been quoted in the section telling Abraham's story in Chapter 16.

An entire sura of 110 verses, #10, is named "Jonah," but there is only one reference in it to the man himself, and that merely states that when his people believed, they were spared the penalty of disgrace. His story is told, very briefly, in Sura 37, and frankly does not make much sense unless one knows the biblical version. So once again I think it's imperative to record the Bible's version in order to understand the Koran's version. The curious reader may jump ahead to that story to see what I mean!

Following is a summary of the biblical story of Jonah, probably written in post-exilic times to counter the extremely nationalistic and vindictive views of Ezra and most of the Jews of that time:

Jonah was told by God to go from his home in Gath-hepher, about three miles from Nazareth (identified in 2 Kings 14:25), to Nineveh (in the northern part of what is now Iraq), to preach against it. Jonah fled instead to Joppa where he boarded a ship going to Tarshish, the modern-day coast of Spain near Gibraltar, at the edge of the known world then.

The Lord hurled a violent wind upon the sea. The sailors panicked and cast lots to find out who was to blame. The lot fell on Jonah so they threw him overboard. He was "rescued" by a whale, in whose belly he lived for three days. He prayed to the Lord and told him he repented of what he had done, so the Lord commanded the fish to spew Jonah upon the shore. This time Jonah did go to Nineveh, a town of 120,000, that took three days to walk across. (*This actually is an anachronism, because in 780* BCE *when this story is supposed to have taken place, Nineveh was a small provincial town. A century later, Sennacherib established it as his royal summer residence and it grew to great size, perhaps still not large enough to take three days to walk across!*)

Jonah prophesied that God would destroy the city in forty days if its people didn't return to Him. The king agreed and led his people back to the Lord. So the Lord did not carry out his threat. This made Jonah unhappy because he really didn't want the Lord to forgive the Ninevites, who were traditional enemies of the Jews. He built a hut east of the city and the Lord caused a gourd plant to grow over his head to shade him from the sun. But the next morning God sent a worm to kill the plant, which made Jonah very angry. The Lord chided Jonah: "You are concerned about the plant which cost you no labor. And should I not be concerned over Nineveh, the great city, in which there are more than 120,000 persons who cannot distinguish their right hand from their left, not to mention the many cattle?"

Now the story of Jonah from the Koran:

Koran 37:140–148—Jonah was also sent with a message. He fled to the laden ship, cast lots, and was condemned. The whale swallowed him for he had done amiss; and had he not devoutly praised the Lord he would have stayed in its belly till the Day of

156

Resurrection. We threw him, gravely ill, upon a desolate shore and caused a gourd-tree to grow over him. Thus We sent him to a nation a hundred thousand strong or more. They believed in him and We let them live in ease awhile. (*The Koran does not say what the message was, where Jonah was supposed to take it, why he had to flee, why and by whom lots were cast, why and by whom he was condemned, how he came to be swallowed by a whale, what he had "done amiss" to deserve such treatment, and what the gourd tree has to do with the story.*)

(2) Job

Job's name comes up in four different suras where Gabriel lists the important prophets, but there is little in the Koran about the man himself or what his affliction was. No reason is given for the ordeal imposed on him except that Satan did it. There are several passages that show the company he keeps. One of them was quoted in Abraham's story in Chapter 16. I shall quote another here:

Koran 4:163–164—We have revealed Our will to you (*Mohammed*) as We revealed it to Noah and to the prophets who came after him; as We revealed it to Abraham, Ishmael, Isaac, Jacob, and the tribes; to Jesus, **Job**, Jonah, Aaron, Solomon, and David, to whom We gave the Psalms. (*Interestingly, Joseph, Lot, and Moses are left out of this list.*)

*In the **Bible** the story of Job is told in a book of forty-two chapters covering over thirty pages. For those readers not familiar with the story, I suggest that they read it since I cannot recount the entire story here and the passages in the Koran are very nearly meaningless without knowing the whole story. So once again I think it wise to briefly summarize the biblical story of Job before we read the Koran's version:*

Satan challenges God to inflict all sorts of misfortunes on Job to see if Job will continue to praise God. God agrees. So Job loses "to the sword" of the Sabaeans all his oxen and their herdsmen, his sheep and their shepherds, his camels and their attendants. Then a great wind comes across the desert and collapses his house and kills all of his sons and daughters. Job blames neither Satan nor God for his misfortunes; rather he throws himself on the ground and says,

"Naked I came forth from my mother's womb and naked shall I go back again. The Lord gave and the Lord has taken away; blessed be the name of the Lord!"

Satan suggests to God that when Job's own body is inflicted with running boils, he will turn away from God. God obliges. But again Job refuses to curse God, even after his wife suggests that he do so. Instead, he says to her, "We accept good things from God; and should we not accept evil?"

Three of Job's "friends" (Eliphaz, Bildad, and Zophar) come and sit with him for seven days without speaking as he sits in an ash heap and scrapes his boils with potsherds. Each friend speaks three times and is answered each time by Job. They all tell Job over and over that he must repent of his sins and God will relieve him of his ordeal. Job continues to claim that he has done nothing that needs to be repented. Job comes across as far from patient.

After Job's final response to the three friends, an angry young man, Elihu, berates the three friends for not being more harsh with Job, and then in a very long speech accuses Job of assuming that he alone is just and even God is unjust. Finally God himself speaks to Job "out of the whirlwind" and accuses him of not understanding just what God has been able to do in creating the world and all the creatures within it. God then speaks to Eliphaz and tells him that he is angry with him and the other two for not speaking rightly of God, and orders them to intercede for Job by sacrificing seven bulls and seven rams as a holocaust. When this is done, God restores prosperity to Job, twice what he had before, and gives him seven sons and three daughters.

Koran 38:40, 44a—And tell of Our servant Job. He called out to his Lord, saying: "Satan has afflicted me with sorrow and misfortune." . . . .We said to him: "Take a bunch of twigs and beat with it; do not break your oath." (*This verse is not explained in the Koran, but tradition holds that Job had sworn to give his wife a hundred blows for failing to help him in some task. Or, perhaps for what she said to him, not quoted in the Koran, but in the Bible [Job 2:9], when Job had been covered with boils from the soles of his feet to the crown of his head: "Are you still holding to your innocence?" she asked. "Curse God and die." So what he did was give her one blow with a hundred twigs. This tradition is often quoted by Muslims as authorizing any similar release from an oath rashly taken.)*

Koran 21:83–85—And tell of Job: how he called on his Lord, saying: "I am sorely afflicted: but of all those that show mercy You are the most merciful." . . . We answered his prayer and relieved his affliction. We restored to him his people and as many more with them: a blessing from Ourself and an admonition to the devout.

Koran 38:41, 44b—We said: "Stamp your feet against the earth and a cold spring will gush forth. Wash and refresh yourself." . . . We found him full of patience. He was a good and faithful man.

There is no counterpart in the Bible to the Koranic verses telling Job to stamp his feet to start a spring flowing. Also, there is no reference to beating his wife.

(3) Ezra

There are only two brief glimpses of Ezra in the Koran, but what does appear is fascinating. It should again be noted that it is quite impossible to understand the following quotes from the Koran *without* knowing the Biblical counterparts. We strongly urge the reader to read not only the book of Ezra, but also Nehemiah.

Koran 2:259—Or (*have you not heard*) of him (*Ezra*), who, when passing by a ruined and desolate city (*Jerusalem*), remarked: "How can God give life to this city, now that it is dead?" Thereupon God caused him to die and after a hundred years brought him back to life. "How long have you stayed away?" asked God.

"A day," he replied, "or part of a day."

"Know, then," said God, "that you have stayed away a hundred years. Yet look at your food and drink; they have not rotted. And look at your ass. We will make you a sign to mankind: see how We will raise the bones and clothe them with flesh."

The last sentence echoes Ezekiel's vision in the book of Ezekiel, Chapter 37: He sees a valley strewn with dry bones which the Lord joins together to form skeletons and then clothes them with flesh, covers them with skin, and breathes life into them.

In Nehemiah 2:11–16, we read that Nehemiah (not Ezra) arrived back in Jerusalem after returning from exile in Babylon, and rode out at night and inspected the ruins of the city and reported to the priests and nobles, "You see the evil plight in which we stand: how

Jerusalem lies in ruins and its gates have been gutted by fire." It was Nehemiah who supervised the rebuilding of the walls of Jerusalem.

However, there may be some historical basis for Mohammed's story of Ezra's resurrection after a hundred years. The Persian king Cyrus, when he conquered Babylon, authorized the first migration of the exiled Israelites from Babylon to Jerusalem in 538 BCE, led by Sheshbazzar. A second wave left under Darius, led by Zerubbabel and Joshua in 521. Ezra led the third migration, under Artaxerxes, in 465–464, seventy-four years after the first wave, which may have given Mohammed the idea that Ezra had been resurrected.

Koran 9:30—The Jews say Ezra is the son of God (*this is not asserted in the Bible*), while the Christians say the Messiah is the son of God (*this is asserted in the Bible*). God confound them! How perverse they are!

Mohammed's claim that the Jews regarding Ezra as a son of God is thought by Christian commentators as a way of showing that the Jews as well as Christians tampered with the Divine Unity.

Muslim tradition holds that when Ezra was raised to life after being dead one hundred years, he dictated to his scribes from memory the whole Jewish law, which had been lost during the Babylonian captivity. We find arguable confirmation of that in the fourteenth chapter of 2 Esdras, a book considered apocryphal by most Christians and Jews.

2 Esdras 14:1–48—(Summary) Ezra is in Babylon and has just received six visions. In the seventh vision, the Lord speaks to him out of a bush and tells him he is about to be taken away from the world of men. Ezra tells God that since Nebuchadnezzar destroyed the law, he (Ezra) would rewrite them. God tells him to take five men (Seriah, Dabri, Shelmiah, Ethan, and Asiel) and God will fill his mind with the law so Ezra can dictate it to the men. In forty days, 94 books were written down. Twenty-four were to be made public but 70 were to be reserved "for the wise among your people."

The early books of the Bible did indeed receive their present form during and immediately after the Exile in Babylon. It was the scribes, perhaps under Ezra himself, who copied and edited the legends, laws and rituals. Ezra may also have been the "Chronicler" who wrote 1 and 2 Chronicles which continues the history of Israel from Joshua's time to the rebuilding of the Temple. Ezra is not credited with writing the Bible, merely restoring it to the condition it was in before Nebuchadnezzar burned the Temple.

The twenty-four books he was instructed to make public are the present-day books of the Hebrew Bible, as well as the Old Testament of the Christian Bible.

The remaining 70 books are the Apocrypha. None are considered canonical by Protestants.

Five are considered canonical by Catholics. They are: Tobit, Judith, Rest of Esther, and 1st and 2nd Maccabees.

Ten were included in the Septuagint, the Hebrew Bible translated into Greek for Greek-speaking Jews in Egypt, Ca. 250 BCE. They are: 1st and 2nd Books of Esdras; The Wisdom of Solomon; The Wisdom of Jesus, Son of Sirach; Baruch; a Letter of Jeremiah; The Prayer of Azariah and The Song of the Three; Daniel and Susanna; Daniel, Bel, and the Snake; The Prayer of Manasseh.

20

People of the Book: Jesus, Son of Mary and Joseph

In the Name of God the Compassionate the Merciful

There are seventeen major references to Jesus in the Koran, plus over thirty brief references such as in lists of prophets. Each of the references tells a part of the story, sometimes disagreeing with the others in details. Furthermore, the story is not told chronologically. So, I have gathered together all the references that are not duplications of other passages and arranged them into a coherent narrative.

This chapter is divided into several sections: the birth story of John the Baptist, the early life of Mary (including her birth, her betrothal to Joseph, her annunciation by Gabriel), and finally the birth, ministry, and life of Jesus.

John, the Baptist:

Because the Koran tells us about John's birth, we begin Jesus' story with that story. The Koran does not tell us about the role that John played in Jesus' life, but we learn from the Bible that John became a holy man, living in the desert, perhaps with the Essenes for a time. He ate locusts and honey and preached repentance to large crowds of people.

John claimed that he had come "to prepare the way of the Lord," that is, he was preparing the world for the coming of the Messiah. Jesus came to him for baptism in the Jordan River before he started his ministry. John clearly saw the spirit of God descending like a dove on Jesus, and heard the voice of God saying, "This is my son, in whom I am well pleased."

None of this is found in the Koran, but still it is fitting to see what the Koran says about John's birth and compare it with passages in the Bible.

The birth story of John the Baptist, from the Koran:

Koran 19:1–7—An account of your Lord's goodness to his servant Zacharias: he invoked his Lord in secret, saying: "Lord, my bones are enfeebled, and my head glows silver with age. Yet never, Lord, have I prayed to You in vain. Grant me, from Yourself, a son who will be my heir."

"Rejoice, Zacharias," came the answer. "You shall be given a son, and he shall be called John; a name no man has borne before him."

There are eleven Johanans, fourteen Jonathans, three Jehonathans in the Bible, all period variations of the New Testament John. Perhaps Mohammed was aware of Luke 1:59–63 in which Elizabeth and Zachariah both opt for the name John over the protests of their family who say, "There is no one among your relatives *who has this name." (Emphasis added.)*

Koran 19:10—"Lord, give me a sign."

"Your sign is that for three days and three nights," He replied, "you shall be bereft of speech, though otherwise sound in body."

Koran 21:90—We answered his prayer and gave him John, curing his wife of sterility. They vied with each other in good works.

The birth story of John, from the Bible:

Luke 1:5–14—(Summary) Zechariah was a priest and his wife Elizabeth was of the line of Aaron. She was barren. Zechariah was in the inner sanctuary of the temple burning incense when Gabriel came to him and told him that his prayer for a son had been heard. The son would be named John.

Luke 1:15–17a—"He will be great in the sight of the Lord. He will drink neither wine nor strong drink. He will be filled with the holy Spirit even from his mother's womb. And he will turn many of

163

the children of Israel to the Lord their God. He will go before him (*Jesus*) in the spirit and power of Elijah . . .''

Luke 1:59–80—(Summary) Zachariah was made dumb until the baby was born and Zachariah was asked what name should be given the child. He wrote, "John," and immediately regained his speech. He sang a long song, telling the role John was to have, including: "And you, child, will be called a prophet of the Most High, for you will go before the Lord to prepare his ways, to give his people knowledge of salvation, through the forgiveness of their sins . . .''

The birth and early life of Mary, from the Koran:

Koran 3:35–37—Remember the words of Imran's wife. "Lord," she said, "I dedicate to Your service that which is in my womb. Accept it from me." And when she was delivered of the child, she said, "I have given birth to a daughter and called her Mary."

In Exodus 6:20, Imran and Jochebed are named as the parents of Moses, Aaron, and Miriam, about 1300 years before the time of Mary, the mother of Jesus. There are two possible explanations: 1) Mohammed made an anachronistic error, confounding Miriam with Mary, "Miriam" being an early variation of Mary, or 2) Mohammed believed that Miriam's soul and body were miraculously preserved for over a thousand years and became Mary, the mother of Jesus.

Koran 3:37—Her Lord graciously accepted her. He made her grow a goodly child and entrusted her to the care of Zacharias. Whenever Zacharias visited her in the Shrine he found that she had food with her.

"Mary," he said, "where is this food from?"

"It is from God," she answered. "God gives without stint to whom He will."

It must be assumed that this Zacharias is the same person who was the father of John the Baptist. What is not clear is the chronology. In the Koranic story just quoted, Elizabeth is presumably already married to Zacharias when Mary comes as an infant to live with them. Christians reading the biblical account will have a problem here, because in the Bible, Mary and Elizabeth (Zacharias's wife) are pregnant at the same time: Mary with Jesus, Elizabeth with John (Luke 1:39–42). And Mary has traveled from her home in Nazareth

164

to *"a town of Judah,"* which is far south of Nazareth. This, of course, can be reconciled, since Elizabeth was *"advanced in years"* when she became pregnant (Luke 1:18). (Nowhere in the Koran is Joseph mentioned, nor Mary's marriage to him.)

The Bible tells us nothing about Mary's background, except to say that she lived in Nazareth. It never names her parents, though Christian tradition claims Davidic descent. But we find in the apocryphal Book of James, or Protevangelium, a story similar in some respects to the one just quoted from the Koran about Mary's early life: In 1:2 and 2:1, Mary's parents are named Joachim and Anne (or Anna), a wealthy and prominent Jewish family in Jerusalem. They guard her purity with extreme care until she is three, when she is sent to the Temple to be raised by the priests. She is nurtured there and fed by an angel until she is twelve, when she is given to Joseph as his betrothed.

The annunciation of Mary:

From the Koran:
Koran 3:44–51—The angels said to Mary: "God bids you rejoice in a word from Him. His name is the Messiah, Jesus the son of Mary. He shall be noble in this world and in the hereafter and shall be one of those who are favored. He shall preach to men in his cradle and in the prime of manhood, and shall lead a righteous life."

"Lord," she said, "how can I bear a child when no man has touched me?"

He replied, "Even thus. God creates whom He will. When He decrees a thing He need only say: 'Be,' and it is. He will instruct him in the Scriptures and in wisdom, in the Torah and in the Gospel, and send him forth as an apostle to the Israelites. He (*Jesus*) will say, 'I bring you a sign from your Lord. From clay I will make for you the likeness of a bird. I shall breathe into it and by God's leave, it shall become a living bird. By God's leave I shall heal the blind man and the leper, and raise the dead to life.' "

Again we find Mohammed echoing a story in the Apocrypha:
Infancy Gospel of Thomas II:1–2,4—The little child Jesus when he was five years old was playing at the ford of a brook and he gathered together the waters that flowed there into pools, and made

them clean, and commanded them by his word alone . . . having made soft clay, he fashioned twelve sparrows . . . Jesus clapped his hands together and . . . said to them, "Go!" And the sparrows took their flight and went away chirping.

From the Bible:

Luke 1:26–35, 38—The angel Gabriel was sent from God to a town of Galilee called Nazareth, to a virgin betrothed to a man named Joseph, of the house of David, and the virgin's name was Mary. And coming to her, he said, "Hail, favored one. The Lord is with you." But she was greatly troubled at what was said and pondered what sort of greeting this might be. Then the angel said to her, "Do not be afraid, Mary, for you have found favor with God. Behold, you will conceive in your womb and bear a son, and you shall name him Jesus. He will be great and will be called Son of the Most High, and the Lord God will give him the throne of David, his father, and he will rule over the house of Jacob forever, and of his kingdom there will be no end."

But Mary said to the angel, "How can this be, since I have no relations with a man?"

And the angel said to her, "The holy Spirit will come upon you, and the power of the Most High will overshadow you. Therefore the child to be born will be called holy, the Son of God" . . . Mary said, "Behold, I am the handmaid of the Lord. May it be done to me according to your word."

The betrothal of Mary to Joseph:

Koran 3:42–44—And remember the angels' words to Mary. They said, "God has chosen you. He has made you pure and exalted you above womankind. Mary, be obedient to your Lord, bow down and worship with the worshipers." This is an account of a divine secret. We reveal it to you (*Mohammed*). You were not present when they cast lots to see which of them should have charge of Mary; nor were you present when they argued about her.

Joseph, Mary's husband, is never named or even alluded to in the Koran. But there is a story in the apocryphal Book of James that explains the lot-casting and the arguments, indicating to Christians that Mohammed had access to that Book. Muslims would say that it was God who knew that and told Mohammed the story through Gabriel.

Apocryphal Book of James 8:3a–9:2—(Summary) Zachariah, in the Holy of Holies, praying about Mary's future, was told by an angel to assemble in the Temple all the widowers in the country. They came. Out of Joseph's rod a dove came forth and flew upon the head of Joseph, clearly indicating that he was to take Mary as his wife. Joseph at first refused to take her, saying he was too old and already had sons. The priests argued with him, saying they had cast lots in choosing Mary from six other virgins and Mary won out. So he accepted her into his household.

We don't know from this story or the Koran whether Mary was pregnant with Jesus before she moved in with Joseph, but it's clear in the Bible:

Matthew 1:18b–21, 24–25—When his mother Mary was betrothed to Joseph, but before they lived together, she was found with child through the holy Spirit. Joseph her husband, since he was a righteous man, yet unwilling to expose her to shame, decided to divorce her quietly. Such was his intention when, behold, the angel of the Lord appeared to him in a dream and said, "Joseph, son of David, do not be afraid to take Mary your wife into your home. For it is through the holy Spirit that this child has been conceived in her. She will bear a son and you are to name him Jesus, because he will save his people from their sins" . . . When Joseph awoke he did as the angel of the Lord had commanded him and took his wife into his home.

The birth of Jesus:

From the Koran:

Koran 19:22–26—Thereupon she conceived him and retired to a far-off place. And when she felt the throes of childbirth she lay down by the trunk of a palm tree, crying, "Oh, would that I had died and passed into oblivion!" But a voice from below cried out to her: "Do not despair. Your Lord has provided a brook that runs at your feet, and if you shake the trunk of this palm tree it will drop fresh ripe dates in your lap. Therefore eat and drink and rejoice."

Koran 19:28–34—Carrying the child, she came to her people, who said to her: "Mary, this is indeed a strange thing! Sister of Aaron, your father was never a whore-monger, nor was your mother a harlot." (*"Sister of Aaron," Muslims say, simply means "virtuous woman" in this context.*)

She made a sign to them, pointing to the child. But they replied: "How can we speak with a babe in the cradle?"

Whereupon he spoke and said, "I am the servant of God. He has given me the Book and ordained me a prophet. His blessing is upon me wherever I go, and He has exhorted me to be steadfast in prayer and to give alms as long as I shall live. He has exhorted me to honor my mother and has purged me of vanity and wickedness. And the Peace of God was on me the day I was born, and on the day of my death and on the day I shall be raised to life."

From the Bible:

Luke 2:1–20—(Summary) Caesar Augustus declared a census: everyone in his realm was ordered to return to his home town to be enrolled. Joseph went with Mary to Bethlehem, where Jesus was born in a stable because the inn was full. Mary wrapped him in swaddling clothes and laid him in a manger. An angel appeared to shepherds and announced the birth of the Messiah. A heavenly host appeared, praising God. The shepherds went to Bethlehem and found Joseph, Mary, and Jesus.

Jesus' ministry:

Very little of Jesus' ministry is mentioned in the Koran, but there are a few scattered references. Some of them follow, with corresponding or disagreeing passages from the Bible:

Jesus as the Advocate:

Koran 61:6–7—Jesus the son of Mary said, "I am sent forth to you from God to confirm the Torah already revealed, and to give news of an apostle that will come after me whose name is Ahmad." *(Ahmad is another of Mohammed's names, meaning "The Praised One.")*

John 16:5-8—*(Jesus speaking)*: "But now I am going to the one who sent me . . . it is better for you if I go. For if I do not go, the Advocate will not come to you. But if I go, I will send him to you. And when he comes he will convict the world in regard to sin and righteousness . . ."

Mohammed believed that Jesus was prophesying that when he ascended to heaven, he would send Mohammed to earth as an Advocate. Now, 700 years later, he has done just that. Christians interpret this to mean that the holy Spirit would come first to the disciples and then all believers in perpetuity.

Koran 57:27—After Noah and Abraham we sent other apostles, and after those, Jesus the son of Mary. We gave him the Gospel and put compassion and mercy in the hearts of his followers. *The four Gospels were all written long after Jesus' death. Muslims believe that Mohammed meant only that Jesus received the revelation of the Gospels from God, and others wrote it down, much as the Koran was compiled.*

There are other passages in the Bible understood by Muslims to refer to Mohammed. E.g., Isaiah 21:7—"If he (the watchman) sees a chariot, a pair of horses, someone riding an ass, someone riding a camel, then let him pay heed." The person riding on the ass is Jesus, the rider on the camel Mohammed.

Another example is found in John 4:24—"God is Spirit, and those who worship him must worship in Spirit and truth." Muslims say that Mohammed is that Spirit because he proclaimed that Jesus was a true man and not God.

Muslims believe that there are other passages in the Bible that refer to Islam. E.g., Matthew 20:1–16—In the parable of the workers in the vineyard, morning, noon, and evening are Judaism, Christianity, and Islam.

Discipleship:

Koran 3:52–54—When Jesus observed that they had no faith, he said, "Who will help me in the cause of God?" The disciples

169

replied: "We are the helpers of God. We believe in God. Bear witness that we have surrendered ourselves to Him. Lord, we believe in Your revelations and follow the apostle. Count us among Your witnesses."

John 8:31—Jesus then said to those Jews who believed in him, "If you remain in my word, you will truly be my disciples . . ."

The son of God?:

Koran 3:79b–80—No mortal (*referring to Jesus*) to whom He has given the Scriptures and whom He has endowed with judgment and prophethood would say to men: "Worship me instead of God." But rather, "Be devoted servants of God . . . Nor would he enjoin you to serve the angels and the prophets as your gods . . ."

Mohammed believed that Jesus never claimed to be equal with God. The Bible states that Jesus did claim this, as is clear in these two passages:

John 14:9—"Whoever has seen me has seen the Father."

John 10:30—"The Father and I are One."

Koran 5:75—The Messiah, the son of Mary, was no more than an apostle: other apostles passed away before him. His mother was a saintly woman. They both ate earthly food. (*Muslims interpret this last sentence to mean that both Mary and Jesus were human, not divine.*)

John 12:44—Jesus cried out and said, "Whoever believes in me believes not only in me but also in the one who sent me, and whoever sees me sees the one who sent me. I came into the world as a light, so that everyone who believes in me might not remain in darkness."

The Lord's Supper (also known to Christians as The Last Supper and The Eucharist):

Koran 5:112–115—The disciples said, "Jesus, son of Mary, can your Lord send down to us from heaven a table spread with food? We wish to eat of it so that we may reassure our hearts and know that what you said to us is true."

Jesus prayed, "Lord, send down to us from heaven a table spread with food that it may mark a feast for us and for those that will come after us: a sign from You. Give us our sustenance; You are the best provider."

God replied: "I am sending one (*a table with food*) to you. But whoever of you disbelieves hereafter shall be punished as no man will ever be punished."

Luke 22:14, 19–20—When the hour came he (*Jesus*) took his place at table with the apostles . . . Then he took bread, said the blessing, broke it and gave it to them, saying, "This is my body which will be given for you; do this in memory of me. And likewise the cup after they had eaten, saying, "This is the new covenant of my blood, which will be shed for you."

The crucifixion and resurrection of Jesus:

Koran 4:156–158—They (*the Jews*) denied the truth and uttered a monstrous falsehood against Mary. They declared, "We have put to death the Messiah, Jesus the son of Mary, the apostle of God." They did not kill him nor did they crucify him, because he was made to resemble another for them.

Koran 3:55–57—They plotted, and God plotted. God is the supreme Plotter. God said: "Jesus, I am about to claim you back and lift you up to Me. I shall take you away from the unbelievers and exalt your followers above them till the Day of Resurrection. Then to Me you shall return and I shall judge your disputes."

Mohammed believed that God took the dead body of Jesus to heaven for three hours while the Jews crucified a man who resembled him. Tradition—not Koran—holds that that man was either Simon of Cyrene, Barnabas, or Judas Iscariot.

Each of the gospels has the crucifixion story in great detail. Here are two key passages.

Luke 23:33–34—When they came to the place called the Skull (*Golgotha*), they crucified him and the criminals there, one on his right, one on his left. Then Jesus said, "Father, forgive them, they know not what they do."

Matthew 27:45–46, 50—From noon onward, darkness came over the whole land until three in the afternoon. And about three

o'clock Jesus cried out in a loud voice, *"Eli, Eli, lema sabachthani?"* Which means, "My God, my God, why have you forsaken me (*a direct quote from Psalm 22:2*)." Jesus cried out in a loud voice, and gave up his spirit.

21

People of the Book: Peter, Barnabas, and Paul

In the Name of God the Compassionate the Merciful

Aside from John, Jesus, and Mary, there are only a few references by name in the Koran to New Testament people. So it is not surprising to find no names given to the characters in the story to be related now. Yet, this vague story, and a story of Seven Sleepers which I'm not going to recount, are considered by both Muslims and Christians to be the only traces to be found in the Koran of Mohammed's knowledge of the history of the Christian church and its spread. It is interesting for Christians to note that the presumed reference to Christian "prophets" is found in Sura 36 (Yā Sīn), the Sura that Mohammed termed "the heart of the Koran," and is read to the dying, at the tombs of saints, and at other important Muslim rituals.

I'm not recording the Legend of the Seven Sleepers because there is no counterpart in the Bible. Furthermore, there is much doubt whether it really does have to do with the early Christian church. For the curious reader, it's in Sura 18:1–26. Gibbon, in *Decline and Fall of the Roman Empire,* devotes two pages to the legend (at the end of Chapter 33). It's an interesting story but not apropos to this study.

Peter, Barnabas, and Paul

Koran 36:12–26—It is We who resurrect the dead. We record the deeds of men and the marks they leave behind: We note all things in a glorious book. You shall cite, as a case in point, the people of the city to which Our messengers made their way. When they rejected both, We strengthened them with a third. (*The glorious book is said to be the New Testament. The city is probably Antioch, to which Jesus—after his death and resurrection—is said by Muslims to have sent two disciples, Paul and Barnabas, to preach the unity of God. The third sent is said to be Peter.)*

They said, "We have been sent to you as apostles."

But the people replied: "You are but mortals like ourselves. The Merciful has revealed nothing: you are surely lying."

They said: "Our lord knows that we are true apostles. Our only duty is to give plain warning."

The people answered: "Your presence bodes for us nothing but evil. Desist, or we will stone you or inflict on you a painful scourge."

They said: "The evil you forebode can come only from yourselves. Will you not take heed? Surely you are great transgressors."

There is no biblical record of a rejection of the apostles in Antioch. In fact, Antioch in Syria became one of the most important cities in early Christendom, second only to Jerusalem.

Peter, Barnabas, and Paul were indeed apostles. But Paul had a problem before he became an apostle. After his dramatic conversion on the road to Damascus (Acts 9:1–19), he tried to gain the confidence of the Christian church in Jerusalem, but they remembered his persecution of the Christians—including his acquiescence to the stoning of Stephen, the first Christian martyr—and literally forced Paul to flee to his ancestral home in Tarsus, Cilicia. Jerome Murphy-O'Connor believes he stayed there for eight to ten years until the church in Jerusalem sent Barnabas to Antioch. We pick up the story there:

Acts 11:23–26—When Barnabas arrived and saw the grace of God, he rejoiced and encouraged them all to remain faithful to the Lord in firmness of heart, for he was a good man, filled with the holy Spirit and faith. And a large number of people was added to the Lord. Then he went to Tarsus to look for Saul (*later Paul*), and when he had found him he brought him to Antioch. For a whole year they met with the church and taught a large number of people, and it was in Antioch that the disciples were first called Christians.

The reference in the Bible that puts Peter and Paul in Antioch is when Paul tells the Galatians about Peter's inconsistency regarding diet:

Galatians 2:11, 12—(*Paul writing*) And when Peter came to Antioch, I opposed him to his face because he clearly was wrong.

For, until some people came from James (*the brother of Jesus, in the Jerusalem church*) he used to eat with the Gentiles; but when they came, he began to draw back and separated himself . . .

22

Heaven and Hell

In the Name of God the Compassionate the Merciful

Unless it be the teachings regarding women, there is probably no more misunderstood and misquoted aspect of Islam than its view of Heaven and Hell. So let's look at what the Koran has to say about those after-life places and compare with the Bible. Biblical agreement or disagreement is nowhere more clear than in these teachings.

There are literally dozens of passages in the Koran, some of them pages long, describing the delights of Heaven—or Paradise, as it is often called—and the tortures of Hell. In contrast, the Bible has very little to say about the actual physical appearance of Heaven and Hell. For example, the Heaven described by John in the Book of Revelation, quoted in this chapter, is widely believed to be metaphorical—but then, who knows?!

Because the passages in the Koran describing Heaven are often intertwined with those describing Hell, it would be very nearly impossible in many cases to dissect them free from each other. So I shall discuss them together. Also, since most of the references are repetitious, I haven't tried to include all of them in this discussion.

But first, hear these comforting words from both the Bible and the Koran:

Koran 93:1–5—By the light of day and by the dark of night your Lord has not forsaken you (*Mohammed*). Nor does He abhor you. The life to come holds a richer prize for you than this present life. You shall be gratified by what your Lord will give you. (*This passage comes from one of the six short Suras that Mohammed revealed when he was in a deep depression, either before the beginning of his ministry or when his success was very dubious.*)

Hebrews 13:5–6—Let your life be free from love of money, but be content with what you have, for he has said, "I will never forsake you or abandon you." Thus may we say with confidence: "The Lord is my helper, and I will not be afraid. What can anyone do to me?" (*Psalms 27:1.*)

Now let's see whether it is be deeds (works) or grace (unmerited love) that one goes to Heaven. The Koran is very clear. The Bible is ambiguous. (This is not a negative criticism; rather, it is an accepted fact among most New Testament scholars.)

Deeds or grace?

Koran 19:76–77, 83—Deeds of lasting merit shall earn you a better reward in the sight of your Lord and a more auspicious end. Mark the words of him who denies Our signs yet boasts: "I shall surely be given wealth and children!" . . . All he speaks of he shall leave behind and come before us all alone.

Romans 3:27–28—(*Paul writing*) What occasion is there then for boasting? It is ruled out. On what principle, that of works? No, rather on the principle of faith. For we consider that a person is justified (*accepted by God as if he had not sinned*) by faith apart from works of the (*Mosaic*) law.

But consider:

James 2:14, 26—What good is it, my brothers, if someone says he has faith but does not have works. Can that faith save him? . . . (*No.*) For just as a body without a spirit is dead, so also faith without works is dead. (*It should be noted that Martin Luther "threw out" the entire book of James because of this passage.*)

And:

Romans 2:5–6—(*Paul writing*) By your stubbornness and impenitent heart, you are storing up wrath for yourself for the day of wrath and revelation of the just judgment of God, who will repay everyone according to his works.

Koran 36:50, 53, 58, 63—The trumpet will be blown and behold they will rise up from their graves and hasten to their Lord . . . You shall be rewarded according to your deeds. On that day the heirs of Paradise will be busy with their joys . . . But to the guilty He will say: "Away with you this day! Sons of Adam . . . This is the Hell you have been threatened with. Burn therein this day on account of your unbelief."

177

Revelation 22:12—(*John's vision of Jesus speaking*) Behold, I am coming soon. I bring with me the recompense I will give to each according to his deeds.

Koran 18:46—God has power over all things. Wealth and children are the ornaments of this life. But deeds of lasting merit are better rewarded by your Lord and hold for you a greater hope of salvation.

1 Corinthians 3:12–15—(*Paul writing*) If any man builds on this foundation using gold, silver, costly stones, wood, hay or straw, his work will be shown for what it is, because the Day of Judgement will bring it to light. It will be revealed with fire.

Judgment Day, or the Day of Doom:

Neither the Koran nor the Bible is ambiguous about believers going to Heaven and sinners to Hell. The following are just a few passages out of many from the Koran and the Bible:

1 Thessalonians. 4:16–17—(*Paul writing*) For the Lord himself, with a word of command, with the voice of an archangel and with the trumpet of God, will come down from heaven, and the dead in Christ will rise first. Then we who are alive, who are left, will be caught up together with them in the clouds to meet the Lord in the air.

2 Thessalonians 1:5a, 9—(*Paul writing*) This is evidence of the just judgment of God, so that you may be considered worthy of the kingdom of God for which you are suffering . . . (Your persecutors) will pay the penalty of eternal ruin, separated from the presence of the Lord and from the glory of his power.

Koran 92:1, 3–11—By the night, when she lets fall her darkness, and by the radiant day! . . . For him that gives in charity and guards against evil and believes in goodness, We shall smooth the path of salvation, but for him that neither gives nor takes and disbelieves in goodness, We shall smooth the path of affliction. When he breathes his last, his riches will not avail him.

Colossians 3:23–25—(*a disciple of Paul writing*) Whatever you do, work at it with all your heart, as working for the Lord, not for men, since you know that you will receive an inheritance from the Lord as a reward. It is the Lord Christ you are serving. For the

178

wrongdoer will receive recompense for the wrong he committed, and there is no partiality.

Koran 68:34–36, 44, 49—With gardens of delight the righteous shall be rewarded by their Lord. Are We to treat alike the true believers and the guilty? What has come over you that you should judge so ill? . . . Therefore leave to Me those that deny this revelation. We will lead them step by step to their ruin . . . Wait then, the judgement of your Lord and do not act like him who was swallowed by the whale.

1 Peter 4:12–14, 17–19—(*Peter writing*) Beloved, do not be surprised that a trial by fire is occurring among you, as if something strange were happening to you. But rejoice to the extent that you share in the sufferings of Christ, so that when his glory is revealed you may also rejoice exultantly. If you are insulted for the name of Christ, blessed are you, for the Spirit of glory and of God rests upon you . . . For it is time for the judgment to begin with the household of God; if it begins with us, how will it end for those who fail to obey the gospel of God? "And if the righteous one is barely saved, where will the godless and the sinner appear?" As a result, those who suffer in accord with God's will, hand their souls over to a faithful creator as they do good. (*The quote is an inversion of Proverbs 11:31, which reads, "If the just man is punished on earth, how much more the wicked and the sinner!"*)

Koran 82:1–3, 19—When the sky is rent asunder; when the stars scatter and the oceans roll together; when the graves are hurled about, each soul shall know what it has done and what it has failed to do . . . Oh, would that you knew what the Day of Judgment is. It is the day when every soul will stand alone and God will reign supreme.

Koran 81:1–14—When the sun ceases to shine; when the stars fall down and the mountains are blown away; when camels big with young are left untended (*that is, do not need care*), and the wild beasts are brought together; when the seas are set alight and men's souls are reunited; when the infant girl, buried alive, is asked for what crime she was slain (*a reference to the common practice of female infanticide*); when the records of men's deeds are laid open, and heaven is stripped bare; when Hell burns fiercely and Paradise is brought near: then each soul shall know what it has done.

The following passages from Sura 84 and Matthew are filled with echoes of each other:

Hell is a place of fire:

Koran 84:4–14—He that is given his book in his right hand shall have a lenient reckoning and shall go back rejoicing to his people. But he that is given his book behind his back shall call down destruction on himself and burn in the Fire of hell; for he lived without a care among his people and thought he would never return to God. (*Muslims believe that the right hand of the damned is chained to his neck, the left hand chained behind his back.*)

Matthew 13:39b–43—(*Jesus speaking*) The harvest is the end of the age, and the harvesters are angels. Just as weeds are collected and burned with fire, so will it be at the end of the age. The Son of Man will send his angels, and they will collect out of his kingdom all who cause others to sin and all evildoers. They will throw them into the fiery furnace, where there will be wailing and grinding of teeth. Then the righteous will shine like the sun in the kingdom of their Father. (*The last sentence is a paraphrase of Daniel 12:3, which reads, "The wise shall shine brightly like the splendor of the firmament."*)

And Heaven will be a place of peace and beauty:

Koran 56:1–11—Such are they that shall be brought near to their Lord in the gardens of delight: a whole multitude from the men of old, but only a few from the latter generations. They shall recline on jeweled couches face to face, and there shall wait on them immortal youths with bowls and ewers and a cup of purest wine (that will neither pain their heads nor take away their reason); with fruits of their own choice and flesh of fowls that they relish. And theirs shall be the dark-eyed houris, chaste as hidden pearls: a guerdon for their deeds. There they shall hear no idle talk, no sinful speech, but only the greeting, "Peace! Peace!"

It should be noted that these promises of the Houris of Paradise are almost exclusively to be found in Suras revealed at a time when Mohammed was 45 and had only a single wife of 60 years of age. In the ten years subsequent to the Hejira, when Mohammed had many wives and concubines, houris are mentioned only twice as part of the reward of the faithful.

It should also be noted that many learned Muslims consider the descriptions of Paradise in the Koran to be, in large measure, figurative, perhaps metaphorical, like those in the visions of John in the Book of Revelation.

The following passage from Revelation is the only description of heaven in the New Testament, and there is none at all in the Old Testament. There are, however, many parables in the New Testament illustrating what the Kingdom of Heaven is like, but I do not consider them apropos to this study.

Revelation 4:1–8—After this I (*John*) had a vision of an open door into heaven, and I heard the trumpetlike voice that had spoken to me before saying, "Come up here and I will show you what must happen afterwards." At once I was caught up in spirit. A throne was there in heaven, and on the throne sat one whose appearance sparkled like jasper and carnelian. Around the throne was a halo as brilliant as an emerald.

Surrounding the throne I saw twenty-four other thrones on which twenty-four elders sat, dressed in white garments and with gold crowns on their heads. From the throne came flashes of lighting, rumblings, and peals of thunder. Seven flaming torches burned in front of the throne, which are the seven spirits of God. In front of the throne was something that resembled a sea of glass like crystal. (*See the story of Solomon and the Queen of Sheba in Chapter 18.*)

In the center and around the throne there were four living creatures covered with eyes in front and back. The first creature resembled a lion, the second was like a calf, the third had a face like that of a human being, and the fourth looked like an eagle in flight. The four living creatures, each of them with six wings, were covered with eyes inside and out. (*The four living creatures are borrowed from Ezekiel 1:10.*) Day and night they do not stop exclaiming: "Holy, holy, holy is the Lord God almighty, who was, and who is, and who is to come." Whenever the living creatures give glory and honor and thanks to the one who sits on the throne, who lives forever and ever, the twenty-four elders fall down before the one who sits on the throne and worship him . . .

Further descriptions of Heaven and Hell:

Koran 56:29–55—We created the houris and made their virgins, loving companions for those on the right hand: a multitude from the men of old and a multitude from the latter generations. (*There is an apparent contradiction here with 56:14 where only a few from the latter generations will be worthy of the houris. But a Muslim commentator, Beidhawi, explains that these multitudes in Verse 29 will be inferior while being numerous.*) As for those on the left hand (wretched shall be those on the left hand!) they shall dwell amidst scorching winds and seething water: in the shade of pitch-black smoke, neither cool nor refreshing. For they have lived in comfort and persisted in the heinous sin (*idolatry*), saying: "When we are once dead and turned to dust and bones, shall we be raised to life? And our forefathers, too?" Say: "Those of old and those of the present age shall be brought together on an appointed day. As for you sinners who deny the truth, you shall eat the fruit of the Zaqqūm tree and fill your bellies with it. You shall drink scalding water; yet you shall drink it as the thirsty camel drinks."

Matthew 25:31–34, 41—(*Jesus speaking*) When the Son of Man comes in his glory, and all the angels with him, he will sit upon his glorious throne, and all the nations will be assembled before him. And he will separate them one from another, as a shepherd separates the sheep rom the goats. He will place the sheep on his right and the goats on his left. Then the king will say to those on his right, "Come, you who are blessed by my Father. Inherit the kingdom prepared for you from the foundation of the world" . . . Then he will say to those on his left, "Depart from me, you accursed, into the eternal fire prepared for the devil and his angels."

Koran 55:38–52—When the sky splits asunder and reddens like a rose or stained leather (which of your Lord's blessings would you deny?), on that day neither man nor jinnee will be asked about his sins. Which of your Lord's blessings would you deny?

The wrongdoers will be known by their looks; they shall be seized by their forelocks and their feet. They shall wander between fire and water fiercely seething. Which of your Lord's blessings would you deny?

But for those who fear the majesty of their Lord there are two gardens planted (Which of your Lord's blessings would you deny?) with shady trees. Which of your Lord's blessings would you deny?

Each is watered by a flowing spring. Which of your Lord's blessings would you deny?

Each bears every kind of fruit in pairs. Which of your Lord's blessings would you deny?

Koran 37:20–21, 35–40, 48—We shall say: "Call the sinners, their spouses, and the idols which they worshiped besides God, and lead them to the path of Hell." . . . On that day they will all share in the scourge. Thus shall We deal with the evil-doers, for when they were told: "There is no deity but God," they replied with scorn: "Are we to renounce our gods for the sake of a mad poet (*Mohammed*)?" Surely he has brought the truth, confirming those who were sent before. You shall all taste the grievous scourge: you shall be rewarded according to your deeds . . . (*But the true servants of God*) shall sit with bashful, dark-eyed virgins, as chaste as the sheltered eggs of ostriches.

Koran 76:5–6, 14–18—For the unbelievers We have prepared chains and fetters and a blazing Fire. But the righteous shall drink of a cup tempered at the Camphor Fountain, a gushing spring at which the servants of God will refresh themselves. They shall be served with silver dishes, and beakers as large as goblets . . . and cups brim-full with jendjebil (*ginger*)-flavored water from a fount called Salsabil. They shall be attended by boys graced with eternal youth, who to the beholder's eyes will seem like sprinkled pearls. When you gaze upon that scene, you will behold a kingdom blissful and glorious.

John 14:1–2—(*Jesus at the Last Supper*) Do not let your hearts be troubled. You have faith in God; have faith also in me. In my Father's house there are many dwelling places. If there were not, would I have told you that I am going to prepare a place for you?

Koran 21:98–106—You (*unbelievers*) and your idols shall be the fuel of Hell; therein you shall all go down. Were they true gods, your idols would not go there: but there they (*idolaters*) shall abide forever. They shall groan with anguish and be bereft of hearing. But those to whom We have long since shown Our favor shall be far removed from Hell. They shall not hear its roar, but shall delight forever in what their souls desire. The Supreme Terror shall not grieve them, and the angels will receive them, saying: "This is the day you have been promised."

On that day We shall roll up the heaven like a scroll of parchment. (*This corresponds to the scroll written upon by each individual's angel, containing the actions of that man's life, which is then rolled up upon his death.*)

In the Bible, the scroll to be rolled up are the heavens:

Isaiah 34:2–4—(*the judgment of God on heathen oppressors*) Their slain shall be cast out, their corpses shall send up a stench; the mountains shall run with their blood, and all the hills shall rot; the heavens shall be rolled up like a scroll, and all their host shall wither away, as the leaf wilts on the vine, or as the fig withers on the tree.

Koran 21:105–106—Just as We brought the First Creation into being, so will We restore it. This is a promise We shall assuredly fulfil. We wrote in the Psalms after the Torah was revealed: "The righteous among My servants shall inherit the earth." (***This is the only text from the Bible that is quoted in the Koran, with only mild paraphrasing:* Psalms 37:29—"The just will possess the land and live in it forever." *The KJV is a little closer:* "The righteous shall inherit the land, and dwell therein forever."**)

Koran 7:44, 46, 60—Then the heirs of Paradise will cry out to the inmates of the Fire: "What our Lord promised we have found to be true. Have you, too, found the promise of your Lord to be true?" "Yes," they will answer . . . A barrier will divide them, and on the Heights there will be the men who will recognize each one by his book. (*Rodwell translates "the Heights" as a "Wall."*) To those in Paradise they shall say: "Peace be upon you!" But they shall not yet enter, though they long to be there. (*This idea may have been borrowed from the Talmud, for the people on the Heights [Wall] never enter either Hell nor Heaven, in a state analogous to Purgatory.*) . . . The damned will cry out to the blessed: "Give us some water, or some of that which God has given you." But the blessed will reply: "God has forbidden both to the unbelievers, who made their religion a pastime and an idle sport, and who were seduced by their earthly life."

This latter passage echoes a parable in Luke's gospel:

Luke 16:19–31—(Summary) A rich man ignores the beggar Lazarus lying at his gate. Both die. The rich man goes to Hell, Lazarus to Heaven. The rich man raises his eyes and sees Lazarus lying in the bosom of Abraham. He asks Abraham to let Lazarus dip his finger in cool water and touch his tongue. Abraham says the chasm

between them prevents anyone from crossing from one side to the other. The rich man asks then that Lazarus be sent to the rich man's brothers to warn them of their fate if they do not change their ways. Abraham answers that since they have ignored Moses and the prophets, they will also ignore even a man raised from the dead. (*Dr. Albert Schweitzer cited this parable as his reason for going to Gabon: he was the rich man, Africa the beggar Lazarus.*)

Koran 22:19—Garments of fire have been prepared for the unbelievers. Scalding water shall be poured upon their heads, melting their skins and that which is in their bellies. They shall be lashed with rods of iron. Whenever, in their anguish, they try to escape from Hell, back they shall be dragged and will be told: "Taste the torment of the Conflagration!"

Koran 67:6–12—When they are flung into its flames, they shall hear it roaring and seething, as though bursting with rage. (*Rodwell translates "roaring" as "braying." Shakespeare used "braying" as one of the clamors of Hell. Milton in describing Hell spoke of "braying horrible discord."*)

And every time a multitude is thrown herein, its keepers will say to them: "Did no one come to warn you?"

"Yes," they will reply, "he did come, but we rejected him and said: 'God has revealed nothing: you are in grave error.' "

And they will say: "If only we listened and understood, we should not now be among the heirs of the Fire."

Thus shall they confess their sin. Far from God's mercy are the heirs of the Fire. But those that fear their Lord although they cannot see Him shall be forgiven and richly rewarded.

Mark 10:47–49—(*Jesus speaking*) And if your eye causes you to sin, pluck it out. Better for you to enter into the kingdom of God with one eye than with two eyes to be thrown into Gehenna, where "their worm does not die, and the fire is not quenched" (*Isaiah 66:24*).

Revelation 21:8—(*God speaking to John in his vision*) "I am the Alpha and the Omega, the beginning and the end. To the thirsty I will give a gift from the spring of life-giving water. The victor will inherit these gifts, and I shall be his God, and he will be my son. But as for the cowards, the unfaithful, the depraved, murderers, the unchaste, sorcerers, idol-worshipers, and deceivers of every sort, their lot is in the burning pool of fire and sulfur, which is the second death.

23

The Resurrection

In the Name of God the Compassionate the Merciful

It would be almost impossible—when dealing with the resurrection—to match the Bible with the Koran verse for verse. In a few places this is possible and I will do so where appropriate. But for the most part I shall present first what the Koran says about resurrection, and follow that with what the Bible says.

As we shall see, both the Koran and the Old Testament define resurrection as an afterlife, somewhere other than on earth, not a resurrection of the physical body. The New Testament also considers resurrection to be an afterlife for everyone except Jesus, for there is no ambiguity in the assertion that Jesus was seen in his physical body by hundreds of people. Whether that body was the physical body that he had before he was crucified is not a subject apropos to this study. I shall let the New Testament speak for itself on that subject!

The Koran

There are innumerable references in the Koran to the Day of Resurrection. As we shall see, most references are to "being returned to God," or "being restored to life." But nowhere does Gabriel disclose just how this is to be accomplished, what exact method is to be used to return everything to God. Nor is it always clear whether the return will be when the person or animal dies, or will be on the Final Day of Doom when the earth and all its contents come to an end. For example, we have seen in the chapter WAR that a man slain in battle against the infidel will surely be admitted to Paradise, but nowhere does it say *when* that will be.

But let us look at some of the passages that made it abundantly clear that the resurrection *will* occur. Some repetition is inevitable, but each passage chosen gives a different meaning or spin to the over-all Koranic concept of the Resurrection.

Koran 2:28–29—How can you deny God? Did He not give you life when you were dead (*incarnation*), and will He not cause you to die and then restore you to life (*resurrection*)? Will you not return to Him at last? He created for you all that the earth contains; then, ascending to the sky, He fashioned it into seven heavens. He has knowledge of all things. (*The concept of seven heavens was probably borrowed from the Jewish Talmud. They are not identified in the Koran, but are listed in the Talmud: the veil, the firmament, the clouds, the habitation, the abode, the fixed seat, the araboth. There is also a Jewish tradition of seven gates to Hell, and seven abodes for the wicked in Hell. Mohammed could have had access to the Talmud because it was closed in its final form in the third century* CE. *Many people in ancient times believed in the seven heavens, and that God was enthroned above the seventh. For example, in Deuteronomy 10:14, Moses is speaking to the Israelites shortly after he found them worshiping the golden calf:* "Think! The heavens, even the highest heavens, belong to the Lord, your God, as well as the earth and everything on it." *Paul believed that Paradise was in the south side of the third heaven, Hell on the north side.*)

Koran 17:13—The fate of each man We have bound about his neck. On the Day of Resurrection We shall confront him with a book spread wide open, saying; "Here is your book: read it. Enough for you this day that your own soul should call you to account."

The Bible's Old Testament also tells of a "book of the Lord," though it is not clear when the book is to be opened:

Exodus 32:32–33—(*Moses praying to God after finding the Israelites worshiping a golden calf***) "If you would only forgive their sin! If you will not, then strike me out of the book that you have written." The Lord answered, "Him only who has sinned against me will I strike out of my book."** (*A similar passage is found in Malachi 3:16–17, written centuries later.*)

Koran 3:105–106—Do not follow the example of those (*Jews and Christians*) who became divided and opposed to one another after veritable proofs had been given them. These shall be sternly punished on the day when some faces will be bright with joy and others blackened.

Koran 6:38–39—All the beasts that roam the earth and all the birds that wing their flight are but communities like your own. We have left out nothing in the Book. They shall all be gathered before their Lord.

Koran 7:57—He sends forth the winds as harbingers of His mercy, and when they have gathered up a heavy cloud, We drive it on to some dead land and let the water fall upon it, bringing forth all manner of fruit. Thus will We raise the dead to life. Perchance you will take heed.

Jesus used the same metaphor with a grain of wheat:

John 12:23–25—Jesus answered them (*Gentile proselytes to Judaism*), "The hour has come for the Son of Man to be glorified. Amen, amen, I say to you, unless a grain of wheat falls to the ground and dies, it remains just a grain of wheat, but if it dies, it produces much fruit. Whoever loves his life loses it, and whoever hates his life in this world will preserve it for eternal life."

Koran 10:3–4—To Him you shall all return: God's promise shall be fulfilled. He gives being to all His creatures, and in the end He will bring them back to life, so that He may justly reward those who have believed in Him and done good works. As for the unbelievers, they shall drink scalding water and be sternly punished for their unbelief. (*The reader may ponder whether "in the end" means on the Day of Doom, or is it a figure of speech meaning "after all"?*)

Koran 17:50–51—"What!" they (*the unbelievers*) say. "When we are turned to bones and dust, shall we be restored in a new creation?"

Say: "Whether you turn to stone or iron, or any other substance you may think unlikely to be given life."

They will ask: "Who will restore us?"

Say: "He that created you at first."

Koran 17:97–98—Those whom God guides are rightly guided; but those whom He confounds shall find no friend besides Him. We shall gather them all on the Day of Resurrection, prostrate upon their faces, blind, dumb, and deaf. Hell shall be their home: whenever its flames die down We will rekindle them into a greater fire.

Koran 19:38, 92—But when that fateful day arrives, woe to the unbelievers! Their hearing and their sight will be sharpened on the day they appear before Us. (*This is an apparent contradiction of the passage above. The reader will recall that Muslims scholars recognize 225 verses that contradict others.*) There is none in the heavens or on earth but shall return to the Merciful in utter submission. He has kept strict count of all His creatures and one by one they shall approach Him on the Day of Resurrection.

Koran 22:17—As for the true believers, the Jews, the Sabaeans, the Christians, the Magians (*probably Persian astrologers*), and the pagans, God will judge them on the Day of Resurrection.

Koran 26:87–94—(*Abraham praying*) "Do not hold me up to shame on the Day of Resurrection; the day when wealth and offspring will avail nothing, and when none shall be saved except him who comes before his Lord with a pure heart; when Paradise shall be brought in sight of the righteous and Hell be revealed to the erring."

Koran 32:5—All will ascend to Him in a single day, a day whose space is as a thousand years by your reckoning. (*This passage seems to say that the resurrection will not occur until the Final Day—which for God may be a thousand years—but this is difficult to reconcile with some of the passages we have quoted in the chapter HEAVEN AND HELL, and with Sura 50:9–12 quoted immediately below.*)

Koran 50:1, 9–12—By the Glorious Koran! . . . We send down blessed water from the sky with which We bring forth gardens and the harvest grain, and tall palm trees laden with clusters of dates, a sustenance for men: thereby giving new life to some dead land. Such shall be the Resurrection. (*This passage seems to imply that Resurrection occurs on a regular basis, not only on the Final Day.*)

Koran 34:7—The unbelievers say: "Shall we show you a man (*Mohammed*) who claims that when you have been mangled into dust you will be raised in a new creation? Has he invented a lie about God, or is he mad?"

Koran 36:8–11—You (*Mohammed*) shall admonish none but those who observe Our precepts and fear the Merciful, though they cannot see Him. To these give news of a pardon and a rich reward. It is We who will resurrect the dead.

Koran 80:18–28—From what did God create him? From a little germ. He created him and proportioned him. He makes his path smooth for him, then causes him to die and stows him in a grave. He will surely bring him back to life when He pleases. (**This seems to imply that the Resurrection is on an irregular basis, not *if* but** *when* God ordains it, and not necessarily at the time of death or on the Final Day.)

Koran 89:21–22—But when the earth is crushed to fine dust, and your Lord comes down with the angels, in their ranks, and Hell is brought near—on that day man will remember his deeds. (*Orthodox Muslims take this passage literally. They say that Hell is brought near by being dragged up by 70,000 chains, each pulled by 70,000 angels.*) (*See also Suras 22:5a, 5c and 75:1–11.*)

The Bible

The Old Testament:

The word "resurrection" does not appear anywhere in the Old Testament. However, contrary to the belief of many Jews and Christians, the Old Testament has quite a few references to an afterlife of some kind. There are only two texts that affirm life after death comparable to that of the New Testament. And there are some passages that seem to indicate a *disbelief* in any life elsewhere after this life is over. Let us then look at these Old Testament references before going on to the very explicit treatment of the resurrection in the New Testament.

First, let's look at the two passages that reflect the same idea as the New Testament:

Isaiah 26:19—But your dead shall live, their corpses shall rise; awake and sing, you who lie in the dust. For your dew is a dew of light, and the land of shades gives birth.

Daniel 12:2–3—(*Daniel is in Babylon, on the banks of the Tigris River, and is seeing a vision of a man dressed in linen, having a body like chrysolite, his face shining like lightning, his eyes like fiery torches. The vision speaks*): Many of those who sleep in the dust of the earth shall awake; some shall live forever, others shall be an everlasting horror and disgrace.

Now, let's look at two very short but very clear references to some form of life after death:

Isaiah 25:18—He (*God*) will destroy death forever.

Hosea 13:14b—Where are your plagues, O death? Where is your sting, O netherworld?

In the story of David and Bathsheba there is a hint by David that he thought that there is an afterlife. Their first child is born, becomes ill, and lives for a week. David fasts during the illness, but when the child dies, he takes food. He is questioned by his servants about this strange behavior:

2 Samuel 12:22–23—He replied: "While the child was living I fasted and wept, thinking, 'Perhaps the Lord will grant me the child's life.' But now he is dead. Why should I fast? Can I bring him back again? I shall go to him, but he will not return to me."

In contrast to David's optimism:

Ecclesiastes 3:19–20—For the lot of man and beast is one lot. Both go to the same place; both were made from the dust, and to the dust they both return.

But later in the same book, we read:

Ecclesiastes 12:1a, 6–8—Remember your Creator in the days of your youth . . . Before the silver cord is snapped and the golden bowl is broken, and the pitcher is shattered at the spring, and the broken pulley falls into the well (*all metaphors for life ending in death*), and the dust returns as it once was, and the life breath returns to God who gave it. (*Perhaps Qoheleth is teasing us with thoughts of immortality by implying that the "life breath" is the soul and it returns to God even though the body returns to dust.*)

In the following passage from Wisdom, we sense a strong belief in some kind of afterlife:

Wisdom 3:1, 3, 6—But the souls of the just are in the hand of God and no torment shall touch them. They seemed, in the view of the foolish, to be dead . . . But they are in peace. For if before men, indeed, they be punished, yet is their hope full of immortality . . . God tried them and found them worthy of himself. As gold in the furnace, he proved them, and as a sacrificial offering he took them to himself.

Job seems to pass through three stages in one short speech: from denial of an afterlife, to uncertainty, and finally to hope.

Job 14:7, 10, 13–14—(*Job responding to Zaphar the Naamathite*) For a tree there is hope, if it be cut down, that it will sprout again and that its tender shoots will not cease . . . But when a man dies, all vigor leaves him . . . Oh, that you would hide me in the nether world and keep me sheltered till your wrath is past; would fix a time for me, and then remember me! When a man has died,

191

were he to live again, all the days of my drudgery I would wait, until my relief should come.

(Jews who introduce the Eighteen Benedictions into their worship will read three times in the Second Benediction words like this: "You, O Lord, are mighty forever, you revive the dead.")

Two men in the Old Testament were taken up bodily into heaven, Enoch and Elijah:

Genesis 5:23–24—The whole lifetime of Enoch was three hundred and sixty-five years. Then Enoch walked with God and he was no longer here, for God took him. (*Since the usual formula, "then he died and rested with his ancestors," is not used here, the Bible is clear that God took Enoch to heaven alive in his earthly body.*)

The writer of the Letter to the Hebrews in the New Testament has no doubt about the meaning of this passage:

Hebrews 11:5—By faith Enoch was taken up so that he should not see death, and "he was found no more because God had taken him." Before he was taken up, he was attested to have pleased God.

2 Kings 2:11—As they (*Elijah and Elisha*) walked on conversing, a flaming chariot and flaming horses came between them and Elijah went up to heaven in a whirlwind. (*The Bible is clear here that Elijah was quite alive when he was carried off to heaven. However it does not say the he was carried off in the chariot as most people believe.*)

*   *   *

There are many references in the Old Testament to a person—usually a king or a prophet or some other noteworthy personage—dying and resting with his ancestors. Note that the Bible never states that they went to heaven in order to be with their ancestors. What is clear, however, is that there are "hosts" in heaven with God. We are tempted to conjecture that these hosts are ancestors gone to heaven, but nowhere does the Bible actually say this. Here are two examples of the formula, followed by two examples of the presence of hosts in heaven:

2 Kings 14:29—Jeroboam rested with his ancestors, the kings of Israel, and his son Zechariah succeeded him as king.

2 Kings 15:38—Jotham rested with his ancestors and was buried with them in his forefather's City of David. His son Ahaz succeeded him as king.

2 Chronicles 33:3–5—He (*Manasseh*) rebuilt the high places which his father Hezekiah had torn down, erected altars for the Baals, made sacred poles and prostrated himself before the whole host of heaven and worshiped them.

Nehemiah 9:6—Then Ezra said: "It is to you, O Lord, you are the only one; you made the heavens, the highest heavens and all their host, the earth and all that is upon it, the seas and all that is in them.

We are teased with the many references to "the holy ones" in heaven. Are they resurrected humans? Here is an example:

Psalms 89:6–7—Who in the skies ranks with the Lord? Who is like the Lord among the gods? A God dreaded in the council of the holy ones, greater and more awesome than all who sit there!

In the story of Jacob and his dream of a stairway to heaven, we have another teaser:

Genesis 28:11–13—When he came upon a certain shrine, as the sun had already set, he stopped there for the night. Taking one of the stones at the shrine, he put it under his head and lay down to sleep at that spot. Then he had a dream; a stairway rested on the ground, with its top reaching to the heavens; and God's messengers were going up and down on it. And there was the Lord standing beside him and saying: "I, the Lord, am the God of your forefather Abraham and the God of Isaac . . ."

The New Testament:

The core belief of Christians is that Jesus Christ died in atonement for the sins of men, was resurrected from the dead, spent about six weeks here on earth, and then went back to heaven where he sits at the right hand of God. There are many references to the resurrection and even more to eternal life as a reward for belief in God and his Son Jesus. There are other references to "rising from the dead" which do not include the words "resurrection" or "eternal life." There are no references in the Bible that clearly state that lower animals will also return to God (See Koran 6:38, quoted above), but many Christians hope—and some believe—that they will!

Beginning with Matthew's gospel and continuing on to Revelation, I shall record some of the references to the resurrection as they appear. However, it should be recalled that this does not mean that they are ordered chronologically. For example, all of the undisputed letters of Paul and most of the other epistles were written before any of the four gospels were written.

Matthew 19:27–28—Then Peter said to him (*Jesus*) in reply, "We have given up everything and followed you. What will there be for us?" Jesus said to them, "Amen, I say to you that you who have followed me, in the new age, when the Son of Man is seated on his throne of glory, will yourselves sit on twelve thrones, judging the twelve tribes of Israel." (See also Matthew 22:31–32, 25:31–34, 27:51b–53, and 28:5–7.)

Luke 14:13–14—(*Jesus speaking*) When you hold a banquet, invite the poor, the crippled, the lame, the blind; blessed indeed will you be because of their inability to repay you. For you will be repaid at the resurrection of the righteous." (See also Luke 18:22, and 20:37–38.)

John 21:18–22—(*Jesus has just driven the money-changers out of the temple*) At this the Jews answered and said to him, "What sign can you show us for doing this?"

Jesus answered and said to them, "Destroy this temple and in three days I will raise it up."

The Jews said, "This temple has been under construction for forty-six years, and you will raise it up in three days?"

But he was speaking about the temple of his body. Therefore, when he was raised from the dead, his disciples remembered that he had said this.

John 3:16—For God so loved the world that he gave his only Son, so that everyone who believes in him might not perish but might have eternal life.

John 5:28–29—(*Jesus speaking*) The hour is coming in which all who are in the tombs will hear his voice and will come out, those who have done good deeds to the resurrection of life, but those who have done wicked deeds to the resurrection of condemnation.

John 11:21–26b—Martha said to Jesus, "Lord, if you had been here, my brother (*Lazarus*) would not have died. But even now I know that whatever you ask of God, God will give you." Jesus said to her, "Your brother will rise." Martha said to him, "I know he will rise, in the resurrection on the last day." Jesus told her, "I am the resurrection and the life; whoever believes in me, even if he dies, will live, and everyone who lives and believes in me will never die." (See also John 6:47–51, 10:24–28; 17:1–3, 20:17–18.)

Acts 17:29–31—(*Paul speaking at the Areopagus in Athens*) Since therefore we are the offspring of God, we ought not to think that the divinity is like an image fashioned from gold, silver, or stone by human art and imagination. God has overlooked the times of ignorance, but now he demands that all people everywhere repent because he has established a day on which he will 'judge the world with justice' (*Psalm 72:2*) through a man (*Jesus*) he has appointed, and he has provided confirmation for all by raising him from the dead. (See also Acts 2:22–24.)

Romans 6:9—(*Paul writing*) We know that Christ, raised from the dead, dies no more; death no longer has power over him. (See also Romans 1:1–4.)

1 Corinthians 15:53–55—(*Paul writing*) For that which is corruptible must clothe itself with incorruptibility, and that which is mortal must clothe itself with immortality. And when this (happens), then the word that is written shall come about: "Death is swallowed up in victory (*Isaiah 25:8*). Where, O death, is your victory? Where, O death, is your sting (*Hosea 13:14*)? (See also Philippians 3:8b–10.)

Hebrews 5:7–9—(*From a letter to Jewish Christians, author unknown, attributed to Paul, or Appollos, or Barnabas*) In the days when he (*Jesus*) was in the flesh, he offered prayers and supplications with loud cries and tears to the one who was able to save him from death, and he was heard because of his reverence. Son though he was, he learned obedience from what he suffered; and when he was made perfect, he became the source of eternal salvation for all who obey him . . .

1 Peter 1:3–5—(*Peter writing to Christians in Asia Minor*) Blessed be the God and Father of our Lord Jesus Christ, who in his great mercy gave us a new birth to a living hope through the resurrection of Jesus Christ from the dead, to an inheritance that is imperishable, undefiled, and unfading, kept in heaven for you who by the power of God are safeguarded through faith, to a salvation that is ready to be revealed in the final time. (See also 1 John 2:24–26.)

Revelation 1:17–18—(*John's vision of Jesus speaking*) Do not be afraid. I am the first and the last, the one who lives. Once I was dead, but now I am alive forever and ever. I hold the keys to death and the netherworld.

24

The Final Day

In the Name of God the Compassionate the Merciful

It is quite clear that Mohammed—and later, his followers—believed
that there would come a Final Day, a Day of Doom, a Day of Judgment. In the chapter dealing with the Resurrection, we noted that it
was not always clear whether the righteous would go to Heaven and
the unbelievers to Hell as soon as they died or whether it would be
later, perhaps even on the Final Day of the world. There is no such
confusion in the passages dealing with the *ultimate* fate of the faithful
and the unfaithful.

There is also no confusion in the Bible about a final accounting
for all people, although it is not called a Day of Doom. Rather, it is
called "the end of the age," or "the day of the Lord," or just "on
that day."

Koran 70:6–18—They (*the unbelievers*) think the Day of Judgement is far off: but We see it near at hand. On that day the sky
shall become like molten brass, and the mountains like tufts of wool
scattered in the wind. Friends will meet, but shall not speak to each
other. To redeem himself from the torment of that day the sinner
will gladly sacrifice his children, his wife, his brother, the kinsfolk
who gave him shelter, and all the people of the earth, if then this
might deliver him. But no! The fire of Hell shall drag him down by
the scalp, shall claim him who had turned his back and amassed
riches and covetously hoarded them.

Koran 74:7—The day the Trumpet sounds shall be a hard and
joyless day for the unbelievers.

Joel 2:1–3—Blow the trumpet in Zion, sound the alarm on my
holy mountain! Let all who dwell in the land tremble, for the day of
the Lord is coming. Yes, it is near, a day of darkness and of gloom,

a day of clouds and somberness. Like dawn spreading over the mountains, a people numerous and mighty! Their like has not been from of old, nor will it be after them, even to the years of distant generations. Before them a fire devours, and after them a flame enkindles; like the garden of Eden is the land before them, and after them a desert waste; from them there is no escape.

Daniel 12:1–2—(*God in the form of a man, speaking to Daniel*) At that time there shall arise Michael, the great prince, guardian of your people; it shall be a time unsurpassed in distress since nations began until that time. At that time your people shall escape, everyone who is found written in the book.

Matthew 13:36–40—Then, dismissing the crowds, he (*Jesus*) went into the house. His disciples approached him and said, "Explain to us the parable of the weeds in the field." He said in reply, "He who sows good seed in the Son of Man, the field is the world, the good seed the children of the kingdom. The weeds are the children of the evil one, and the enemy who sows them is the devil. The harvest is the end of the age, and the harvesters are angels. Just as weeds are collected and burned up with fire, so will it be at the end of the age."

Matthew 24:29–31—(*Jesus speaking to the crowds*) Immediately after the tribulation of those days, the sun will be darkened, and the moon will not give its light; the stars will fall from the sky and the powers of the heavens will be shaken. And then the sign of the Son of Man will appear in heaven, and all the tribes of the earth will mourn, and they will see the Son of Man coming on the clouds of heaven with power and great glory. And he will send his angels with a loud trumpet blast and they will gather his elect from the four winds from one end of the heavens to the other.

Koran 73:11–15—Leave to me those that deny the Truth, those that enjoy the comforts of this life; bear with them yet a little while. We have in store for them heavy fetters and a blazing fire, choking food and harrowing torment: on the day when the earth shall quiver with all its mountains and the mountains crumble into heaps of shifting sand.

2 Peter 3:8–10—(*a pseudonymous letter once attributed to the apostle Peter, to Christians being confronted by false teachings*) But do not ignore this one fact, beloved, that with the Lord one day is like a thousand years and a thousand years like one day. The Lord

does not delay his promise, as some regard "delay," but he is patient with you, not wishing that any should perish but that all should come to repentance. But the day of the Lord will come like a thief, and then the heavens will pass away with a roar; the elements will be dissolved by fire, and the earth and everything done on it will be found out.

Koran 80:31–42—But when the dread blast is sounded, on that day each man will forsake his brother, his mother and his father, his wife and his children: for each one of them will on that day have enough sorrow of his own. On that day there shall be beaming faces, smiling and joyful. On that day there shall be faces veiled with darkness, covered with dust. These shall be the faces of the sinful unbelievers.

Isaiah 27:12–13—On that day, the Lord shall beat out the grain between the Euphrates and the Wadi of Egypt (*the valley of the River Nile*), and you shall be gleaned one by one, O sons of Israel. On that day a great trumpet shall blow and the lost in the land of Assyria (*the ten "lost tribes" carried off to Assyria*) and the outcasts in the land of Egypt shall come and worship the Lord on the holy mountain, in Jerusalem. (*The "outcasts" may be the remnant of Israelites left behind when Moses led the majority out of slavery.*)

Matthew 24:15–21—(*Jesus speaking*) When you see the desolating abomination spoken of through Daniel the prophet standing in the holy place (let the reader understand), then those in Judea must flee to the mountains, a person on the housetop must not go down to get things out of his house, a person in the field must not return to get his cloak. Woe to pregnant women and nursing mothers in those days. Pray that your flight not be in winter or on the Sabbath, for at the time there will be great tribulation such as has not been since the beginning of the world until now, nor ever will be. (*The "desolating abomination" predicted in Daniel 9:26–27 was the erection by Antiochus IV Epiphanes in 167 BCE of a statue of Zeus in the Temple in Jerusalem. But Jesus here is predicting the Roman destruction of the Temple in 70 CE.*)

1 Corinthians 15:51–53—(*Paul writing*) Behold, I tell you a mystery. We shall not all fall asleep, but we will all be changed, in an instant, in the blink of an eye, at the last trumpet. For the trumpet will sound, the dead will be raised imperishable and we will be

198

changed. For that which is corruptible must clothe itself with incorruptibility, and that which is mortal must clothe itself with immortality.

Koran 77:29–36—Woe on that day to the disbelievers! Begone to that hell which you deny! Depart into the shadow that will rise high in three columns, giving neither shade nor shelter from the flames, and throwing up sparks as huge as towers, as bright as yellow camels! Woe on that day to the disbelievers! On that day they shall not speak, nor shall their pleas be heeded. Woe on that day to the disbelievers! Such is the Day of Judgement.

Koran 78:17–26—Fixed is the Day of Judgement. On that day the Trumpet shall be sounded, and you shall come in multitudes. The gates of heaven shall swing open, and the mountains shall pass away and become like vapor. Hell will lie in ambush, as a home for the transgressors.

Koran 88:1–13—Have you heard of the Event which will overwhelm mankind? On that day there shall be downcast faces of men broken and worn out, burnt by a scorching fire, drinking from a seething fountain. Their only food shall be bitter thorns, which will neither sustain them nor satisfy their hunger. On that day there shall be radiant faces of men well pleased with their labors, in a lofty garden.

Koran 14:47–50—On the day when the earth is changed into a different earth and the heavens into new heavens, mankind shall stand before God, the One, who conquers all.

Revelation 21:1–8—Then I (*John*) saw a new heaven and a new earth. The former heaven and the former earth had passed away, and the sea was no more. I also saw the holy city, a new Jerusalem, coming down out of heaven from God, prepared as a bride adorned for her husband. I heard a loud voice from the throne saying, "Behold, God's dwelling is with the human race. He will dwell with them and they will be his people and God will always be with them (as their God). He will wipe every tear from their eyes, and there shall be no more death or mourning, wailing or pain, (for) the old order has passed away." The one who sat on the throne said, "Behold, I make all things new."

Koran 39:67–71, 73—The Trumpet shall be sounded and all who are in the heavens and on earth, shall fall down fainting, except those that shall be spared by God. Then the Trumpet will be blown again and they shall rise and gaze around them. The earth will shine with the light of her Lord, and the Book (*records of each person's good and bad deeds*) will be laid open. The prophets and the witnesses shall be brought in, and all shall be judged with fairness: none shall be wronged. Every soul shall be paid back according to its deeds, for He best knows all that they did. In throngs the unbelievers shall be led to Hell . . . But those who fear their Lord shall be led in throngs to Paradise.

1 Thessalonians 4:13–18—(*Paul writing*) We do not want you to be unaware, brothers, about those who have fallen asleep, so that you may not grieve like the rest, who had no hope. For if we believe that Jesus died and rose, so too will God, through Jesus, bring with him those who have fallen asleep. Indeed, we tell you this, on the word of the Lord, that we who are alive, who are left until the coming of the Lord, will surely not precede those who have fallen asleep. For the Lord, himself, with a word of command, with the voice of an archangel and with the trumpet of God, will come down from heaven, and the dead in Christ will rise first. Then we who are alive, who are left, will be caught up together with them in the clouds to meet the Lord in the air. Thus we shall always be with the Lord. Therefore, console one another with these words.

Koran 83:4–5, 20–21—Truly, the record of sinners is in Sijjīn. Would that you knew what Sijjīn is. It is a sealed book. (*Sijjīn is a prison in Hell (which lends its name to the registry of bad deeds.)* . . . *The record of the righteous shall be in Illiyyūn. Would that you knew what Illiyyūn is. It is a sealed book, seen only by the favored. (Illiyyūn is a lofty apartment in Paradise which lends its name to the registry of good deeds.)*

Koran 7:187a—They ask about the Hour of Doom: when will it come? Say: "None but my Lord has knowledge of it. He alone will reveal it—at the appointed time. A fateful hour it shall be, both in the heavens and on earth. It will but suddenly overtake you (*Mohammed*).

Mark 13:32–33, 36–37—(*Jesus speaking to Peter, James, John, and Andrew on the Mount of Olilves*) But of that day or hour, no one knows, neither the angels in heaven, nor the Son, but only the Father. Be watchful! Be alert! You do not know when the time will come . . . May he not come suddenly and find you sleeping. What I say to you, I say to all: "Watch!"

Koran 52:1–12—By the Mountain (*Sinai*), and by the Scripture penned on unrolled parchment; by the Visited House (*the Ka'bah*), the Lofty Vault (*the sky*) and the swelling sea, your Lord's punishment shall surely come to pass. No power shall ward it off. On that day the heaven will shake and reel, and the mountains move and pass away. On that day woe betide the unbelievers, who now divert themselves with vain disputes.

Koran 22:1–5a—Men, have fear of your Lord. The catastrophe of the Hour of Doom shall be terrible indeed. When that day comes, every suckling mother shall forsake her infant, every pregnant female shall cast her burden (*abort*), and you shall see mankind reeling like drunkards although not drunk: such shall be the horror of God's chastisement.

Koran 5:109–112—One day (*the day of Doom*), God will gather all the apostles and ask them: "How were you received?" They will reply: "We have no knowledge. You alone know what is hidden."

John 6:37–40—(*Jesus speaking to the crowd on the shore of the Sea of Galilee*) "Everything that the Father gives me will come to me, and I will not reject anyone who comes to me, because I came down from heaven not to do my own will but the will of the one who sent me. And this is the will of the one who sent me, that I should not lose anything of what he gave me, but that I should raise it on the last day. For this is the will of my Father, that everyone who sees the Son and believes in him may have eternal life, and I shall raise him on the last day.

25

A Prayer of Mohammed

In the Name of God the Compassionate the Merciful

There are dozens of references to prayer in the Koran, as we have seen in Chapter Three, THE FIVE PILLARS OF ISLAM. But there are only two actual prayers recited by Mohammed. One is the Exordium, quoted in Chapter Two. The other is found in Sura 3:190–194.

Mohammed leads into it with these words: In the creation of the heavens and the earth, and in the alternation of night and day, there are signs for men of sense; those that remember God when standing, sitting, and lying down, and reflect on the creation of the heavens and the earth, saying:

Lord, You have not created this world in vain.
Glory be to You!
Save us from the torment of the Fire.
Lord, those whom You will cast into the Fire
You will put to eternal shame: none will help the evil-doers.
Lord, we have heard someone calling to the true faith, saying:
"Believe in your Lord," and we believed.
Lord, forgive us our sins and remove from us our evil deeds
and make us die with the righteous.
Lord, grant what You promised through Your apostles,
and do not hold us up to shame on the Day of Resurrection.
You never break Your promise.